The Story of Green & Black's

Craig Sams has an impeccable history as a health food advocate. He founded Whole Earth Foods, starting with the UK's first macrobiotic restaurant, Seed, and moving on to launch a range of organic products. He was chairman of the Soil Association from 2001–8. Josephine Fairley is a former glossy magazine editor whose quest has always been to combine outer and inner beauty. Craig and Josephine founded Green & Black's together in 1991 and sold the company to Cadbury Schweppes in 2006. Craig remains president of the company and, among other things, he ensures the original principles of sustainability and organic production are being held. Craig and Josephine are now concentrating on new ventures that embody their passion for sustainable living and wellbeing, including The Wellington Centre, an integrated health clinic, and Judges, an organic bakery and wholefood store, both in their home town of Hastings, East Sussex, and Carbon Gold, a company that produces the soil improver biochar.

Praise for *The Story of Green & Black's*

'A fairy tale for those of us who dream of taking a prolonged pit stop from the rat race in a quest for a more fulfilling 9 to 5 . . . a blueprint for the new generation of ethically minded entrepreneurs . . . packed full of marketing and business insights.' *Marie Claire*

'A wonderful story . . . It's also an insight into the elevated world of the organic and fair-trade glitterati. It's a world I admire. We have come to understand the work of these people and of the Soil Association, and it should be more widely publicised. This book helps with that process; it not only gives us what seems to be an open account of the Green & Black's story, it puts it into context . . . a great book.' John Vincent, *Management Today*

'There are some inspiring passages on motivation, enterprise, passion and the conundrum of trying to run an ethical business in an unethical world . . . This is a good book which should be read by all budding entrepreneurs, particularly those with a social conscience.'
Spectator Business

'Both absorbing as a story in its own right and full of useful take-aways. Whether it's due to the nature of the Green & Black's story itself or the combination of Josephine Fairley's journalist background and Craig Sams' pioneering entrepreneurial background, this book avoids the pitfalls that many fall into . . . the later stages of the book act as a textbook case study on all aspects of the entre-preneurial process.'
Director

'With motivational advice for any would-be entrepreneur and essential tips like the seven recommended steps to taste chocolate properly, this book is as rich and satisfying as the product it celebrates.'
Waterstone's Books Quarterly

'The book is a fascinating look in the world of two determined ethically minded entrepreneurs. An inspiring read, that will make you think twice about what you eat.'
Ulster Tatler

Published by Random House Business Books 2009

2 4 6 8 10 9 7 5 3

First published in Great Britain in 2008 as *Sweet Dreams* by
Random House Business Books

This updated edition first published in Great Britain in 2009 by
Random House Business Books
Random House, 20 Vauxhall Bridge Road,
London SW1V 2SA

www.rbooks.co.uk

Addresses for companies within The Random House Group Limited can be found at:
www.randomhouse.co.uk/offices.htm

The Random House Group Limited Reg. No. 954009

A CIP catalogue record for this book
is available from the British Library

ISBN 9781905211463

Typeset in Dante MT by Palimpsest Book Production Limited,
Grangemouth, Stirlingshire

Printed and bound in Great Britain by
Clays Ltd, St Ives plc

Craig Sams and Josephine Fairley

The Story of
GREEN
&BLACK'S

How two entrepreneurs turned an ethical
idea into a business success

rh

BUSINESS
BOOKS

This book is dedicated to Justino Peck, Cayetano Ico, Cirila Cho, Ines Coc and all the Maya men and women cacao growers and to the memory of Gregor Hargrove.

Contents

Prologue   1

Part One: Before Green & Black's

1   Craig's Story   7
2   Jo's Story   25

Part Two: Green Meets Black

3   A Very Short History of Chocolate   45
4   The First Bar   57
5   Maya Gold   80
6   New Lines and False Trails   101

Part Three: Growing Pains

7   Organic Goes Mainstream   129
8   The Black Hole   153
9   Under New Management   175
10   Hurricane Iris   190

Part Four: The Final Chunk

11   Selling On or Selling Out?   211
12   Toledo Cacao Fest 2007   225

Epilogue   235
Index   249

Prologue

It was a dark and stormy night. No, really: the night was as dark as the 70% cocoa solids chocolate the two of us wanted to launch. The rain was lashing at our Portobello Road window. It was March 1991. And we had nothing better to do on a soggy Saturday evening than come up with a name. (Well, of course we did, but sometimes in this world you have to put business before pleasure . . .) We were snuggled up under the duvet with a yellow legal pad and a pen. The challenge: to come up with a name for an intense, tastebud-teasing chocolate – the world's very first organic chocolate.

Names are everything. Quite often they can be make or break for a brand. We had no idea, then – not a clue – that the chocolate we were naming would become a global by-word for deliciousness and ethical business. If we had, we'd probably have been too paralysed with fear to come up with anything at all. We batted a few suggestions back and forth: Eco-Choc; Bio-Choc. Though they gave a clue as to the chocolate's environmentally friendly credentials, they weren't about to get anyone salivating, frankly. Then Jo remembered the confectionery brands of her childhood: Callard & Bowser; Barker & Dobson; Charbonnel & Walker. Somehow, the ampersand in the middle told a story, made the companies sound established, trustworthy and as if they'd been around for a hundred years.

'Green & . . .' (the green seemed right – it gave a subliminal eco-message). Somehow, 'Black' went with it perfectly. Black: the sexiest colour of all. Black: a design classic. Black: synonymous with style. And our soon to be launched chocolate was such a dark shade of brown, it was almost black. Green & Black's. Ta-dah! It sounded perfect. Intriguing, too. We've lost count of the number of times we've been asked, 'Is there a real Mr Green and Mr Black?' Answer: no. It's us. A wholefood entrepreneur and organic pioneer, Craig Sams, and a former magazine editor, Josephine Fairley. But somehow, that simple '&' sign made the brand sound like we had been artisan chocolatiers since 1876. We knew we had it. Green & Black's. It just sounded right. (And we do know that if we'd stuck with Eco-Choc, we wouldn't be writing this book now.)

Craig started sketching on the yellow legal pad. The typeface had to be a little retro and gold, of course, to imply luxury. Why not have the wrapper a deep shade of brown, a clue to the darkness within? Somehow, a ribbon and a seal felt right, too. And let's put the organic logo – which at the time was from Nature et Progrès, the French certification body – inside the seal. There, that looks smart . . . luxurious – not earthy and wholefoody. No offence to wholefood-lovers – after all, Craig was the first person to bring brown rice and tamari into this country, in the 60s. He'd built an empire in the natural food trade. But we felt that this delicious chocolate had potentially wider appeal than just to committed vegetarians, vegans and wholefoodies.

It seems unbelievable, now. The whole creative process took all of ten minutes. We went downstairs to input it onto Craig's Macintosh and print it out on his (hah!) state of the art 170-dots-per-inch, one page per minute, £1,400 inkjet printer – and on Monday morning phoned George Smith, who fine-tuned all the packaging designs for Craig's company Whole Earth Foods. Incredible as it seems, back then, all packaging designs were done by hand – in George's case, with watercolours and ink – before being handed to the printer.

We had absolutely no idea that what we were doing was going to be more than a fun challenge; something we could do together. A project that mirrored our beliefs, which would ensure there was always something scrumptious to snack on in our kitchen cupboard, and – who knows? – might eventually make money. We could never have imagined that one day, our brand (with that all-important ampersand) would be cooler than Prada (according to the Coolbrands survey in 2006) bigger than Marmite (in sales value), be one of the UK's Top 100 Food Brands and be enjoyed from Melbourne to Miami via Manhattan and Manchester. Or that it would change thousands of lives in the developing world – at the same time as it would change millions of people's perception of chocolate from a sweet snack to a sensual gastronomic experience.

1

Craig's Story

I've been a champion of natural and organic foods all my adult life and I have dedicated my career to spreading the word about healthy eating. Long before Green and Black's, I opened the UK's first macrobiotic restaurant, and from there, with my brother Gregory, went on to set up Whole Earth, a company dedicated to organic, no added sugar foods. I often wonder how I got started on this road – perhaps the roots lay in my early life. When I sit back and think about it, I realise that some quite unusual things happened to me at a young age, and they must have affected my view of the world. If I were a musician, this might be a list of my influences.

My roots are in farming. I was born on a farm in Nebraska in 1944, when 30% of America's population lived on the land. Now it's less than 1%. Chemical fertilisers, pesticides and machinery replaced all those people, including me. My earliest American ancestor was Lars Ole Dugstad, who, in 1841, was one of a small band of Norwegian pioneers who first ploughed and farmed 80 acres of the virgin Koshkong Prairie in Wisconsin – described by one of them as 'blessed with wild flowers in more different colours than there are in the rainbow'. A year earlier most of the native Winnebago Sioux had agreed to move westward from their woodland homes in Wisconsin and eventually they were given a permanent 40,000-acre home on the Winnebago Indian Reservation in eastern Nebraska. By chance, Lars's son Ole decided to leave

Wisconsin and seek land further west and ended up buying a 160-acre farm in Nebraska on the edge of that reservation. That's where I was born. I was a product of the land I was born on; my mother was raised on the food that was grown on the farm, including the chickens and eggs my grandfather specialised in. His chicken houses held 500 hens, the peak of intensification at the time; anything more was considered cruel and unclean. Now chicken houses can hold 10,000 or more hens at a time.

My family moved around – a lot. When World War II ended my dad, Ken, a Marine sergeant, went to college in California at UCLA and we lived in Westwood Village when it was un-developed and consisted largely of open green fields in a wild Californian/Mediterranean type countryside. As five year olds, we kids played close to nature, thinking nothing of picking up garter snakes or king snakes and draping them round our necks. Later we moved to San Diego, where nature was again on our doorstep with dense canebrakes of native bamboo through which we'd carve out hidden pathways and secret rooms. When we stumbled across a Gila Monster lizard we knew to steer clear because of its venomous poison. But I was plugged into the urban world as well – I'd spend hours on our porch recording the different types of cars that passed along the road outside our house: Packards, Studebakers and Kaisers as well as Fords, Chevrolets and Chryslers.

My parents, in their own way, were natural-living pioneers. My dad had a stress-related digestive disorder, probably Crohn's Disease, that arose from his time on Saipan in 1944, where he was wounded while trapped under Japanese shellfire for several days before naval cover arrived to relieve them. In the late 1940s they gave him sulfa drugs and the new-fangled antibiotics to try to cure him, but nothing did the trick and he had wasted away to a shadow of his former self, losing about 50 pounds in weight. In desperation, he went to see a Japanese doctor based in Hollywood, who advised him to go on a diet that excluded sugar, meat, dairy products and white flour and that included brown rice and wholewheat bread. Within a few weeks, Ken was gaining weight and functioning normally and went on to do a masters degree in English at UCLA. Food had worked as medicine when all else had failed. From then on we never had white bread, white sugar or white rice. If he relapsed, our mother, Margaret, would only cook vegetarian meals till he was better. She also became adept at cooking Middle Eastern specialities such as *tabboulleh*, hummus and *kibbeh*, all nutritious wholegrain-based foods that she had learned to make from her Syrian mother-in-law, my grandmother Shafiqa.

We were snatched from the warm and sunny idyll of Southern California when my dad got a job as a historian for the US Air Force, who were just establishing bases in England. On a wintry morning on 12 December 1951, he met us as we disembarked from the ocean liner *Ile de France* at Plymouth. I had my first train journey en route to London. Ken was living in West Ruislip, where we stayed for a few months. I would catch newts and frogs in a little stream near our lodgings at the house of Mrs Spurdens and her daughter Veda, who were vegetarians and nature-cure enthusiasts. They introduced Ken to yoga and meditation. He was more interested at an intellectual than a practical level, but it trickled down to me and my brother Gregory: we were too young to know anything different so we didn't see this sort of thing as odd or abnormal.

In 1953 Veda took nine-year-old me on a youth hostelling trip to Holland. There had just been serious flooding and we took a bus from Vlissingen along the dike-top road towards Bergen-op-Zoom, looking at houses that had water up to their upstairs windows. I was profoundly alarmed at seeing that flood; no one could tell me when or even whether the waters would subside. At Scheveningen, further up the coast, we walked along the beach without touching the sand because large jellyfish heads, like stepping stones, studded the beach where the storm had driven them ashore.

Another strong memory is from 1952. We were sitting in our classroom when the entire room went dark. A heavy fog had settled over London. We were sent home early and for the next few days the city hardly moved. Walking along the street one could barely see a lamp post or even tell if you were on the road or the pavement. Traffic was at a standstill. Some estimates suggest that at least 10,000 people died from air poisoning. We kept the windows shut and, when I went out, I folded a handkerchief and held it over my mouth and nose. There would be little black spots on it where it had covered my nostrils.

I also remember walking to school one wintry day in 1953 when some friends emerged from a shop with a bag of sweets. It was the first day they had stopped being rationed and therefore the first day that a kid could go into a sweet shop and buy themselves a treat. Kids would arrive at school with a bag of sweeties and share them round – suddenly our sugar consumption skyrocketed. As a child I never took sugar for granted, always seeing it as something special and exotic rather than the commonplace it has become.

We moved to Bayswater, and I'd bike along to the Heath & Heather (now Holland & Barrett) shop in Kensington High Street to pick up a loaf of wholewheat bread, often having gnawed off the heel by the time I got home. My school in Hampstead was called St Mary's Town and Country School. It functioned, to some extent, as a refuge for teachers from A. S. Neill's much more progressive Summerhill who yearned for a class where they could actually teach something to the children. Frau Boehm, our German teacher, introduced us to Bircher muesli at lunch one day in 1954 and we also had it at breakfast at our school camp, which was near Thaxted in Essex. It was real muesli, made overnight so the raisins were swollen back to their original grape size and the oats had gone through a minor lactic fermentation, becoming creamier and slightly sour. Once we got over the unfamiliarity of it, all the kids loved it.

After school I'd go home and meet my local friends and we'd decide whether to go and play in Kensington Gardens: riding our bikes, playing cricket with a tennis ball or fishing in the Serpentine. Alternatively, we'd play on a large bomb site just off Westbourne Terrace, where the shells of bombed buildings with dangling pipes and staircases to nowhere conjured up imagined explosions and visions of a wartime that was still less than a decade behind us. One bomb site, just off Bayswater Road, had a petrol station on the corner, and during the Suez crisis queues of cars stretched all the way to Notting Hill Gate as desperate motorists sought to buy vital supplies of fuel.

I remember the people who fed the ducks and swans that nested around the Serpentine. I saw urchins who not only stole the swans' and ducks' eggs from their nests but also gathered up the pieces of bread to take home for their dinner. Their neighbourhood, just north of Harrow Road, was a desolate zone of terraced houses and streets covered in broken glass.

Every two years during the summer we would go back to the US for an extended leave. This was a chance to visit relatives in Pennsylvania, Nebraska and California and for Gregory and me to revisit our American roots. In 1956 we went to Nebraska and I remember being horrified to see hillsides with deep gullies gouged out of them, where masses of earth had just been washed away from the fertile but delicate loess soils of the eastern part of the state. It didn't help that this was near a town called Craig, in which I took particular pride. In those days kids with my name were rarer than hen's teeth, but I had a whole small Nebraskan town named after me, albeit one raddled by soil erosion. My uncle Floyd Doxtad explained to me about erosion and also how modern farmers would contour plough sideways along the hillsides which created ridges that helped contain the soil. Of course sometimes this didn't work, but it helped to hold back the losses. When I went back to junior high school, my science project was a demonstration in front of the class, using two boxes of soil, one contour ploughed and one ploughed straight down. From a jug I poured an equal amount of water over each tilted box and then we measured the silt in the overflow. I got an A+ for that project.

In high school I joined Debate Club and we would debate against other schools. Sometimes we wouldn't know which side of an argument we'd have to take until just before the event. This forced us to consider what the other person was thinking. It helped broaden my mind, but also gave me a useful negotiating tool; if you know what the other person wants then it's much easier to optimise a deal.

For a twelve-year-old, I'd seen a lot more than the average kid's share of flooding, bombed-out buildings, urban poverty, rationing, petrol queues, killer fogs and horrendously eroded farmland. Combined with our peripatetic lifestyle, never living in one place for more than a year or two at most and attending thirteen different schools in twelve years, I suppose I grew up in a less secure frame of mind than most children. I also had an easy familiarity with foods that most people still considered exotic, such as wholewheat bread, muesli, bulgur wheat, tahini and brown rice.

In 1957 we moved to Nebraska and I became a paperboy. After school, while the other kids would hang around a soda fountain and listen to the latest hits on the jukebox I would pick up my papers from the *Omaha World Herald* printworks and deliver them on my round. I paid for the papers, sold them within my territory between 24th and 27th Streets and Dodge and Leavenworth. I collected the money, and my profit depended on having a lot of customers and good credit control. It was a great education in the basics of business. Then I broke my arm at karate practice and had to pay my friend Jimmy Wickencamp to deliver for me and I handled the sales and cash collection. Even when my arm was better I kept up the arrangement; I had discovered outsourcing, a skill I have nurtured ever since. I developed the philosophy that 'Somebody, somewhere can do almost everything I can do better and cheaper than I can.' Finding that person meant I was free to concentrate on my strengths, such as they were.

In 1960 we moved back to London and in my senior year at the American high school in Bushy Park my big project for my much loved English teacher, Mrs Edna Leigh, was a carefully researched paper on George Bernard Shaw. Shaw's robust arguments for his lifelong vegetarianism were forthright and convincing. I was impressed that he only died at the age of ninety-four as the result of complications from falling out of an apple tree he was pruning. His linking of meat-eating and war and his identification of longevity with a wholesome diet registered positively with me and influenced my diet, though I wasn't a strict vegetarian. For the Sams family an evening out in 1961 would often be to go to the massive Vega Restaurant, just off Leicester Square. We'd fill our plates with a wonderful variety of salads, grab a few slices of wholemeal bread and enjoy good, mostly raw, vegetarian food. The Vega closed in the late 1960s and is now an Angus Steak House.

When I was offered a scholarship to the Wharton School of Finance and Commerce at the University of Pennsylvania, Mrs Leigh brushed a tear from her eye. She was far from delighted to be seeing me off to the sausage factory of business school instead of to Harvard where I would probably have ended up with a degree in English or English Literature. My yearbook entry listed my career ambition as 'market research' and I wanted nothing more than to get into the world of marketing.

In September 1961 I went off to Penn, but not before we had one last visit as a family to our relatives in the States. Uncle Floyd took me and Gregory to the Sioux City stockyards, where we saw, up close and personal, his steers getting the bolt through the head. Because Floyd was one of their biggest suppliers, he had access to all areas. He took us up the outside stairs and opened a door where we saw the moment of kill from a distance of no more than five feet away. Then we watched the stripping down of the carcass into its component parts, men with knives, covered in blood and other unmentionable material and I decided that the mild flirtation I'd been having with vegetarianism should get more serious.

At Penn I announced that I was vegetarian on the first day of my freshman year. In the freshman commons they had no idea what to do with me. So, in order to get any decent nutrition, I had to supplement my diet with wholewheat bread and peanut butter from the local grocery. I applied to eat in the self-service cafeteria, normally off-limits to freshmen. The dean was worried about liability: what if he let me have vegetarian food and I were to die of malnutrition? To cover his ass, he insisted that I obtain letters from my parents, from the principal of my high school and from our family doctor to confirm that I could eat a vegetarian diet. In the end, paperwork supplied, I got to eat in the cafeteria.

Meanwhile I got a small business going, selling peanut butter and jelly sandwiches to other students in the freshman dormitory. It was a distraction from my studies, but I learned a few key principles of small business that were never going to be covered in the Wharton curriculum.

I joined Phi Kappa Sigma, Penn's oldest fraternity and a WASP house. In my sophomore (second) year I lived in the frat house and I was the 'Kappa' – I ran the kitchens, working with Saul, our sixty-year-old chef. We planned menus, ordered ingredients and managed the finances and budget for the frat house's breakfast, lunch and evening meals. I liked feeding people, but I stopped being vegetarian.

At the end of my junior year I took a year off from university and spent the summer and autumn in Formentera, a small and (then) completely unpaved and unspoiled island just south of Ibiza in the Mediterranean. There we lived on bread, figs, rice and beans. A vegetable other than an olive was a luxury, everything was grown on the island; the wholewheat bread was made from locally grown and milled wheat; fish was the main source of protein. It was idyllic and cheap, but in November 1964 I returned to London and in February 1965 I headed south to Istanbul and points east. I had $200 in my pocket, all the necessary visas in my passport to get as far as Pakistan and I started by hitchhiking to Dover. During the day I would hitchhike, at night I'd take trains thereby combining accommodation with travel. I'd met a friend on the Orient Express (then a real train, not a rich person's toy) and in Istanbul we pigged out on the incredible pastries and smoked a lot of hashish. The connection between blood sugar, dope and diet really sank in at that point. We'd smoke, giggle, then within an hour or two rush down to the nearest pastry shop and stuff ourselves with huge plates of baklava. I travelled overland via Damascus, Baghdad, Bushehr, Shiraz, Baluchistan and Quetta to Karachi.

In Karachi I began to feel unwell and by the time I reached Jaipur, in India, I was not well at all. Some Peace Corps volunteers I met there suggested I might have hepatitis, as my urine was copper brown and my poo was white. I went to a hospital in Delhi, had a vitamin B12 injection and stayed one night before checking out and heading to Peshawar, then to Kabul. Because I also had dysentery, I went on a diet I had learned in Iran: *noon* or wholemeal unleavened flatbread with unsweetened tea. It cured the dysentery and I was pleased to note that the hepatitis symptoms also lessened considerably – at least enough to enable me to travel back to London in April. Back at Penn in the autumn a few friends in the bohemian Powelton Village neighbourhood where I lived were into the Zen macrobiotic diet and they persuaded me to give it a whirl. Here was a diet that pushed all my buttons: wholegrains were at the centre, it was a way to be vegetarian without being undernourished, and it was committed to organic food. Macrobiotics saw organic agriculture and food as the essential foundation on which social justice, environmental integrity and human health could be built. It gave power and responsibility over one's own well-being, and longevity to the person who practised it. Not only that, it was also, in the 1960s, seen as way of feeling good that was an alternative to repeated use of psychedelic drugs, which most of my contemporaries were beginning to realise were only a temporary short cut to enlightenment, not a permanent pathway.

So, by the age of twenty-one I was tuned in and turned on to healthy eating, organic farming, the politics of food, alternative medicine, oriental philosophy, enlightenment, sustainability, the environment, food-service management and the power of food and farming to bring about real change in society. Little of this had to do with my Wharton courses, which were mostly a waste of time because I had little desire to join the ranks of suits at General Motors or Dupont, which were just a couple of the companies eagerly offering jobs to Wharton grads.

In the 1960s, music, fashion, environmental and political attitudes were in ferment and flux and the macrobiotic approach to diet fitted neatly into the overall lifestyle and philosophy that was being created. The reactions were vicious. A cover story in *Reader's Digest* in 1966, written by Dr Frederick Stare, a professor of nutrition at Harvard University, was entitled 'Macrobiotics – The Hippie Diet That's Killing Our Kids'. The American Medical Association viewed as quackery the statements in macrobiotic publications that cancer and heart disease had dietary causes and could be prevented and even cured by dietary modification. Their concern led the FBI to visit Irma Paul's macrobiotic bookshop on 5th Avenue in New York in February 1966 and to remove for further study several books and pamphlets on sale. I had visited the shop the afternoon after the raid and a rather glum Irma stated that she could not sell me any books until she heard back from the FBI. A few days later they returned, removed all the books and carted them away to be incinerated. This convinced me of the power of the macrobiotic philosophy and of what profound changes it could bring to our state of health, our food and farming.

That evening I visited the Paradox Restaurant in the East Village, which had recently been founded by Michel Abehsera, a pioneering macrobiotic cook and author of the seminal cookbook *Zen Macrobiotic Cooking*. As I surveyed the scene the hairs stood up on the back of my neck and I had a moment of destiny – my future was to be doing something like this. I was due to graduate from Penn in a few months' time and I had already been accepted into the Peace Corps, all set to go to their facility in New Jersey where I would be trained to teach English language to Moroccan kids. But I decided to go to London instead and open a macrobiotic restaurant modelled on the Paradox. I began, in October 1966, by importing macrobiotic books such as *Zen Macrobiotics* and *The Macrobiotic Guidebook for Living* and these went on sale at Indica Books, jointly owned by Barry Miles and Paul McCartney. I also sold them, along with macrobiotic foods such as *tabboulleh*, brown rice rissoles and falafel, at the UFO Club. This had a fortnightly 'happening' featuring bands like the Pink Floyd, Procol Harum and the Incredible String Band. It was a venue where the emerging alternative culture gathered and where trends in music and fashion took hold, so it was the ideal place for me to sell macrobiotic food.

In January 1967 I was offered the basement kitchen of Centre House, an early new-age centre on Airlie Gardens, just off Notting Hill Gate. What was originally a macrobiotic study centre quickly morphed into a busy restaurant. We got busier and busier until, after a particularly loud evening where Graham Bond brought his Simon and Marijke-painted Hammond organ into the restaurant and jammed until late, the residents of this quiet area successfully lobbied for our ejection. Meanwhile, I was also importing embroidered sheepskin coats from the Ghazni province of Afghanistan and putting them on sale at a boutique on King's Road called *Granny Takes a Trip*. The Beatles, who were regular customers there, bought one each and were seen out and about wearing them, sparking the worldwide craze for these garments. They wore my jackets inside out for the cover picture of *Magical Mystery Tour*. Along with hand-dyed silks by Aedan Kelly and hand-embroidered kaftans from Tunisia's finest makers, my clothing enterprises helped to set the styles that characterised the British psychedelic look. I also imported hand-woven shoulder bags and Khamba boots made by the Tibetan refugees in Dharamasala in India. My biggest venture, to import Russian army surplus uniforms, met with sympathetic consideration from the military attaché at the Russian Embassy but didn't make it past the bureaucracy back in Moscow, who responded with a firm *'nyet'*.

My heart, however, was in promoting healthy food and when an opportunity for a larger restaurant on Westbourne Grove appeared, I grabbed it. In July I formed a limited company called Yin-Yang Ltd. My brother joined me in the business and together we worked to develop the market for macrobiotics. He published *Harmony* magazine, a groundbreaking introduction to the macro-biotic philosophy and, with our mother Margaret, developed superb food in Seed, our new restaurant. Seed became an almost legendary hip – and hippy – macrobiotic watering hole, where brown rice and organic vegetables formed the backbone of the menu. Despite today's dour and ascetic image of macrobiotics, our restaurant rocked, both with progressive music and a groovy clientele drawn from the alternative scenes of music, the arts and fashion. Yoko Ono, who had studied and practised macrobiotics in Japan, was one of our earliest customers. When she later hooked up with John Lennon, their presence there, along with that of many other celebrities, made it a must visit destination.

In 1969 we decided to open Ceres Grain Shop, Britain's first natural foods shop, to deal with the strong demand for our ingredients from restaurant customers who wanted to cook macrobiotic and organic food at home. Just a year later, Gregory and I launched the Harmony Foods range of products, with the key one being Britain's first organic brown rice (whole rice as we called it), along with pre-packaged aduki beans, millet, buckwheat, three kinds of miso, tamari soya sauce, *hiziki* and *kombu* seaweeds, *umeboshi* plums, *kuzu* arrowroot, tahini sesame cream and, quirkily, patchouli oil (which was pretty much the signature scent of the era).

In 1972 we took over the former eel and pie shop next door to our Ceres Grain Shop on Portobello Road and opened Ceres Bakery, where all our products were made with organic wholegrain flours, without any sugar or white flour and where we pioneered the development of sourdough and naturally leavened breads. Gregory built up a network of organic producers who supplied the organically grown grains. He would mill the grain on our stone mill and supply it, sometimes still warm, to the bakery, where we baked bread to supply our burgeoning wholesale business which extended all over London. We had our own little mill in the bakery where we experimented with grinding peanuts and made peanut butter for sale in the shop. We launched it under the Harmony brand in 1972. Like many natural food companies on the other side of the Atlantic, we found that a yummy product like peanut butter had a wider appeal than aduki beans and millet, though it was disdained by purists as borderline macrobiotic. In 1976, after being featured on the BBC's widely watched *Nationwide* programme when we were making fresh peanut butter at the first Mind and Body Exhibition at Olympia, Harmony peanut butter was stocked by Waitrose and Safeway. This opened our brand out to a wider audience than the specialist natural food stores. We were a £3-million business and expanding in all directions.

Macrobiotics was the driving force of the natural food industry in the 1960s and 1970s and macrobiotic principles were at the heart of the evolution of the natural food diet. Macrobiotic specialties provided a unique attractor that drew regular customers to natural food stores. In 1977 I created the first fruit-juice-sweetened jams and these launched the whole 'no sugar added' category. Apple juice, however high its glucose or sucrose content might have been, was not called sugar and was therefore an acceptable sugar substitute in jams and soft drinks. It offered a guilt-free way to enjoy sweet foods, but from a strict macrobiotic point of view, they were a bit of a cheat. We felt uncomfortable marketing them under the purist Harmony brand so we launched them under another brand we had registered: Whole Earth. Now, combined with Ceres Bakery, producing organic wholemeal breads, our organisation produced all the ingredients of the classic peanut butter and jelly sandwich – natural style.

The business thrived on innovation or, at least, innovation provided the fingernails by which we held on as the business surrendered territory after territory. It was not enough to be the first with brown rice, miso, wholemeal sourdough breads, brewed soya sauces such as *shoyu* and tamari, aduki beans, natural peanut butter, no sugar added jams, organic baked beans and carbonated fruit-juice drinks. It was not enough to have led the way in adding fruit-juice concentrates in place of sugar in recipes, creating the no sugar added category. There was always someone bigger and stronger who waited until an innovative line got big enough, then did whatever it took to capture the market. Whitworths and Tilda captured the brown rice market, Allied Bakeries captured the wholemeal flour and bread market with their Allinsons brand, Weetabix Alpen captured the muesli market and Robertson's and the French government-subsidised St Dalfour captured the no added sugar jam markets.

Nonetheless, by the late 1980s Whole Earth peanut butter had become a multi-million-pound brand. It had a respectable 20% of the branded peanut-butter market, second to Nestlé's Sun-Pat. Then, in 1989, perhaps inevitably, Nestlé launched Wholenut. The label artwork had the earthy feel of Whole Earth, the name sounded similar to Whole Earth and the nuts were unblanched, just like Whole Earth's. Nestlé launched a £5 million advertising campaign, determined to kick Whole Earth out of the category and capture the healthy part of the market for itself. When we visited supermarket buyers you could sense their sympathetic concern for our future – they had seen the storyboards for Nestlé's TV campaign and knew that our days on their shelves were numbered. It was like being a spectator at your own funeral. At Whole Earth I fought back with a £20,000 spend on tube cards on the London Underground and we managed to keep our supermarket listings. We had some help from Nestlé. Their Sun-Pat Wholenut had been developed and launched too quickly, it was claggy for some reason and tasted slightly rancid because the nuts had spent too much time in storage before being ground. Wholenut wasn't finally withdrawn from the market until 1994, but the shock of its launch in 1989 convinced us at Whole Earth that we needed to strengthen our position.

In 1988 the first organic peanuts had become available and we had already launched the first organic peanut butter. We rushed to capture this niche. With Nestlé, KP, Skippy and their big budgets all crowding into the sector, any corner they were less likely to venture into offered some hope of survival. Tesco stocked Whole Earth organic peanut butter in 1990 and it sold surprisingly well, merchandised on the main shelves alongside the other peanut butters, long before they created a separate section for organic foods. Organic peanut butter was our back-up niche survival strategy while we waited for the Sun-Pat Wholenut story to play out.

Then, in 1990, a shipment of our organic peanuts failed its testing for aflatoxin, a mould residue. This was unacceptable and the peanuts had to be rejected. It took seven weeks for a replacement container from Paraguay to arrive. The resulting out of stock situation tested Tesco's patience – they were wasting shelf space on a product Whole Earth were unable to supply. We got the boot. Undaunted, we started looking for a more reliable peanut supplier – our organic peanut butter exports to Germany and Holland were still growing and we needed nuts. This quest led nowhere until, in February 1991, Lisbeth Damsgaard, who owned Urtekram, our Danish peanut butter distributor, told me about a French aid project in Togo, West Africa, where an agronomist, André Deberdt, had been working with Ewé tribespeople in the highlands of southwest Togo to grow certified organic (by Nature et Progrès – France's counterpart to the Soil Association) pineapple, mango, guava, oil palm, peanuts and cacao. The tropical fruits were the project's main success. They were dried in solar driers (adding value at source) then shipped to Europe where they were sold to manufacturers of organic mueslis and snack bars. I contacted André and asked him to send me a sample of peanuts. Regrettably they tested at unacceptable levels of aflatoxin and I called Deberdt to tell him that they could not be used. There was no solution – this was an endemic problem with peanuts from that region.

He mentioned that the farmers also grew cocoa and offered to send a sample of chocolate made by a French laboratory that specialised in micro-scale manufacture. Remembering a bar of Lindt chocolate with 70% cocoa solids I'd tasted in Spain two years previously, I asked him to send over a sample. It was completely delicious, even more so than I had remembered. I had to restrain myself from eating the whole bar because I wanted Jo to taste it when she got home. I could see how it could be an exciting new product, but I wasn't sure how it would fit into our Whole Earth Range. In 1987 we'd had a huge party at the Groucho Club to celebrate Yin-Yang/Whole Earth's twentieth year, and our advertising and letterheads proudly boasted 'Twenty years of no added sugar'. It was not going to be easy to break what was at that point a twenty-four-year record, just for one product.

70% – the Magic Number

Craig: In October 1988, at the airport on the way home from Bio-Cultura, Spain's organic trade show in Madrid, I stumbled across a bar of Lindt 70% chocolate. Gregory was a fan of Bendick's Sporting and Military chocolate, the highest cocoa solids chocolate you could get in Britain at that time (around 50%). It was his one concession to sugar in his diet. So I bought him a bar and then, on an impulse, bought another for myself. And opened it. And ate it. I didn't eat sweets or chocolate, but this was a revelation – the low sugar content balanced the bitterness of the cocoa beans and made for a very pleasant and (almost) guilt-free experience.

Its deliciousness stuck in my memory. So, a few months later, when in Zurich for an IFOAM (International Federation of Organic Agriculture Movements) conference, I sought out the Lindt product in various chocolate shops (it's a Swiss brand), including the massive chocolate shop at the airport. I drew a blank – and there was no equivalent high-solids product in any other brand. It seemed that Lindt's 70% recipe was for sale only in Spain, where people are closest to the unsweetened cocoa tradition of the Americas. I had kept the wrapper, and was prompted to write to Lindt & Sprungli and say how much I'd enjoyed the chocolate and to ask (beg?) them to tell me where or how I could obtain it in the United Kingdom. Failing that, could I buy it by the case by mail order? I mentioned that there were plenty of people like myself who avoided sweet things in general – but would be drawn into the chocolate market if they offered a 70% solids product in Britain.

Fortunately the consumer relations people at Lindt were too busy to respond to what they probably saw as a rather eccentric request. It's the old story: when you ask for something you can't find you're told there's no demand for it. It was not until 1995, four years after the launch of Green & Black's, that Lindt finally reacted to my helpful suggestion of seven years earlier. They jumped right in and launched a 70% solids Excellence bar in Tesco, then rolled it out to the other supermarkets. Lindt was quickly established as our main competitor. Fortunately the premium end of the chocolate market was growing so quickly that even though they took sales away from us, we still had a job on our hands to keep up with surging demand for Green & Black's.

2

Jo's Story

I was much too young to be a hippy, to my great regret, but I did flirt with the style, spending the summer of 1967 (aged eleven) walking barefoot with flowers in my hair in our back garden in suburban Bromley. No, my route into ethical living and organic food was long and circuitous, but it probably began in 1971, when I started putting bricks in loo cisterns.

A borrowed, dog-eared, long since lost book called something along the lines of *The Consumer's Guide to Saving the Planet* sowed the seeds of eco-consciousness. It was 1971, the year that Friends of the Earth was founded, and green consciousness was spreading its branches from its 1960s hippy roots. The book instantly inspired me (then a fifteen-year-old schoolgirl) to want to do my bit – recycling and re-using wherever possible. This was considerably easier said than done in darkest suburbia, where there were few planet-saving gestures I could make. I could persuade my mother to drive to the bottle bank to recycle her Mateus Rosé bottles. I could rummage through the local Oxfam to fill my wardrobe (though in the days when you could stumble upon glorious 1930s chiffon frocks in your nearest charity shop, that was no hardship). And I could save water by going around putting bricks in loo cisterns at home and at school.

Lots of loos at school meant lots of water saved, I reasoned. Alas, this piece of direct action was regarded more as vandalism than conservation. My classmates certainly didn't share my green leanings (I always did feel a misfit), and my solitary eco-gesture earned me a place on the 'punishment' chair, just outside the staff room, where I was subjected to the ritual humiliation of having to explain my 'crime' to every single teacher who entered and exited this inner sanctum. I was a bit of a regular on the punishment chair but felt extremely indignant about this particular incident, and did my best to explain myself. They weren't having any of it.

Nor were my parents. Politically, ecologically, environmentally, my parents and I couldn't have been further apart – although we got on fantastically well, considering. My father, for instance, as the science editor for ITN's *News At Ten*, was Mr High-Tech himself – reporting on each and every space mission, medical breakthrough and robotic invention to millions of viewers on a regular basis, during the heyday of the nightly TV news show. Later, he worked as a consultant for the Chemical Industries Association – ominously known as the CIA – for British Nuclear Fuels and for various drug companies. (In fact, early on in my relationship with Craig, manning the Whole Earth stand in the Soil Association's tent at the Royal Show – highlight of the agricultural calendar – I realised that, bizarrely, I could hear my father's voice in the background. I followed the familiar intonations, and discovered it came from the British Nuclear Fuels portakabin, next door to our tent, once again emphasising the chalk and organic cheese nature of our father–daughter relationship.)

And my mother? Organic she most certainly was not (if she even knew what the word signified). Her pursuit of flawless horticultural beauty meant that no greenfly or black spot on her roses was safe from her arsenal of toxic chemicals. Her obsession with pesticides and fertilisers is one reason I later became so passionate about organics. She died at fifty-five from a rare bone-marrow cancer, though I'm convinced that 'potting shed' would have been a more accurate cause of death. (Most of the chemicals my mother used have now been withdrawn.)

We lived in a sprawling, comfortable home which my mother maintained at approximately the temperature of one of the tropical houses at Kew. Unlike guests to our house now – who've been known to pile on jumpers to keep hypothermia at bay – you could have had Christmas dinner in a bikini at 149 Hayes Lane. Our lifestyle was a model of post-war excess: double cream in the coffee, double gin in the G & Ts, lavish and dressy parties, two cars in the drive and almost everything shiny bright and new. Though we lived a good 15 miles from Harrods, my mother knew the store like the back of her hand – and the name of the Harrods driver whose green delivery van was always turning up at the foot of our drive to deliver food, wine, Christmas crackers and birthday presents – anything that had taken my mother's fancy. The fridge and freezer were always crammed full and the lid would barely fit on the sweetie tin, which was constantly replenished. Unsurprisingly, under these circumstances, my sweet tooth developed very early on: Penguin biscuits, Twixes, Kit-Kats – and plenty of bars of Cadbury's Bournville, which I always preferred to the 'glass and a half in every bar' sweetness of Dairy Milk. Our carbon footprint was probably the size of Kent.

The best thing my parents did for me, though, was send me to a good school. Actually, Bromley High School didn't really know what to do with me. I loathed it, and they in turn were exasperated by me. I had an irritating habit of paying absolutely no attention in class ('the dog ate my homework' night after night), but somehow – just – I scraped through most of my exams, and even got As in the subjects whose teachers I liked. But I was banned from my history class for spending one entire lesson on top of the stationery cupboard, as a dare, and the highlight of my day was our lunch hour levitation sessions in the cloakrooms, during which six of us pooled our collective kinetic powers and ultimately succeeded in lifting Dorcas Bird above our heads on just two fingers – just one digit at either end of her long, lean body. Fact.

But as far as I'm concerned, no child should have to go to the same school from four to sixteen; no wonder I found it stultifying. All I could think of, as I flicked through the pages of my beloved *Vogue* magazine (which I'd been buying with my pocket money since 1969), was my escape from suburbia. I fantasised about wearing the clothes, living *la dolce vita* and hanging out on yachts with playboy figures like Prince Egon von Furstenburg and Lord Lichfield. (I'm not quite sure how I reconciled the idea of speed-boats and haute couture with the greener side of my nature, but at fifteen, life is full of philosophical conflicts.) My planned exit route, however, was fairly humble: I aspired to become a secretary. (Back in 1972, that was a valid female ambition. Which tells you everything about how far women have come in just over thirty years.)

During my last term at Bromley High School for Girls though, there came a defining moment in my life. My religious knowledge teacher, Mrs Wootton, was also the school careers teacher; somehow, a discussion about the scriptures had segued into a conversation about what we all planned to do when we left school. (Shamefully – as far as my teachers were concerned – I was due to leave at sixteen, while most of my classmates were headed for Oxford or Cambridge.) Jackie Chapman was going to become a doctor. Stephanie Dodsworth wanted to teach. And I? 'I want to be a secretary,' I announced. Mrs Wootton narrowed her eyes. 'Jo Fairley,' she retorted, 'if you ever make so much as a Girl Friday, I'll eat my hat.' (A Girl Friday, for those of you who are under thirty-five was – in a nod to Robinson Crusoe's right-hand Man Friday – a general office helper, who'd run around after their boss doing errands. Girl Fridays were a legacy from Swinging London, and had as much to do with wearing a mini skirt and looking decorative in the office or sliding elegantly in and out of an E-Type Jaguar as being able to touch-type or minute a meeting.)

With that put-down, she unwittingly ignited rocket fuel under my hitherto dormant ambitions. I became fiercely determined to prove her wrong. When I was invited back a few years ago to talk to the sixth form, and later be guest of honour at the school prize giving (dearly wishing either of my parents had been around to witness this most unlikely of scenarios, and that Mrs Wootton was still alive so I could stand over her and watch her eat her bloody hat), I wasted no time retelling the story. Actually, I think her put-down was a pretty unforgivable thing to say to any teenager. And I sometimes wonder, if I'd been a less confident and rebellious fifteen-year-old, whether I'd have fallen for her doomsaying – and would have set my career sights way lower. And how differently my life might have turned out if I had.

With my new-found determination to become much, much more than a Girl Friday, I did a year's secretarial course at the Langham Secretarial College just off Park Lane. I graduated with a secretarial diploma and a prize for Pitman's shorthand (I chose a book of Rod McKuen poetry, which is pretty sad); I felt ready to become secretary to a prime minister, at the very least. Sadly they didn't seem to have a vacancy at Number 10, so I applied for the job that seemed to offer the most holidays: as a secretary in the geography department of London University, where typing papers on the geomorphology of deserts for crusty old professors on a manual typewriter, with a view out of my window of a brick wall, rapidly began to do my head in.

I did a stint working for a wonderful firm of solicitors in Knightsbridge – Brian Sandelson & Co. (I was known as Mr Treasure's Treasure'). I loved it; and was given lots of responsibility and allowed to prepare property conveyances all on my own, which would probably have freaked out the clients (an eighteen-year-old with six O Levels – including art – doing their conveyancing!), but it built my confidence hugely. (And, besides, for anyone with a window-shopping gene, Sloane Street was heaven on a stick.)

After a couple of years, a friend told me about a vacancy in a fashion company in Maddox Street, in London's West End, working for a very glamorous but unlikely pair of knitwear entrepreneurs – one Cuban, one from a Greek shipping dynasty – at a time when their designs were starring on the fashion pages of every magazine I opened. I remember the excitement of our 'as featured in *Vogue*' striped chunky mohair pullovers completely selling out in one department store, despite it being the middle of the 1976 legendary heatwave. (Unlike chocolate, of course, wool doesn't melt when it gets hot.)

The glamorous bunch of young girls who worked there were invited to Tramp nightclub most evenings by our Cuban boss's coterie of stellar, fun-loving friends: everyone from Harry Nilsson to Keith Moon via George Best and Lionel Bart. I'd always been baffled when José invited his rock star mates downstairs to 'see the cashmere'; we didn't *make* cashmeres. It wasn't till years later that I discovered the answer from a former work colleague: what José was selling began with a 'c' but it most definitely was *not* knitwear. I doubled as secretary, house model (I'm only five foot five but, luckily, platform soles were in fashion) and helped out our PR, Joy Goodman, running round WI with armfuls of knitwear. One day, fashion editor Jane Procter (who later went on to become editor of *Tatler*) swung by to look at the summer collection with a copy of the ad industry bible *Campaign*. I spotted the fact that a new magazine was starting up, and needed staffing from tea boy to editor, and applied to be a secretary in the fashion department. Carlton Publishing's dynamic wunderkind founder Terry Hornett spotted something my school careers mistress clearly hadn't, and redirected me to the features department of *Woman's World* – the new magazine – instead.

For three caffeine-charged weeks, it was just me and the genius features editor, Howard Robinson (later, sadly, the first person I knew who died of AIDS). After a fortnight or so, Howard handed me a press release and said, 'Write that up for me.'

I replied: 'But Howard, I can't write.'

'Don't be so f***ing wet,' was his response, 'everyone can write.'

I believed him. I put fingers to keyboard and began my first paragraph. Actually, précis had been my best subject at school: taking the salient points of information from a longer piece of writing and condensing them into something shorter and more readable. Howard taught me the importance of a catchy first line, a snappy title and keeping copy punchy enough so it held the reader's attention – all invaluable writing skills, which would one day help me craft that first, attention grabbing press release for Green & Black's. I got endless practice – and if it didn't make perfect, at least it removed the terror of committing words to paper. There was always Tipp-Ex.

Before long, Howard had flounced out and I worked under Bridget Rowe, the editor (later to edit the *News of the World*), basically as a baby word-factory turning out an article a day; everything from how to build a compost heap to a national knicker survey, for which I had to ring dozens of high-profile women (from politicians to movie stars) to ask them where they bought their lingerie; incredibly, most of them responded, and I learned not to blush while discussing thongs and push-up bras with the likes of Suzi Quatro. One of the most excruciating moments was having to stand up at a press conference and ask Yul Brynner if it was true that bald men were sexier – in front of 200 other journalists. Looking back, it was all fantastic training: it made me bold enough to ask anyone anything, and taught me not to be scared of anyone, even Bette Davis, who I was dispatched to interview at a hotel near Pinewood Studios, where the screen legend was making one of her last films. She looked like an old tortoise of about 137 to my nineteen – but still had that steely glare and gravelly voice. When I got the name of one of her films wrong, she all but slapped my wrist. She actually addressed me throughout as 'young woman.' Not much could faze me, after that.

At twenty-three, Terry called me into his office. 'I need your help.' It turned out he needed a new editor for *Look Now*, *Woman's World*'s baby-sister publication. 'What sort of person are you looking for?' I asked him. He rattled off a list of attributes: young, creative, fashion-conscious, finger on the pulse. I joked: 'What you really want, Terry, is someone just like me.' And was completely floored when he said yes, and he'd like me to start in the morning.

So I turned up, willing – but completely, quakingly terrified – on my first day as Britain's youngest-ever magazine editor. (Tina Brown, then at *Tatler*, was older than me by a couple of years.) I realised: I didn't know how to edit a magazine, and spent the first month bluffing my way through with a copy of *Publishing Terms* given to me by my father, which helped me speak the lingo. I even edited entirely by sign language for the first week, having lost my voice (I think it was psychosomatic). I found I could spot a potential cover photograph, on the light box, and after four years turning out around 7,000 words a week, I certainly knew a good story when one landed on my desk. A funny thing happened: as my first issue was put to bed and we started on the next, I realised I *did* know how to edit a magazine: it was actually a mechanical process, and once I'd mastered the vocabulary, I was free to be creative in the job.

For me, failure is never really an option. I'm someone who wears her sleeves permanently rolled up in anticipation of getting on with a job – fuelled in no small part, I'm sure, by the desire to prove wrong the many people who tried to write me off at school. And, if Nike hadn't already claimed it as their own, my personal motto would probably be 'Just Do It'. I've had my fair share of moments of blind terror, but the secret is not to let on.

After three happy years at *Look Now*, I was head-hunted by

IPC Magazines to edit *Honey*, one of the magazines I'd read in class at school when I really should have been doing Latin declensions. I hadn't forgotten about being 'green', but right then, pretty much all I could do was send the occasional conscience-salving cheque to Friends of the Earth and (by now) drive my own empties to the bottle bank. Meanwhile, like many high-flying people (I never worked less than twelve-hour days), I was spending an ever-bigger chunk of my salary cheque on therapies like aromatherapy, shiatsu and reflexology to bust the stress that came with the job.

I really didn't enjoy editing *Honey*: hated working in an anonymous high-rise, hated working in a corporate culture where we had meetings to plan the meetings we were going to have, hated the sick building syndrome which gave me six colds in the first six months. Instead of being the most senior creative person on the team, I was on the lowliest rung of management. The last six months of my editing career were spent arguing for a bigger budget for *Honey* to mount some kind of promotional campaign that would fend off an assault by the soon to be launched *Elle*. Six months of banging my head against a brick wall, pleading with my publisher to be taken seriously when I told him that this hotly anticipated launch would steal my readers. Lo and behold, 30,000 of them defected almost overnight. My publisher, Colin Reeves-Smith, called me into his office and announced he'd be cutting my budget, because my circulation had dipped (as I'd predicted it would!) 'I can't edit this magazine on a smaller budget,' I protested.

'Well, if you can't, we'll have to find someone who can,' said Colin.

'Fine, but I'm not resigning,' I told him. He offered me a year's salary to stand down, and it was all I could do not to yelp in triumph. He gave the job to an unknown called Glenda Bailey; for the *Honey* staff (a feisty lot who I'd had to work hard to bring round to my

side), it was an editor too far. After five months, it was *Honey* R.I.P.
By then, I was a free woman, and I've never had a job since.

Instead, I became a freelance journalist. Sitting on the other side
of the desk had given me an unrivalled insight into what editors
want: copy that's on time, snappy and sticks to the brief like glue,
and I was rushed off my feet with assignments within days. I still
am a freelance journalist, to this day. It suits my leaf in the wind
career approach; I believe in being flexible enough to grasp oppor-
tunities, even unlikely ones, as they appear. I still write because I
like not quite knowing what I'm going to be doing next week. I've
covered everything from Sumo wrestling to polo via Romanian
orphans, accompanying Anita Roddick through Romania.

Anita and I first met in 1990, on an assignment to Mexico and
Texas, where I was shadowing her to write an article for the *Sunday
Express* magazine. I had been entranced, as millions of us were,
by the story of how she started the Body Shop, concocting products on her kitchen table using fresh fruit and veg, while husband
Gordon was trekking the Andes on a horse, leaving their two small
daughters, Justine and Sam, in her loving care. The idea that you
could grow a global business – become a self-made millionairess
(and there weren't many of those about) – from such humble,
fresh banana-y beginnings inspired thousands of women round
the world, I'm sure, to roll up their sleeves and start a business of
their own.

Not surprisingly, I had been a bit nervous about meeting this
human dynamo, by now a global business icon. Within five minutes,
after arriving looking like a brightly coloured tumbleweed, Anita
had mislaid her passport at least four times, confessed to a paralysing
fear of flying, and laughed uproariously at her own scattiness. She
was irresistible. She nattered on about human rights, her darling
daughters, Gordon, world music, Amazonian rainforest devastation, sculpture, global politics, Italian food and 387 other topics for
eight straight hours until we landed at Houston airport, by which

time we were firm friends. We were met by a vision of devastation at the aloe plantations we'd gone to visit, which had been blackened by frost for the first time in history (an early warning of climate change, perhaps?), and throughout the trip she showed huge empathy for the farmers, whose income would be so badly affected by the damaged harvest. But after Houston, we tagged on a mad daytrip to Mexico, where she shopped for Britain: glassware, sombreros, basketwork, all of which she lugged back to the UK herself. And we never stopped laughing.

A few years later, I joined Anita on another trip – to Romania, with Sam and Justine, her daughters. We spent much of the time moved to tears by the hideous plight of the orphanage children. Body Shop revolutionised life at several of them, sending out clothing, toys and staff volunteers to transform these forgotten orphanages from indescribable squalor, to bright, light, airy and stimulating places to live. One of my lasting memories of Anita will be when we toured the local villages in a Body Shop truck with supplies of toiletries. She was raging at the injustice of a country where rural people hadn't had access to soap for fifteen years, while lobbing bottles of Blue Ice Shampoo to the back of the desperate crowd. Not for Anita the chauffeur-driven corporate limousine or the private jet. I loved how she didn't give a hoot about roughing it on a Romanian train with toilet facilities that defied description (let alone use), alongside women with live chickens poking out of their handbags. Anita, Justine and I laughed all the way to Bucharest, with our legs firmly crossed.

Anita was one of my major heroes – and ultimately became a great supporter of Green & Black's, my friend and my mentor, and someone I'll miss for evermore. She was endlessly encouraging and supportive when we first set up the company (as well as boosting sales somewhat by consuming considerable quantities of our dark chocolate).

I was enjoying my writing career; it's wonderfully creative – and exciting. Other assignments saw me flying to Kenya for lunch with anthropologist Richard Leakey and back the same afternoon (please, Planet Earth, forgive me; nobody had heard about carbon footprints or off-setting in the mid-90s.). I've been insulted by Joan Collins and twinkled at by Tom Hanks and Pierce Brosnan, who was dressed in his James Bond dinner jacket at the time. I've sat in the front row at Chanel fashion shows, I've seen champagne being made. What's not to like? (Even the Joan Collins episode gave me a story to dine out on for years.)

But I started to ask myself what – aside from entertaining readers – I was actually contributing to the world? In the late 1980s, the first tender green shoots of eco-awareness began to emerge in the mainstream – sparked mostly by the shocking burning of the Amazon rainforest, which was covered widely in the media. After the 'greed is good' spend, spend, spend 1980s, many ordinary people woke up to the pressure that we were placing on the earth's fragile resources – the forests, our water supply, oil reserves – and although it was a long, long while before anyone mentioned carbon footprints, they began to be aware of the impact they were making.

By the late 1980s, eco had even become chic. It wasn't all earth shoes and macramé your own yoghurt this time round (sorry, Craig). I'd see BMWs and VW Golfs at the bottle bank, not just 2CVs. Celebrities were taking up the green cause, extolling the virtues of organic food or recycling or campaigning against animal testing. Paul and Linda McCartney helped launch a range of washing products called Ark, for a new environmental charity. Sting and Trudie Styler were campaigning to save the rainforest. And *The Times* – who I was writing a news column for, on the women's page – asked if I'd do a weekly green column instead. I covered everything from the world's first 100% recycled bin bag (hot news back then), to New York discos combining eco-activism with urban nightlife and launches of greener cosmetics. At last, I felt, I could make a difference, inspire other people to make the small, green gestures that together could add up to big changes.

Just to make me busier than ever, magazines wanted stories about intriguing green people, too – for instance, *Not The Nine O'Clock News* comedienne (now sex psychologist) Pamela Stephenson, who founded a charity called Parents For Safe Food, which campaigned for safe, chemical-free food for families. Her crusade was to have the most toxic pesticides on the planet – the 'dirty dozen' including lindane, aldicarb, maneb, mancozeb – banned, globally. Pamela was worried about the impact these pesticides had on growers, certainly, but her real concern was that they ended up in baby food and on children's plates. A passionate organic foodie long before most people knew what organic meant, Pamela had asked if I'd write their campaign literature (I was more than happy to oblige, with some technical input from food-miles guru Professor Tim Lang). Pamela enlisted the support of her ritzy friends, from Twiggy to Olivia Harrison (George's wife) and Gael Boglione (who now owns Petersham Nurseries) to highlight specific issues, and – briefed by Tim on the technical side – I'd capture in a few hundred words their support for that particular aspect of the pro-organic campaign.

And then there was Craig . . . An old friend, a once upon a time boyfriend. We'd met in an Islington hallway some years before; I was leaving the party, just as he arrived – which always says just about sums our relationship up – and he grabbed my arm. 'I don't know who you are, but don't leave.' (How romantic is *that*?) I was focussed on my editing career, he was trying to build Whole Earth, and the timing just wasn't right. But we'd stayed in touch, via friends (I used to go kite flying with Craig's dad, Kenneth). I bumped into Craig at the Groucho Club in 1988, where we were both members, and proposed him as a story idea to *ES Magazine*, then being edited by my best friend Maggie Alderson. The accompanying photograph shows Craig looking very, very tanned in a Hawaiian shirt, sitting at his computer on the Astroturfed roof outside his office. (Not much has changed there.)

As green credentials go, they didn't get much better than Craig's. He'd been selling organic food since long, long before I was plopping bricks in school loo cisterns. In short, a kindred (earth) spirit. Second time around – after I'd interviewed him for the article – we fell in love. Actually, it wasn't instant. We were such good friends, I didn't want to spoil a good thing. Most Saturdays, I'd pick him up in my car and we'd drive to visit a mutual friend – Jane Stonehouse – in hospital, where she was recovering from a stroke. He'd invite me back to his place for a 'cup of tea' and I'd politely decline, citing urgent duties elsewhere. One day, I took my agent and friend, Kay McCauley, round to visit him in Notting Hill. When we left, she asked me if he and I had a thing going. When I said we didn't, she couldn't understand it; I was thirty-three and Kay clearly considered me on the shelf. I told her Craig and I were just good friends, whereupon she shook me by the shoulders and said, 'Jo, if you don't even CONSIDER this guy, I'm never speaking to you again.' Between that and other friends telling me that if I didn't start sleeping with him soon, they would, I got the message. I got an olive tree in a pot for his roof deck and had it delivered. He rang up to thank me and we went off to Wales for a weekend visiting rehabilitated coal mines – more romantic than it sounds.

After a year I moved out of my Fulham flat and into his maisonette above the Whole Earth offices at 269 Portobello Road. We were (still are) incredibly happy, despite on the surface having nothing in common. I can only cook with a recipe book in one hand and a wooden spoon in the other; he throws open what (to me) looks like an empty fridge and rustles up a three-course meal. I love shopping (even if I'm not buying); he'd rather go to the dentist, frankly. He likes jazz and (to me) arcane rhythm 'n' blues; I own the complete works of Carly Simon. I've rarely seen a movie where I wasn't captivated by the plot; Craig has a ten-minute rule whereby if he isn't gripped, he'll go home rather than throw wasted time after wasted money. But we had many friends in common. I got on very well with his kids, Rima and Karim, who'd first known me as their dad's friend and never seemed to feel threatened by my shift in status to lover. And since we both love to grow things, together we created a wonderful roof terrace above Portobello Road – me nurturing flowers, Craig in charge of the raised beds where he produced a staggering seasonal range of home-grown veg and fruit, from spuds to lettuces, beans, apples and kale. It was quite a sight from the Hammersmith & City Line that thundered by and, for most of the summer, we were self-sufficient.

A year or so after I moved into Portobello Road, like some truffle-snuffling pig I'd discovered my first square of what became Green & Black's on Craig's desk, lurking under some paperwork. It was all that remained of a prototype bar of velvety, dark chocolate. As a lifelong chocolate-lover (I always joke that if I went on *Mastermind*, my specialist subject would be 'The History of British Confectionery from 1956 to the Present Day'), my quest for satisfaction had lured me into *confiseries* the world over. I'd even written about chocolate, occasionally, for magazines and newspapers like the *Evening Standard*. But as this square of dark chocolate melted on my tongue, I knew my hunt for chocolate heaven was over: 70% cocoa solids (the highest percentage on the UK market was 50%, back then); real vanilla (as opposed to synthetic vanillin flavouring) and – most importantly – organic. The first in the world. As a journalist, I knew the news value in this.

There was just one problem: Whole Earth's company credo was no added sugar. Cleverly, Craig had invented all sorts of ways to sweeten foods without using sugar – in particular, using apple-juice concentrate. (Try adding apple-juice concentrate to cocoa and it'll coagulate but never harden. So that was a non-starter.) What's more, launching chocolate wasn't in the budget or the business plan. But I nagged him. And nagged him. (Possibly a risky strategy since we weren't actually married at that point.) But eventually, Craig came up with a suggestion: if I was so keen, I had to find the wherewithal to launch this chocolate myself. He'd do the all-important distribution and sales – after all, Whole Earth was perfectly set up for that, with a small sales team and all the warehousing and distribution in place. I'd have to do the marketing and PR, and – importantly – come up with the £20,000 cash for the first consignment. And there was, of course, another challenge. The chocolate needed a name. Which is how come, one rain-soaked Saturday night – when we might normally have had passion on our minds – we took to our bed with that yellow legal pad, instead. And conceived Green & Black's.

Role Models

Jo: Everyone needs heroes and role models, especially in business: they can inspire you to keep going when the going gets tough (and inevitably, there will be times when it does). I have a few, the first of whom is Martha Stewart – the world's first self-made billionaire. Yes, she went to jail for some less than savoury behaviour over shares. But mostly, she got where she is by hard graft, a sense of style, grit, determination – and perfectionism. There is nothing wrong with wanting perfection, or control freakery: it's caring about every last detail of what you do. Another of my heroes is Madonna – what a brand! – and my favourite story about her concerns a recording session, when she'd worked late into the night laying down a track for a new album. Next morning when she pitched up, the sound engineer said, 'Listen to this: I played around with it after you'd gone.' Madonna fixed him with her steeliest gaze. 'This is _not_ a democracy,' she pronounced.

I also hugely admire an artist called Beatrice Wood, who was still working as a potter right up to her death at the age of 105. (She never stopped caring about how she looked, either, slicking on signature red lipstick each morning and sliding on an armful of Navajo silver bangles.)

But my all-time hero is my late friend Anita Roddick. Her memorial service in 2007 was one of the most emotional evenings imaginable, with figureheads from some of the charities she supported – Greenpeace, Friends of the Earth, Amnesty International, with Craig and Patrick Holden representing the Soil Association – all rallying us to continue her work, under the banner 'I Am An Activist' (the phrase projected onto the huge screen in Westminster City Hall). Justine Roddick – who I shared that journey with in Romania – blubbed her way through a video tribute to her mother ('I'm known as the family cryer; I cry at _Coronation Street_,' she began), which encouraged us to pick up the phone and speak to our loved ones, as she had to Anita the day before she collapsed. (They'd clearly had a wonderful chat, which had been a huge comfort to Justine.) And then Sam – always the rebellious, riotous younger daughter – made a rousing final speech which she concluded by saying, 'People keep asking me if I'm going to step into my mother's shoes. Well, the answer is no: her shoes are MUCH too small for me. But I am going to wear her knickers – which are much bigger, and much easier to fill!' At the end of a poignant evening, how we all laughed with Sam before setting off to walk along the Embankment to the National Theatre, carrying lanterns and candles and vowing to sign up to www.iamanactivist.org the minute we got home, to continue banging the drum against injustice, poverty, sex trafficking and so many of the other causes close to Anita's heart. Anita inspired me and millions of others with her vision that it is possible to do business and do good at the same time.

Part Two

GREEN MEETS BLACK

3

A Very Short
History of Chocolate

When we bought the first consignment of 2,000 cases of Green &
Black's chocolate, what seemed most exciting about it was that it
was something new: 70% cocoa solids and organic. A UK market
dominated by sweet milk chocolate had never seen anything like
it. But, of course, the history of chocolate stretches back much
further than Penguins and Lion Bars, and it's fair to say that it
became increasingly important to us as the company grew.

Botanists still can't agree where cacao originated: some say in
the Amazon region, others in Central America, still others say both.
This quest for the botanical epicentre of cacao reflects the fact that
there are two main kinds: the Amazonian variety with large deep
purple beans and the Central American variety which is paler and
has smaller beans. The Central American variety was the mainstay
of the ancient Olmec civilisation and the Mayan civilisation that
flourished in its wake. During the Classic Period from 300–900 AD
the Maya developed a whole ritual around the gods of cacao
and the use of drinks made from cacao was central to their culture.
The Aztec invaders who conquered Mexico adopted this cacao
culture and established an imperial trading relationship with the
Maya, whose empire had been built primarily on trade.

Cocoa beans were used as currency – one of the few instances of money truly growing on trees – they performed the function of capital, in much the same way as cattle were once used in Europe. The beans are still used as small change in village markets, when coins aren't to hand. Archaeologists suggest that Lubaantun, in the heart of the cacao-growing area of Belize, may once have been a ceremonial centre, perhaps the Bank of the Maya, where cacao was traded. Small terracotta cocoa pods have been found there. Just as a dollar bill or a sovereign was once redeemable for a certain quantity of gold or silver, these terracotta cocoa pods may have been redeemable for a specific amount of cocoa beans.

The diet of the Central American civilisations was based on the 'three sisters': maize, beans and pumpkins. Meat was infrequent, alcohol was rare and dairy products nonexistent. Cacao supplied stimulation and protective nutrients and was therefore highly prized as an essential component of the diet.

In the wild cacao trees grow to a height of 10–20 metres, which means they live in the middle storey of the rainforest, a very difficult niche to fill. The tree gets by with a lot less sunlight than most plants, and exhibits a frugality and intelligence of function that enables it to live and reproduce in extremely deprived conditions. It tends to do best on hillsides, where glancing light increases the otherwise sparse availability of sunshine. That's why it's so successful in the Maya Mountains and the upper Amazon, where mountain slopes allow light to cut through the canopy at an angle. In the wild it is often found in stands, when it manages to colonise an area.

The cacao tree actually flowers on its main trunk and leading branches – which is always a surprise to people, who seem to expect pods to hang like apples or pears. The flowers are pollinated by midges which breed on the rotting debris of the forest floor. The pollinated flower forms a pod, or 'cherelle', which grows directly out of the trunk or branch. It is as hard as wood and contains thirty or so seeds surrounded by a sweet, juicy, milky pulp. As the pod ripens the seeds begin to germinate, still inside. Enzymes in the seeds convert the stored nutrients in each seed into simple food to nourish the growing plant. When the shoots and roots are a few millimetres long the pod falls to the ground and rolls away from the parent tree. The pod then forms a protective barrier over the thirty or so seedlings, like a shield. Eventually the shoots lift the pod up and it falls over and off, but by then the seedlings have got a good start. If they are all successful they gradually merge into one unified, multi-trunked tree. So the extraordinary cacao tree has evolved in a way that is extremely rare in nature.

In domesticating cacao, the Maya made few changes to the wild tree. Mayan legend states that it was matriarchal horticulturalists, the grandmothers, who domesticated, bred and created many of the world's most commercially important plants. These gifts of the Maya to the rest of us include maize, amaranth, pumpkins, kidney beans, avocados, papaya, guava, chilli peppers, chicle (chewing gum), vanilla, tobacco and dahlias, so it is perhaps not surprising that they could effect precise changes in developing the *criollo* cacao tree. *Criollo* simply means local in Spanish. The cultivated tree differs from the wild one in three main ways: its pod is softer and easier to open with a stone or a knife, the tree grows to a limited height, 3–5 metres as opposed to 10–20 metres, making pruning and harvesting easier; the seeds, which are creamy coloured in wild cacao, are more purple in colour. This reflects a greatly increased content of healthy flavonoids and other phenolic compounds.

The Maya cultivated cacao in forest gardens in which every tree had a function. As a result, the trees that offered shade for the cacao also provided thatching and building material, fodder, oil seeds, wood, medicines, fruit and allspice. Careful management of the shade ensured that the cultivated cacao didn't grow too quickly but thrived in a healthy and controlled environment that closely replicated the natural wild environment of the tree.

When Europeans established cacao plantations in the 1800s they were not interested in the economic value of shade trees, but still ensured there was sufficient shade to prevent diseases and maintain fertility. By the 1960s pesticides had been developed that enabled growers to bypass nature's constraints and allowed the increased use of chemical fertilisers.

Nowadays cacao plantations are laid out on three basic patterns. The oldest are in Belize and were planted on the whole pod basis. The farmer would simply prepare a space in the forest and then plant a germinating mature pod. Once the tree had emerged he would allow all the seedlings to grow up together and then prune them selectively to maximise yield. Yields are low at about 400 kilos per hectare, but this is enhanced by high yields from other forest products – making for true biodiversity.

Another system grew up in the last century and is plantation-based. The cacao was planted in rows 5 metres apart, and the trees were grown from individual seeds. This leaves sufficient space between the trees to allow for tall shade trees to be grown, which are then managed to provide the perfect level of light. Yields are about 500 kilos per hectare, with other economic benefits if farmers also plant mahogany and red cedar as the shade trees. Other valuable products that can be grown alongside include allspice, mangoes and cohune palm for thatch and timber for house building. Over a twenty-five-year period the income from hardwood can greatly exceed that from cacao and increases each year. Unfortunately, because of forest-protection laws and land-tenure uncertainties in many areas, smallholders often do not plant these high-value trees in case they are confiscated by the national government.

The most modern method is also the most intensive and is more suitable for large plantations. The trees are closely planted at 2.5 metres apart. The only shade comes from small and economically valueless shrubs and also from the top part of the cacao tree itself. Fertility comes from regular applications of nitrogen. Yields are

around 800 kilos per hectare, double the least intensive forest system of cacao-growing. But there is no other income from the land. Disease is rampant and requires constant control with expensive chemicals. The fungal diseases witches' broom, monilia and black pod are common and devastating and becoming more virulent. One quarter of Brazil's cacao-producing capacity was wiped out when they adopted this method because the sprays could not keep up with the rapid spread of disease from this over-intensification.

More than most processed foods, the quality of a good bar of chocolate depends heavily on the careful harvesting, fermentation and drying of the cocoa beans. If this part of the process isn't done properly, it can be covered up with flavourings or with increased roasting times and temperatures, but it will always lead to a compromise on quality, so everything depends on the farmers who grow and process the cacao after harvest.

The pod takes five to six months to ripen and must be picked before the seeds have germinated – but as close as possible to this point. It's a real art. When you're a grower in 90-degree heat several miles from home there is a temptation to pick pods that are underripe, to save having to go back a few days later. Getting the moment of harvest right makes all the difference to every subsequent step of making a bar of chocolate.

Once the pods are harvested they begin to germinate, which triggers the release of those fabulous enzymes that later help develop greater depth of flavour. This is followed by the all-important fermentation process. The germinating beans, in their sweet-sour pulp, are packed up and left to ferment for five or six days. On plantations the beans are put into large tanks, but in smallholdings they are packed into small boxes or piled on banana leaves and then covered with more leaves. The farmer will occasionally test the temperature in the heap and move the beans round to ensure that it never gets too hot. This process is vital to drawing out the complex flavours which make really good chocolate so exquisitely seductive.

Chocolate Tasting Technique

1. Sniff the chocolate for a preview of its flavour.
2. Pinch your nose to cut off the aroma so you just experience taste and texture.
3. Place the chocolate in your mouth. Let it rest there for a few seconds to taste the base notes of bitterness, sweetness, acidity and astringency. Acidity is a by-product of fermentation, but too much is a sign of rushed fermentation. Astringency is also a sign that fermentation was too hurried and the enzymes that turn simple phenolic compounds into more mellow-tasting complex ones didn't have enough time to do their work.
4. Stop pinching your nose and note the aromas that unfold.
5. Spread the chocolate around your mouth by chewing it five or so times. This releases the secondary flavours and aromas.
6. Gently press it against the roof of your mouth for a few moments to get it up on your palate, where your nose takes over from the inside. The smell goes up your retro-nasal passage, reaching the same odorant receptors that have already enjoyed the sniff earlier.
7. Now let it melt slowly and feel the texture – which should be totally smooth, with no grainy bits.

Try to capture as many flavours as you can – it helps to associate them with flavours you've already experienced, and it can help to write them down: raspberry, red wine, toffee, coffee – and so it goes on. With so many different flavours in a single piece of chocolate, it's no wonder different people pick up on different flavours, recognising some while missing out on others. The same thing happens with wine tastings – the human brain has its limitations!

The next stage is to dry the seeds. The enzymes are still actively developing the flavour of the cocoa, which is why drying should not be rushed. In big plantations they dry the beans in ovens, whereas small farmers lay them out in the sun. The beans are dried until they have only about 8% moisture left. It's easy to tell when the moisture is at that magic level: you hold a bean between your thumb and index finger next to your ear and squeeze it. It gives a little snapping sound when it's dry enough.

The quality of the cocoa beans has a direct impact on the next stage: roasting. The better the beans, the shorter the roasting time and the lower the roasting temperatures can be. The advantage of good fermentation and drying is that all the roaster has to do is to tease out and develop the good flavours inherent in the beans rather than roasting them to drive bad flavours out.

Once the beans are roasted they are ground down to a small particle size, so tiny that you can't feel any grit on your tongue. Then sugar is added – anywhere from 15–50% of the quantity of cocoa solids (or even more) and the mixture is conched for several hours or until it's ready. A conch is a machine like a dough mixer that moves the liquid chocolate around, developing its texture. Sometimes this can take half a day or longer. As it's turned, every tiny particle of chocolate becomes wrapped in its own film of cocoa butter. This liquid chocolate is then poured into the moulds that give a chocolate bar its characteristic shape. If you want to make drinking cocoa, you add no sugar to the pure ground cacao and instead of conching you squeeze it under a hydraulic press that drives out the liquefied cocoa butter and leaves behind the solid material as 'cake.' This is the cocoa powder that is used in drinking chocolate – but actually, it still contains at least 12% cocoa butter.

In Mexico, hot chocolate made with water, cocoa, sugar, spices and corn meal is always drunk on the Day of the Dead, when souls return from another world, temporarily reborn into this one. It coincides with our own Halloween. There are many present-day cultural associations of cocoa with fertility and regeneration. Hot chocolate is a symbol of human blood, much like wine in Christianity. In the bad old days of human sacrifice, the Aztec priests would wash the blood off the sacrificial obsidian knives with hot chocolate and give the resulting drink to those waiting to be sacrificed to calm their nerves.

When the Spanish, led by Hernando Cortes, conquered Mexico, they found that cocoa was central to trade and to the culture of the Aztecs. The emperor Montezuma was alleged to consume little besides an unsweetened chocolate drink based on cocoa, maize and spices, including chillies. The chocolate was made frothy by pouring it from one cup to another. The Spanish in Mexico adopted this custom and it was particularly popular among Spanish women, who drank chocolate warm and sweetened – instead of with chillies – and frothed to a foam with a little wooden tool called a *molinillo*. From Spain chocolate was sold to other European countries, supplied in the form of little unsweetened tablets of ground cocoa, similar to the rations carried by Aztec warriors. The tablets were cooked with hot water and sugar.

The Portuguese were the first to grow cacao outside the Americas when they began to cultivate it in Sao Tomé, an island off the coast of the Congo, which soon became Europe's major source of cocoa. In Victorian Britain drinking cocoa was seen as a healthy and temperate alternative to alcohol, particularly gin, which was wreaking havoc among the population. Quaker companies such as Rowntree, Cadbury's and Fry were kings of the cocoa market and were the forerunners of today's social purpose businesses. However, the virtual slave-labour conditions in Sao Tomé alarmed these companies and in the early 1900s William Cadbury set about establishing new plantations in Ghana and by 1908 Cadbury's and other British companies had stopped importing from Sao Tomé.

The first modern cocoa powder was made in Holland by Conrad van Houten in 1828. He patented a hydraulic press to squeeze the cocoa butter out of ground cocoa beans and also developed the process of 'Dutching' – the use of sodium bicarbonate to alkalise the cocoa and develop its taste and solubility. Because this cocoa powder was much less oily it was more suitable for preparation with milk. Then came Joseph Fry's breakthrough in 1849: he cleverly made the very first moulded chocolate bar. In 1868 a Swiss chemist, Henri Nestlé, developed a process for making powdered dried milk. A decade later – in 1879 – another Swiss, Daniel Peter, added powdered milk to chocolate to make the first milk-chocolate bar. But chocolate was still rough-textured and it was Rudolphe Lindt, in Switzerland, who came up with the conching method that makes it smooth and delectably palatable. Extraordinarily, there have been few other technical developments since that pioneering time and a chocolate factory today operates on much the same basis as it did a hundred years ago.

The English developed a different way of making milk chocolate to the Continentals. This involves cooking fresh liquid milk with cocoa mass and sugar to make a toffee-like crumb, and then drying it by evaporation. The crumb is then used as the base for making the characteristic British chocolate – of which Dairy Milk is the most celebrated example. This produces a more munchable chocolate, with a thicker texture. Continental chocolate, by contrast, tends to melt in the mouth. Munchable chocolate clearly struck a chord with the British public and the twentieth century saw bar after bar of chocolate confectionery launched on an increasingly chocolate-crazy market.

By the late 1970s, 2.5 million tonnes of cocoa beans were being turned into chocolate annually, with per capita consumption in Europe at nearly 2 kilos per head, America at 1.2 kilos per head, and the rest of the world at much lower levels. This booming demand was met by growers in West Africa, Malaysia, Brazil and other countries in South and Central America. By far the most important international supplier was the Ivory Coast, who supplied half the world's cocoa. In 1977, the price shot up to $5,000 a tonne, its highest-ever level, as demand raced ahead of supply and speculators piled on the agony. The response of America, Britain, Holland, Germany and Switzerland was to fund massive aid programmes recommending methods of intense farming that would create a global overcapacity in cocoa. These methods, however, also triggered high levels of fungal infections such as witches' broom, monilia and black pod, which were controlled by costly chemicals such as DDT, dieldrin, lindane and other organochlorine pesticides. These would be sprayed on the cacao trees by farm workers – often women: being petite, they fitted under the trees easily, so they could spray up into the leaf canopy, using backpack sprays. Protective clothing wasn't supplied in many cases and, even when it was, would you slip into a rubber suit and headgear when the temperature was nudging 90 degrees?

Lindane has been linked with breast cancer, with tiny traces detectable in some chocolate bars on sale; it also evaporates in humid tropical conditions, travels into the upper atmosphere and has been found in polar bears a long, long way from the rainforest, having presumably fallen in snow or rain in polar regions. It has been long since banned in Europe. Dichlorvos, a commonly used organophosphate pesticide in cacao producing areas, has been found to be particularly toxic to children who are more sensitive to chemicals which affect cell division. Like most other chemicals, it kills more than its target pests and is highly toxic to birds, honey bees and fish.

In cacao-growing areas, where pesticides are frequently used, skin conditions and lung diseases are commonplace. In addition, at one point on some plantations the rate of birth defects was so high that in extreme cases plantation owners would insist female workers be sterilised before they were offered jobs, or would only employ women past childbearing age, to avoid any risk of a legal case if too many babies were born with abnormalities. Even where these chemicals have been phased out, traces remained in the soil. Of all food crops grown, more pesticides are used on cocoa than any other. Only cotton is dosed with higher levels of pesticides; of course, we don't put cotton in our mouths. (The environmental impact of non-organic cotton – which is nowadays frequently grown from genetically modified seed – is still horrendous.)

Massive global demand for chocolate was having a devastating effect on the environment, and on the farmers who grew the cacao. By 1991, the industry was ready for a shake-up – and our 70% cocoa solids, organic chocolate bar could be just the thing to do it. It tasted delicious, it didn't hurt the environment, it didn't hurt the producers and it didn't have any pesticide residues.

Healthy Chocolate?

Chocolate is choc-full of feel-good chemicals, and healthy ones too:

Polyphenols – these are the antioxidants found in red wine, green tea, grape seed and bilberries, and are also present in chocolate. A single 20g bar of dark chocolate contains 400mg of polyphenols, the minimum daily requirement.

Anandamide – this substance locks onto the cannabinoid receptors – the same ones that respond to cannabis. It won't make you high, though, as it stimulates the receptors differently. Instead of inducing the short-term forgetfulness and 'cool' of cannabis it induces increased short-term memory and warm sentimentality.

Phenethylamine – this is the substance found in elevated levels in the brains of people who are in love. The association of chocolate with Valentine's Day and romance has sound chemical foundations.

Methylxanthines – cocoa's theobromine and theophylline are kinder stimulants than caffeine. They provide less speedy stimulation than coffee because they take time to break down into caffeine. However, eating dark chocolate just before bedtime can be a recipe for insomnia. Theobromine has a long history of medical use in lowering blood pressure – many of the heart health benefits of cocoa may come from this rather than flavonoids.

Magnesium – cocoa is the plant world's most concentrated source of dietary magnesium. Falling magnesium levels create the symptoms of premenstrual tension, hence the premenstrual craving many women feel for chocolate. Magnesium helps keep bones strong and blood vessels relaxed.

Copper – an important co-factor in preventing anaemia and in ensuring that iron makes effective haemoglobin. The Mayan view of hot chocolate as blood is more than a metaphor – it has chemical foundations.

Cocoa butter – the perfect emollient for the skin, far better than the petroleum jelly substituted for it in cheap body-care products. It melts at precisely human body temperature. That's why people love the mouthfeel of chocolate. As the cocoa butter melts, it acts as a heat exchanger on the palate, cooling the tongue as it goes from a solid to a liquid state. Cocoa butter stays liquid at normal body temperature, thereby avoiding the blocking of arteries and cholesterol imbalances that hydrogenated fats can cause.

4

The First Bar

By August 1991 we were all ready to go. We had our bar. We had our name. And then we swiftly discovered that the fastest way to trigger a heatwave is to buy 2 tonnes of something that melts at approximately 23 degrees Centigrade. Almost immediately, we had to put the chocolate into controlled-temperature storage, and wait until the thermometer dropped before we could start any kind of sales drive. Luckily, Craig took it all in his stride and kept us both calm during this nerve-wracking time. 'Welcome to the world of business,' he said, with a smile.

Even before we had finished designing the packaging for the bar, we'd shown the chocolate to some wholesalers in the health food trade. Not all of them were ready for a product like this. Back in 1973, Whole Earth had helped form a group of pioneering natural food shops and wholesalers called the Natural Foods Union and one of their points of difference from the existing health food shops was that they focussed on whole foods and didn't sell anything containing sugar – not even brown sugar. So some of the largest and most important wholesalers, such as Community Foods, simply said 'No'. They wouldn't change their no sugar policy just for Green & Black's. Whole Earth Foods already had an arrangement with Community that they would be master wholesalers of the Whole Earth range, covering smaller wholesalers and consolidating shipments for export customers for whom it was just too fiddly

If You Don't Do It . . .

Jo: Starting any new venture is a leap of faith. It needs courage and daring. What gave me the nudge to part with £20,000 – a fortune! – of savings was the memory of a postcard I'd bought on Carnaby Street, twenty years before, when I was about fourteen, of a man poised at the edge of a diving board. 'If you don't do it, you'll always wonder what would have happened if you had done it,' the motto read. For years, until I lost it in an office move, I'd kept it pinned above my desk for inspiration, and it had always pushed me to be a little bit braver than my normal, cautious self. I like to put sayings and images that will inspire me up on the wall facing me, and look at them regularly during the working day. (Pre-Palm Pilots, I'd also write them down in my Filofax.) When times are tough, those few words can give you the drive to continue, or restore your faith, or even inspire you to take the plunge – off that diving board – in the first place.

to deal with a lot of separate suppliers. We reminded Community of this and pointed out that if they didn't stock Green & Black's then we'd have to go back to dealing direct with this group of customers – and this would put an end to their master distributor arrangement. On reflection, they accepted that the no sugar policy may have had its day and agreed to stock our chocolate. This made it readily accessible for all the London-area retailers who used Community Foods' cash and carry warehouse (which is conveniently located at the junction of the North Circular Road and the M1 motorway).

The retailers seemed to be excited by our new product – and we weren't really surprised. We knew they were looking for ways to spice up their offerings – and, in many cases, throw off the brown rice and lentils image the industry had (not always fairly) acquired. At that time, the only 'chocolate' most health food stores sold was actually carob, a Mediterranean bean with a sweet pod and a vaguely chocolatey flavour. It had become popular in the health food market because it was caffeine free. Unfortunately, though, it was taste free too, and any true chocoholic who tries carob is in for a big disappointment.

Craig knew the health food market really well, and after all those years of substituting apple juice or malt extract for sugar, he instinctively knew that we had to be up front about launching a product that contained the very ingredient he had been avoiding for decades. We decided to be clear and honest. So on the back of the wrapper we printed the following statement:

PLEASE NOTE: This chocolate contains 29% brown sugar, processed without chemical refining agents. Ample evidence exists that consumption of sugar can increase the likelihood of tooth decay, obesity and obesity-related health problems. If you enjoy good chocolate, make sure you keep your sugar intake as low as possible by always choosing Green & Black's – the chocolate with the least sugar, the most cocoa solids and organic too! We have conscientiously avoided ingredients like artificial vanillin flavourings and hydrogenated fat, an artificial fat sometimes described as vegetable fat. Green & Black's chocolate gives you less sugar and no hydrogenated fat – for real value.

No other chocolate bar or product containing sugar has ever done anything like it, but we both firmly believe that this made a big difference to our target customers: we were helping them make an informed decision about whether or not to choose our chocolate.

The Whole Earth infrastructure was invaluable in getting the product off the ground, too. Whole Earth had a couple of sales people, who were already seeing buyers (mostly in the natural-food world) and could present the chocolate when updating them on Whole Earth's own launches. The chocolate itself was stored in Manchester at Duerr's, Whole Earth's peanut butter and jam manufacturers (except during heatwaves when it was rapidly whisked into cold storage), and was distributed from there. Would it have been possible to start Green & Black's from scratch, without these nuts and bolts being secured? Absolutely. But it would have been harder work and much more expensive to set up the supply chain. As newcomers, we'd have had to knock louder on wholesalers' doors or spend additional money at trade shows, to get them to sample our wares.

In reality, getting the product into shops is only half the battle. The real struggle is always in persuading consumers that they should actually eat it. Advertising is one route, but it's not cost-effective: today, a whole-page ad in a glossy Sunday supplement can cost you as much as £45,000 (and that's without any special positioning – right-hand pages are pricier, as are inside covers, with the back cover most costly of all). You have to sell a shedload of chocolate to get a decent payback, and in any case, we firmly believe that public relations is way, way more powerful than advertising. If you can persuade a third party – a journalist – to write or talk on air about your product, it is infinitely more effective than an ad. Jo's background in journalism gave her a unique insight into how public relations worked from the other side of the table, as it were, and she knew that press releases are a writer's lifeblood. A few journalists are in fact completely passive: without the avalanche of press releases crossing their desks, they wouldn't know where to start to find a story. We knew it was key to write something exciting that would capture their attention.

We wanted to get across the news element: it was the first organic chocolate in the world. It had a really high cocoa content. And above all, it was delicious – which few people would have been expecting, for something so 'worthy'. Yes, we wanted to convey the ecological message about forest clearance, and the problems of pesticide use – but essentially, we had to appeal to people's taste buds, as well as their consciences. So the very first press release read like this:

Guilt-Free Chocolate? Well, Almost . . .

Chocolate that's guilt free? Well, Green & Black's first organic chocolate comes pretty close. From a social, environmental and quality point of view, Green & Black's is great news. Unlike most contemporary chocolate production, the cocoa beans that go into this delicious 100g bar are grown without the use of fungicides, herbicides or pesticides – which are increasingly being shown to take their toll on the health of cacao plantation workers, who suffer from a wide range of agrochemically linked diseases such as lung and eye problems.

Intensive cacao farming has led to the devastation of forests so that trees can be planted close together. The trees on the virgin plantations in Togo from which our beans come are allowed to grow in the shade of other, taller forest trees, so that no forest felling is necessary for cultivation. No other chocolate, then, is so kind to the environment. Do ideologically sound products always taste delicious? In our experience, no. But Green & Black's is an extremely high-quality product whose flavour rivals that of even the most celebrated chocolate brands.

Containing 70% cocoa solids, it is blended with raw cane sugar and pure vanilla – not the artificially produced vanillin favoured by most chocolatiers. And the high percentage of cocoa solids means that Green & Black's is relatively low in sugar – about half as much as most chocolate.

Composing the release was only the first part of the marketing story. When we sent it out, we made sure it was accompanied by a bar or two of the chocolate. It's been a key part of our philosophy from day one never to skimp when it comes to giving chocolate away. We've given away so many slabs and squares over the years that we actually have a saying: 'The first bar is free!' And we certainly made sure to spread them around to all the tastemakers we could think of.

Jo had great contacts in the media and they certainly helped, but the chocolate would have been news even without them. The key was to take the time and trouble to make sure the chocolate reached its media destination. It sounds so basic, but we knew it was vital to find out names (rather than just food editor) and spell them correctly on the parcel. The package looked sexy from the word go: we used shiny brown carrier bags (no point delivering something in a crumpled envelope or manky Jiffy bag so the pleasure factor's already diminished). We had attractive folders printed with chocolate squares (not a million miles from the design for the cover of this book), and the same seal and ribbon as on our bars. We knew journalists keep nice folders for their paperwork, so there was always a chance that ours would hang around on their desk for quite some time, subtly reminding them of our existence. And – wherever it was possible – we made sure to hand deliver our precious product, thus maximising the chances of it landing on the right desk, and not being munched en route by the post room.

Emily Green, then at the *Independent*, was the first to pick up on it. We could have kissed her. 'Right On, and It Tastes Good, Too . . .', ran the headline on 22 September 1991 – our first press coverage, coinciding with the moment when we were finally, post-heatwave, able to launch Green & Black's in the natural food trade. 'Organic chocolate goes on sale throughout Britain for the first time this month,' wrote Emily. 'Green & Black's Organic Chocolate comes from plantations in Togo, West Africa, which have been kept completely free from pesticides and chemical fertilisers and are certified as organic by the French equivalent of our Soil Association, Nature et Progrès. Sceptics who might assume that any such chocolate, coming from outside established chocolate channels, would be "right on" but fairly gruesome on the palate, are in for a surprise . . .' 'A sure-fire hit with lovers of long, dark chocolate . . .' 'A powerful, military-style chocolate with a potent, almost coffee flavour . . .' And the 600-word eulogy to Green & Black's wasn't just a tastebud-tantalising rave, but looked in depth at the issues of pesticide residues in chocolate, covering such topics as plantation poisonings, birth defects and chronic illness among workers. If you'd been passing Jo's office as she read it, you'd have seen someone virtually doing small cartwheels of delight; the piece got us off to a flying start with the press.

Taste magazine followed, a day or two later: 'Question: what's green, black, organic, carries a health warning on the wrapper and tastes wonderful?' And so it went on. *The Sunday Times* covered us ('The right-on hostess can now plan the right-on pud', etc., etc.), *Today, New Woman, Elle* ('For guilt-free chocolate eating, Green & Black's Organic Dark Chocolate contains less sugar than most brands, and the cocoa is grown without chemicals. The result is a rich chocolate that satisfies any cravings.'). Pretty soon we had a small sheaf of press cuttings to our name. And it hadn't cost us a penny, if you don't count several cases of chocolate and some cab fares for deliveries. Eventually Jo even wound up in *Tatler* in a fashion feature about women with links to chocolate (with a Fry and a Cadbury or two), wearing a fetching brown hat on the top of which was perched a live rabbit!

The launch was a spectacular success, and we knew we must be on to a good thing when we very quickly started getting competitors. Competition is scary and irritating, but it can be the sincerest form of flattery. A few months after the launch of Green & Black's, for instance, Valrhona brought out a range of single estate chocolate bars, made in the same bean to bar, artisanal way as Green & Black's. We were very envious of Valrhona's incredibly clever idea for launching their product into new markets. They gave their distributors the seed money to set up a chocolate society, which would extol the virtues of high-cocoa chocolate.

To all intents and purposes, each society was independent, and would enlist the support of food writer chocophiles and chocolatiers like Chantal Coady, of the groovy King's Road chocolate boutique Rococo, to take part in tastings. But for absolutely no seed money at all, we piggy-backed on this. In order to maintain an reputation for independence, the *Chocolate Society Journal* would do tastings of other high-quality chocolate bars, so that it wasn't Valrhona, Valrhona, Valrhona. At that time, in terms of competition, there was us – and that was it. So we'd be tasted alongside Valrhona's bars and compared – favourably. And every time a food writer 'discovered' this new wave of intensely flavoured, dark chocolate – often introduced to it by the chocolate society – they'd write about Valrhona and about Green & Black's. Getting another person – be the writer, chef or enthusiast – to recommend your product is so much more powerful than writing your own puff pieces.

We were incredibly fortunate to have so many angles from which to approach publicity: the 70% story, being organic, the environmental benefits, the fact that we were taking care to look after our suppliers. We sent out a press release every four to six months. Even without a new product to unveil, we'd mail out a release to remind the press we existed, perhaps piggy-backing on a survey about chocolate someone else had done – any new peg that would ensure we kept the message fresh. (Though it's important not to do it so often that bored food writers toss your carefully crafted press pack straight in the bin. Since we always included chocolate with a release, however, that was less likely to happen.)

One angle we found incredibly useful was provided by a French author called Michel Montignac, who published a runaway bestseller in 1989 called *Dine Out and Lose Weight*. It was the first book to mention the glycemic index, which measures how quickly the carbohydrates in food are absorbed into the bloodstream. It was also the first diet book to tell people that they could eat chocolate, so long as it was dark and had 70% cocoa solids. While refined sugar scores 70 on the index, and rice and potatoes score 60, dark chocolate scores a measly 22, meaning that it makes its way into the bloodstream very slowly indeed. Why? Because in dark chocolate – and it really only applies to the 70%-plus varieties – the sugar is bound up in the cocoa and the cocoa butter – and there isn't very much of it. This, incidentally, is why many diabetics are able to enjoy small quantities of Green & Black's without upsetting their blood sugar levels.

Another angle that worked to our advantage came from the Women's Environmental Network, which was then run by a feisty, no-nonsense campaigner called Bernadette Vallely. We hadn't realised that WEN was launching its own chocolate campaign, on the back of a book by a diligent researcher called Cat Cox, entitled *Chocolate Unwrapped: The Politics of Pleasure*. (A tiny bit dry and decidedly academic by choc-book standards, but incredibly well-researched and with almost fifty pages of references to back up her claims.) At every opportunity WEN had been spreading the word about the less savoury side of chocolate production: the exploitation (especially of women), the use of chemicals, the environmental damage wreaked by large-scale cacao growing. Trouble was, women didn't really want to hear this unrelenting bad news about their favourite food group and PMT-buster, and so WEN were thrilled to bits to discover that now, they could share the less than pretty stories in *Chocolate Unwrapped*, while relaying the good news that there was now a chocolate women *could* enjoy, guiltlessly. And it was called Green & Black's. It was a no-brainer to give them as much chocolate as they wanted, which they would sample whenever they could: at green fairs, or campaigning events or eco-meetings. *Chocolate Unwrapped* proved a very useful tool, when we were talking to more serious

Charitable Connections

Jo: I have tried to support the Women's Environmental Network (WEN) in any way ever since I became aware of their campaigning on environmental issues that have a particular impact on women – from chocolate to sanitary protection, local food to nappies, cosmetics to packaging waste (theirs was the first campaign I ever encountered that encouraged shoppers to unwrap their groceries and leave a small mountain of paper and plastic at the checkout). I'm convinced of the importance of giving back. It's karma. 'Do as you would be done by' was a favourite saying of my mother's and frankly it's true in life, business and relationships generally. Can you expect good things to happen to you, if you crap on everyone else? I don't think so. So I was chuffed to bits when WEN asked me to become a 'matron' in 2006, and to speak on their behalf at various meetings, including the 2007 Tory Party Conference Climate Care Clinic. (Not surprisingly, WEN don't have 'patrons'.) I'm horrified that this feisty group of campaigners has had to suspend a lot of their valuable work due to lack of funds – which is simply a reflection of the fact that larger, noisier, more financially stable charities have lassoed the environmental agenda. (If you'd like to help them, visit www.wen.org.uk.) There are several very painless ways to boost WEN's bank balance: for instance, by shopping on-line at John Lewis, Natural Collection, Marks & Spencer or Green People via a link from their website, on which WEN will get a commission. Isn't the internet wonderful?

journalists. We didn't have to tub-thump about exploitation, or pesticide use, or people who had been displaced from their land to make way for large-scale cacao planting; we just handed them a painstakingly referenced book.

With publicity working so well, the chocolate made some inroads into the health food trade, and we were pleased and encouraged.

Repeat orders were coming in from wholesalers. A few samples were dispatched to chocolate buyers in supermarkets, but nobody really expected much of a response: organic was very, very new, and still had very much a wholefoody image; 'luxury' and 'organic' weren't words ever uttered in the same sentence. Then one afternoon, about six weeks after the launch, the Green & Black's hotline rang on Jo's desk. 'Hello, this is Sainsbury's,' said the voice. 'One of our directors has had a bar of your chocolate at a dinner party, and we'd like to submit it for the next range review.' We were so excited and – in Craig's case – baffled. 'No, no, no, it doesn't happen like that,' he said. 'You go knocking at a supermarket's door for two or three years, and eventually, you get your foot inside and get to see a buyer!'

Our MD, Alan Wills (who had come to us from Rank Hovis MacDougall and had a track record in sales), followed up, discreetly pointing out that actually, we'd already sent some chocolate to Sainsbury's, but hadn't heard a squeak. We dispatched some more samples, and got the nod: Sainsbury's was the very first supermarket to stock Green & Black's – one of the very first branded organic products (as opposed to lettuces, carrots or spuds) to go on their shelves. At that time, Sainsbury's was numero uno in the supermarket stakes – market leader. Every other supermarket wanted to *be* them, But luckily, they didn't pin us down to an exclusive contract which meant we had leverage with the other supermarkets: Safeway soon wanted to stock the chocolate, too.

It was a few years later that we found out exactly how our big break had come about: it was actually Lady Sainsbury who'd spotted the chocolate when it was served to her at a dinner party, and she'd pointed out to her husband that he really ought to stock it on Sainsbury's shelves. We count ourselves very lucky to have had such a wonderful champion – but luck only gets you so far, and the rest is pure hard graft. Or, to quote American footballer

The Benefits of Naivety

Jo: I had never been in business before Green & Black's. Other than working as a secretary, a journalist and an editor, I'd never done anything else. No Saturday jobs. No holiday jobs. So it is hardly surprising that my attitude to business was, shall we say, a little naive. There are some advantages to this naivety, though; you don't know what you're *not* meant to do. For instance, when small shops started to ring my 'batphone' (the Green & Black's line) to ask if they could stock the chocolate they'd been reading about in the press, I didn't say: 'Sorry, but it's too much trouble to take a single case of chocolate to the post office and mail it to Valvona & Crolla, in Edinburgh.' (One of the greatest delis on the planet, as it happens.) When Jean-Charles Carrarini called from Villandry, on Marylebone High Street, to ask where he could get the chocolate, I didn't tell him that I'd get back in touch when I had a wholesaler who could cover his area at some point way off in the future, which is what tends to happen. (As I know only too well, first hand, because nowadays I'm always trying to source new products for my own shop, and frequently get fobbed off with a line like that.)

No, I immediately packed two cases of dark chocolate in the boot of my car, parked on a double yellow line and delivered it myself to Jean-Charles, with an invoice for (I think) £22.46. He gave me cash. Actual money. Now, this is not something that you ever get to see, as a writer – it's all bank transfers and cheques. (And I equate being a journalist with being a butterfly catcher: you're just trying to capture an idea for long enough to pin it down on paper.) I drove home from Villandry in a complete froth of excitement and ran upstairs like a six-year-old who's just been given her first pocket money. 'I *love* business,' I announced to Craig, beaming. 'You buy something for one price, you sell it for another, and *you get to keep the money in-between.*'

Langston Coleman, 'Luck is what you have left over after you give a hundred per cent'.

By kismet (and there has been a lot of that, in Green & Black's history), Jo later got the chance to tell this story to Sir David Sainsbury himself – at Highgrove, the Prince of Wales's organic country estate in Gloucestershire, where the prince was hosting a reception for VIPs (Sting and Trudie Styler, Paul and Linda McCartney, the Marchioness of Worcester and other high-flyers) who potentially might be persuaded to support the Soil Association.

We lined up outside the ravishing sandstone Georgian house, shuffling past the muddy wellies (so neatly lined up) to take our turn shaking hands with HRH. As luck would have it, Jo was standing next to Sir David Sainsbury, who was then running the supermarket chain; they got chatting, and Jo thanked him for the fact that his shops had been first to stock our chocolate, telling him the story about that call, out of the blue, from the buyer. Jo got to Prince Charles just ahead of Sir David, did the customary neat curtsey to the prince, and – on looking at her badge – HRH lit up: 'Ah, Green & Black's – you make that marvellous chocolate.' OK, so it wasn't quite like being given a royal warrant on the spot, but if we could have wished for anyone to overhear the Prince of Wales heaping praise on our product, then the man controlling our most important supermarket outlet at that time would have been pretty near the top of the list.

Even when you have a great product, as we did, you have to work to make sure people actually taste it. We knew, with the chocolate, that tasting is believing. From the very beginning, we thought the best way to market Green & Black's was to get it into as many mouths as possible; it spoke more eloquently about its own deliciousness than we ever could in even the floweriest of press releases. One brilliant way was to take space at trade fairs, in particular BioFach in Germany and the Natural Products Expos on both coasts of America and in London. These fairs have the highest number of visitors because every key buyer and retailer converges in that location, at one time, looking for new products to introduce to their customers and keep them excited. The fairs are an excellent opportunity to get your product tasted by the people who really count.

At the beginning, Green & Black's didn't have its own budget for trade shows, so we piggy-backed on our sister brand, Whole Earth's, stand, with a little booth in the corner where we'd stand getting repetitive strain injury breaking up squares for tasting. (We didn't have a budget for exhibition staff, so that left us to man the stand for nine hours straight each day.) On one occasion, in Wiesbaden, we spent the four days surrounded by bouncing plastic tomatoes hanging on elastic: Whole Earth's German sales contact, 6 foot 8-inch Thorsten (who'd organised the stand) thought it would be fun and original to string it with hundreds of fake tomatoes to catch people's eye, with tags asking: '*Warum humpf die tomaten?*' ('Why are the tomatoes bouncing?' Answer: 'Because they're so happy to be going into Whole Earth Ketchup' of course!) But it served the purpose: people were intrigued, thought the stand was amusing, wanted to know more – and while they were there, we could sneak them a square of Green & Black's. In a sea of corn chips, ketchup and muesli, it usually went down a treat.

Anaheim. Wiesbaden. Mannheim. Frankfurt. Nuremberg. Baltimore. Harrogate. Olympia. And so on. Join Green & Black's, see . . . the inside of an exhibition hall. But it had to be done. It's where we made contacts, killing lots of birds with one stone, and – in our case – slowly starting to build overseas markets for our chocolate: Sweden, Denmark, Finland, America, Australia, New Zealand . . . It was all pretty haphazard, no big quantities, and loads of hassle (and when our venture capital came in, the number-crunchers were probably right to take a red pen and cut the list of export markets in half), but it was hugely heartening to get feedback that our chocolate potentially had a market beyond the UK's borders.

Trade shows were key to cracking the American market. The USA is so vast that from a distribution point of view, it's like a jigsaw puzzle, with no one distributor covering the whole country. We tried to focus on the most receptive territories: the East Coast (from Boston to Baltimore), the West Coast (Seattle to Los Angeles) and Colorado, which is really the hippy heartland and target market for all brands organic. Despite exhibiting at the Natural Products Shows on both coasts, we made slow, halting progress with a few hundred cases shipped here, a few hundred there. We only really got Green & Black's off the ground in the USA when we were approached by a charming couple, Ronnie and Lillian Dick, who had discovered our product at the International Food Exhibition at Earl's Court.

True WASP New Englanders, Ronnie and Lillian were based in Newport, Rhode Island. Anglophiles who had built a small business – Belgravia Imports – they travelled often to the UK sourcing British products and introducing them to the US: Village Bakery baked goods, Bottle Green drinks, Tracklements Preserves, Wendy Brandon jams (and now Burnt Sugar, the fudge people). They'd found a niche: foraging for products that appealed to their own very discerning palates, which they felt they could rave about to buyers back home. Ronnie, who used to work in the shipping world, was highly experienced in business and technically retired, but (like us) slowing down isn't really in his DNA. Belgravia was a venture that he and Lillian, his second wife, could enjoy together – and when it came to Green & Black's, it was love at first bite. They were small and so were we. They were prepared, unlike the big distributors we'd talked to, to take a few hundred cases at first and believed they could sell the chocolate at a decent quality premium, unlike other importers we'd met who said we were too pricy.

Ronnie and Lilly soon became as utterly passionate about Green & Black's as we were, which meant that if we couldn't personally see buyers at Wholefoods Market or Wild Oats in the States, or turn up for the Fancy Food Show in New York, we knew they'd be damned good ambassadors in our stead. We had faith that if we could get the chocolate on the shelf, it would sell – even at that premium price. So did Ronnie and Lillian, and it was the start of a great business relationship and a friendship that endures to this day.

In a very, very small way, some early adopters had given us a toe-hold in the US market. Katherine Tiddens – a member of Social Venture Network – was owner of a beautiful, before-its-time eco-store in New York's so-trendy SoHo, called Terra Verde and, after sampling our chocolate on a buying mission to a show in Germany, wanted to stock it in her store alongside the unbleached towels, the organic mattresses, the green paints. There was no other way to get it to her than to ship it direct, so we did, knowing that Terra Verde would be a terrific shop window for the chocolate in Manhattan, even if we wouldn't make a cent out of having it show-cased there. Soon after the launch of Maya Gold it became her bestseller. The first Christmas Katherine had it on her shelves, we got a call to say she'd just put 200 bars in Sting and Trudie's Christmas gift baskets, which they'd order from Terra Verde and send to all their friends. Cue excited squeals in the Green & Black's office (NB Craig does not squeal).

Terra Verde also helped us get Green & Black's into the store that Jo considered to be the most important in New York: Dean & DeLuca. Not so much a shop, but a deli legend. In the 1980s, on a business trip to New York, Jo had been browsing in Dean & DeLuca, marvelling at her first sight of fiddlehead ferns on their shelves. A small Italian man came up to her. 'Are you from England?' (It's really that obvious, unfortunately.) 'You look like you might know a thing or two.' Giorgio DeLuca – as he turned out to be – proceeded to pump her for advice on whether to go into a business partnership with Terence Conran, who was interested in setting up a store in London. Yes, he absolutely should, she told Giorgio, over a freshly frothed cappuccino. Perfect match: great design, great taste, great potential for co-branding. For whatever reason, though, the marriage never happened. Instead, Terence Conran's sister Priscilla set up Carluccio's with her husband Antonio, which sort of became the grocery arm of Conran's, and is now hugely successful. But Giorgio and Jo stayed in vague contact – close enough for her to drop off some Green & Black's samples, when she was in Manhattan. He liked it. But the only way to get it to him was to send Dean & DeLuca's stock to New York in the same package as Terra Verde's. So Giorgio would actually walk the half block from Prince Street to Katherine's store, to pick up his delivery of Green & Black's. But you know what? It still gives us a huge thrill to see Green & Black's on the shelf of Dean & DeLuca's (much larger) Broadway store even now. As gourmet showcases go, there's still nowhere finer to aspire to, in the whole US of A.

Trade shows cost money. Manpower. They are completely bloody knackering. (We can promise you: there is no beer in the world that will taste better than the first cold lager of the evening as you slump into your seat in the bar after you've got back to your hotel.) Sometimes, you have to drive there, death defyingly, across several countries (we have chilling memories of one drive through Luxembourg in sheeting rain, with about six-inch visibility), or upset your body clock by flying across time zones, just for the privilege of living for four days on show food (in our case, a diet of corn chips, salsa, chocolate and anything else we could scrump from our fellow exhibitors), never seeing so much as a shaft of daylight.

But we found they are worth it, every time: you get to peek at what the competition is up to. You get to make those contacts.

And certainly, we ended up bonding with some of our fellow exhibitors, forging some great 'we're all pioneering this organic thing together' relationships. A good friend we made in those days is Gary Hirshberg, founder of Stonyfield Farm yoghurt, which we got to see grow from a tiny New Hampshire farm-based company into a brand that was eventually swallowed by the French dairy giant Danone. Unlike many owners who sell out and find it impossible to work with the new owners, he has maintained Stonyfield's integrity and taught Danone a thing or two about ethical business. Which, when you sell your ethical business, is what you really hope for. (That, and possibly your first holiday in a long, long time.)

A few years ago, we were guests with Gary at Clarence House, for a Soil Association cocktail party hosted by the Prince of Wales. Afterwards, Ben and Zac Goldsmith hosted a delicious dinner up the road at Annabel's, which some of the guests went on to. As we sat tucking into Annabel's bitter-chocolate ice cream (now, there's a recipe we'd kill for), in our palace-worthy finery, Gary turned to us and smiled. 'Who'd a thunk it, eh?' And truly, when we were starting out – breaking up squares of chocolate (us) and handing out tubs of frozen yoghurt (Gary) to thousands upon thousands of potential buyers/stockists/consumers/the occasional freeloader – if you'd told us that one day, we'd be chatting about our experiences with HRH in his gorgeous drawing room, well, you could have knocked us down with one of the Prince of Wales's signature three feathers.

The Crystal Skull of the Maya

Craig: One of the realisations many entrepreneurs have in business is that the universe moves in mysterious ways. I've often wondered if Maya Gold – a cornerstone of Green & Black's success – was almost mystically brought about by my very first, slightly off the wall trip to Belize in 1987. OK, this isn't the type of thing you learn about in business school, but ask any independently minded businessperson, and he or she will almost certainly tell you there was a big dose of kismet and serendipity – and even chance and magic – in their success story. (Anita Roddick always maintained that the Body Shop was 'a series of happy accidents'.) And whether or not you believe in the power of crystal skulls, Mayan mysticism and superstition (and I'd never admit that I do!), I've always felt this is where Maya Gold really began – at the moment I first encountered cacao. So fasten your seatbelts and suspend your disbelief.

In 1987 – long before Maya Gold (or even my relationship with Jo) was a twinkle in my eye – I was invited to Belize to take part in an event called the Harmonic Convergence. It arose from a book by José Argüelles called *The Mayan Factor*, which was a detailed analysis of the extraordinary Mayan calendar. The Harmonic Convergence, so Argüelles explained, marked the end of a 468-year hell cycle: a moment when major constellations and planets were all aligned, heralding an end to endless wars and human destructiveness.

The Maya believed that our era began in 3114 BCE and that the 5125-year period since then would end on 20 December, 2012 – the dawn of a new 5125-year era of more harmonious and spiritual existence. (It's creeping up on us!) So, on 17 August 1987, the date of this Harmonic Convergence, people gathered at Glastonbury Tor, Stonehenge, Chaco Canyon, Machu Picchu, Palenque and various other sacred sites round the world to hold hands and experience the convergence – building links that would develop and strengthen over the following two and a half decades. I headed for the Maya Mountains of southern Belize, and a spiritual site – a mystical Mayan temple called Lubaantun – at the invitation of my cousin Anthony Conforti.

Anthony, a TV producer in Albuquerque, New Mexico, had hooked up with John Francis, an Apache/Lebanese financier, to go to Belize and film the Maya performing their Deer Dance on that all-important date, 17 August. Their cameraman was Malcolm Electric Warrior, a Jicorilla Apache. Now, the legendary Deer Dance captures all the stages of Mayan (and human) evolution in a four-day event that culminates in the cosmic marriage of heaven and earth – where a 100-foot-long straight tree trunk is raised up on cords and inserted into a large hole in the ground, representing the union of the male principle with the female principle. The sexual connotations were obvious, but the spiritual element, according to the Maya, was equally significant. The coming era of change is anticipated in the Deer Dance's final stages – and underlines the reality that change can go either way, and it's what you do with an opportunity that counts.

Some years earlier Anthony had befriended Anna Mitchell-Hedges, a Canadian woman who, in 1926, at the age of just seventeen, had discovered a priceless Mayan artefact: a perfect crystal skull. Anna had accompanied her adoptive father, the English adventurer and explorer, Austin Mitchell-Hedges, on one of his 'archaeological' expeditions to Belize. He was looking for the lost world of Atlantis in the Caribbean, but was also partial to a spot of grave-robbing on the side. In practice this meant he would take his motor cruiser along the coast, go up river and 'excavate' promising-looking Mayan ruins. He'd then take the booty back to England, sell or borrow against the best bits to antiquity dealers and collectors and use the funds to finance further expeditions. The League of Nations banned such 'archaeological' practices in 1927, putting a stop to this plunder, which was getting out of hand.

When Anna (along with an English noblewoman called Lady 'Mabs' Richmond-Brown) was with Austin at a dig at Lubaantun, Anna saw something glint beneath some stones. The next day she was lowered down on a rope and emerged with a crystal skull, perfect in every respect, with a separate articulated jaw. Glamorised as the 'Crystal Skull of Doom' in literature, it stayed in Anna's possession for the rest of her life – she died, aged 100, in November 2007. She told Anthony that she wanted to return the crystal skull to the Maya, subject to the condition that its safety could be assured. The

Maya also wanted it back, believing it to be one of thirteen original crystal skulls that existed from ancient times. Anthony's aim, with his film, was to raise awareness of the cultural importance of this treasure and organise support for its return. There was a legend that the crystal skull must be in its rightful place before the cosmic events of 2012.

Anthony and I hooked up in Belize City, loaded all the gear into a 4x4 and headed south down the perilous, unpaved Hummingbird Highway to Punta Gorda. This sleepy coastal town of rundown shacks and houses on stilts was the market town for the Mayan villages in the foothills of the Maya Mountains – which are about 10 to 20 miles inland – and is a Garifuna (the local tribe) fishing town. We made our HQ at Nature's Way Guest House, run by Chet Schmidt, an old hippy who had had an eerily similar life to mine: he had visited the macrobiotic Paradox Restaurant in New York's East Village in 1967, a year after me, then opened a similar place in Berkeley.

Interpreting the Deer Dance for us was Leonardo Acal, a young farmer from the village of San Pedro Columbia, just across the Columbia river from the hill on which stood Lubaantun (Falling Stones), where Anna Mitchell-Hedges had found the notorious and controversial 'Crystal Skull of Doom'. Orphaned at the age of seven, Leonardo had been adopted by the Maya elders and trained in their lore. He could recite over twenty-seven hours of oral history that he had memorised by rote. Leonardo was the last repository of Kekchi Maya tribal culture; a spiritual and sensitive man, he was also a hard-working farmer who would walk several miles to his patch of land (called a milpa) where he grew corn, beans and squash and then bring back a heavy load of produce for his family in the village.

The Deer Dance culminated on 20 August 1987, the fourth day after the Harmonic Convergence. The dancers were enlarging the hole symbolising the female Earth energy into which the cosmic pole of maleness would be inserted and then they would climb the pole to garner little prizes at the top. The celebrants were greasing the pole with a slippery lard mixture. Hanging round waiting for them to finish their preparations, I engaged in a chat with Maximo Bolon, a local farmer. I asked him if the farmers grew peanuts, because I was interested in organic peanuts for my Whole Earth peanut butter. They did. I asked him what chemical fertiliser or herbicide they used and he responded immediately: 'We don't use any chemicals on our crops – we Maya are the best farmers in the world.' He then also mentioned that they grew cocoa and offered to take me to a plantation just outside the village.

The climax of the dance was several hours away, so we set out into the bush and, as we crested a ridge, he pointed at the towering forest canopy in the valley below. 'There it is.' I looked at the trees and asked, 'Those are cacao trees?' Maximo laughed and explained that the cacao trees were below the canopy. I went down the hill and into the forest and there they were: cacao trees in an orchard through which a cool, clear stream tumbled from its source over a small series of waterfalls and meandered around moss-covered rocks. The trees had red and yellow pods, with smaller grey-green pods still to mature. I had never seen cacao before and was overwhelmed by its beauty and the beauty of the orchard in which it grew. Maximo picked a ripe pod and split it with his machete. I tasted the sweet, aromatic pulp that covers the beans, then broke a bean open and savoured the bitter and astringent taste of raw unfermented unroasted cocoa. I was hooked, but I wasn't really sure on what. Whole Earth Foods was a sugar-free company, so that evening I scribbled in my notebook a product idea: a chocolate spread, using palm oil from the local cohune palm trees, sweetened with apple-juice concentrate. I cooked up a plan where farmers could sell 'rainforest credits' for maintaining the shade of the rainforest over their plantations. I even came up with a name: Maya Maya. (It wasn't till I looked at the notebook again years later that I remembered those early chocolatey musings. It felt quite spooky, actually.)

At that time Hershey were still offering $1.75 per pound for cocoa, which translated to £1,286 per tonne. I cooked up a plan to set up something called the Rainforest Agricultural Trust, issuing 100-year bonds to cover the cost of funding rainforest plantations where mahogany and cedar trees would be planted and protected, while cocoa would generate income. Our suppliers would be the Maya Mountains Organic Farming Association. I estimated that for a $289 per tonne premium for organic cocoa, the income from every tonne would enable another 2.6 acres of rainforest to be created, planted, owned – and generate income for the village selling it.

It was a half-baked scheme but I even sketched out a logo for the MMOFA. My friend Charlotte Black, a Scottish stockbroker, researched details of some Scottish forestry schemes to help me work out the new (to me) economics of forestry. However, more urgent matters demanded my attention. My minority shareholders in Whole Earth were a Liverpool flour milling firm called Wilson King, and they had taken responsibility for making Whole Earth's jams, peanut butter and breakfast cereals. After a series of quality control disasters I decided it was time for a divorce. Demerging with Wilson King took up all my time and resources. The ideas that several years later were to become an integral part of the Green & Black's modus operandi didn't get off the ground. Perhaps it was a good thing: the time and tide weren't quite right then.

And success in business really is all about timing: the right product, at the right time, in the right place. It's a sort of harmonic convergence of its own. (Whether or not you're being helped by the cosmic forces of an ancient treasure – which I sometimes do wonder about, in my crazier moments!)

5

Maya Gold

The sales of our 70% chocolate bar had gathered momentum very rapidly: fifty-four cases in August 1991, 107 in September, 913 in October then quickly into the thousands. We got through the first shipment, ordered double the amount and planned with cautious optimism for spectacular sales growth. We had a wonderful product with no competition in its territory of high cocoa solids, organic, ethically sourced and priced under £2 for a 100g bar.

The supermarkets would wait to see how sales were going before they competed with own-label. We were in a strong position because, at that point, there were only two sources of organic, properly fermented cocoa in the world. Togo produced the best, for us, and there was also organic cocoa from Bolivia – but its flavour didn't sit well on most palates. Rapunzel in Germany used it in the chocolate they made with dried molasses in place of sugar – the molasses concealed the problems with its flavour. We had an excellent supply chain and skilled and conscientious Ewé tribespeople in the forested highlands of western Togo who were expert in growing and fermenting cocoa. Their *forastero* cocoa had a well-rounded flavour that helped establish our 70% dark chocolate as both agreeable and intense.

Nobody else could gain access to this valuable resource: the huge complexity of dealing with a remote African community and of obtaining certification for the organic crops they grew meant there was little or no chance that some more powerful company could horn in on our source of supply.

But then, in 1993 things in Togo began to turn nasty and violent. After losing the election, General Gnassingbé Eyadéma decided that, as he still controlled the army, he would not give up the presidency. Riots ensued; Eyadéma sent the troops into the middle-class suburbs of Lomé – the capital; they fired their rifles into the streets and houses. Seven thousand refugees ran for the border and crossed into Ghana. The French sent in the paras to restore order and cut off aid until Eyadéma settled down. Without aid there was no money to pay the dock workers, so they went on strike or just went home, leaving Green & Black's shipment of cocoa to languish on the docks. We were desperate for more cocoa for our next production run, so the organic beans that were awaiting shipment had to be packed in containers, airlifted out of Togo and flown to the Chocolaterie d'Aquitaine factory in Bordeaux, who contract manufactured for us and had kept a production slot open for this emergency shipment. As soon as the chocolate came off the line it was taken to Bordeaux airport and put on the first plane to Gatwick, where we had a van waiting. It just got to Sainsbury's depot in time for its 2.30 delivery slot and we avoided a delisting that, at that time, would have been a potentially fatal blow. There is no greater sin in the grocery business than to leave a customer with an empty space on their shelves where your product should be. They lose customers to their competitors when this happens and in consequence show no mercy to the incompetent supplier who failed them. We knew it was unecological to fly those beans from Africa, but if our business had collapsed, the growers wouldn't have had a market for their beans. (That's why issues of air miles – and foreign organic growers – have so many people chewing their pencils over a policy of organic sustainability.)

We were really shaken by the anxiety and expense of the experience – and it was at this point that Craig recalled the trip he'd made to Belize in 1987 when he and his cousin Anthony Comfort were making a film about the crystal skull of the Maya (see page 75). There was clearly the potential in Belize to find an alternative supplier for organic cocoa and, so, in May 1993, we contacted Diego Bol, who was headmaster at the Toledo Community College in Punta Gorda town and who came from one of the main cocoa-producing villages in the foothills of the nearby Maya Mountains. He reported that things had been going downhill for the local producers and he put us in touch with Justino Peck, the chairman of the Toledo Cacao Growers Association (TCGA). Peck confirmed that the farmers were in trouble as they were having difficulty repaying loans they had taken out in the 1980s, when agronomists from the Overseas Development Administration, USAID and the Peace Corps had encouraged them to purchase hybrid seeds, fertiliser and pesticides. In order to secure the loans, reservation land, which had previously been held in common, had to be alienated and put in individual title, then held as collateral by Belize Bank.

Owning land is not part of Mayan culture. The 250,000 acres of reservation land the farmers lived on had been given to the Maya by Queen Victoria, and a further 100,000 acres had been more recently designated as the Columbia River Forest Reserve, which according to a 1952 agreement between the Maya and the British authorities was to be left pristine and untouched. All farmland was held as public property, and in each village the *alcalde*, or mayor, who was elected by the villagers annually, would decide who farmed where. Aid workers came into this environment to encourage farmers to grow cacao, promising mega profits, but when young farmers wanted start-up loans the bank demanded collateral in the form of title deeds to the land. When they asked the *alcaldes* and the village elders for these they met with unbending resistance. Bitter disputes broke out, dividing villages and families. When the young farmers told the aid workers of their problems the USAID people said, 'Tell the old people they are fools – you'll be poor for ever if you don't own your own land.' Eventually the young farmers prevailed and they got title deeds they could deposit at the bank as security for their loans to buy seeds and chemicals.

Aid workers were able to promise mega profits because the Hershey Hummingbird plantation had committed to purchasing fermented dried cocoa beans at a price of BZ$1.75 per pound (US$1 is roughly equal to BZ$2). But then, completely unexpectedly, Hershey pulled out in 1990, leaving the farmers in the hands of middlemen buyers who progressively reduced the price they were paying from BZ$1.75 to BZ$1.25, then to BZ$0.90, then to BZ$0.70 and finally to a humiliating BZ$0.55. At this price most farmers could not afford to spend the time to harvest and process their cacao and production dropped by more than half, just as the trees were finally reaching maturity. At the same time, the bank was applying pressure for repayment of their outstanding loans and many farmers had to seek work as migrant labour, picking oranges or cutting sugar cane on plantations to the north, in order to service their debt. It was a classic example of how tribal land can be alienated from its traditional inhabitants and users and be brought into the public non-tribal market. In the nineteenth century unscrupulous American merchants sold whisky on credit to Indians, then cleared the debt by taking reservation land in place of cash, until in 1934 the US Congress legislated against the alienation of reservation land. No such protection existed in Belize.

We were keen to work with the cacao farmers in Belize, and wanted a relationship of mutual commitment like the one we had with the farmers in Togo. We had been the first company to use our packaging to describe the conditions under which our cacao was grown, to talk about the growers and their lives. Every bar of our 70% solids dark chocolate referred to the growers in the rainforest highlands of Togo. Having a chocolate bar in which they had a share by dint of the very name of the product, was our half of the commitment to work together.

Craig had been working on a flavour blend of spices and citrus that he had used in a Whole Earth product called Spicy Apple Juice which aimed to be a 'drinkable apple pie'. With a few tweaks to make the citrus aspect more punchy, the mix blended well with chocolate. What was particularly exciting was that the result was similar to the traditional Mayan *kukuh* that was prepared and drunk during the ceremonials of the Deer Dance, where cocoa, enhanced with the flavours of allspice, tzbek vanilla and limonoids from *Choisya ternata* tea combined to make a spiritual sacrament. (*Choisya* is also known to gardeners as mock orange.)

The name we came up with for this new chocolate bar was Maya Gold, reflecting the prosperity that cacao had once brought to the Maya, when cocoa beans were the medium of their trade and the main source of their trading wealth. We wanted an image for this product that would distinguish it from our bestselling 70% dark, and realised we would need something eye-catching. Craig found the perfect illustration in a book on Mayan art: a black and white picture of Tlaloc, the Toltec rain god who was the counterpart of the Mayan rain god Chac. The Toltec were a satellite culture to the Maya in the tenth century. The black and white illustration wasn't very sexy-looking, though. Certainly wasn't going to leap out at you across a crowded supermarket, beside the Twixes, the Rolos and the Cadbury's Dairy Milk. Excited by his recent purchase of Photoshop software and having scanned in the picture, Craig painstakingly began to colour in Tlaloc into the wee small hours. The detail on the drawing was so fine, he would do it night after night.

He claimed, afterwards, that it was like a meditation: while turning the raindrops blue and orange and red, he was creatively visualising the product's success.

It was worth the effort, because the resulting image was very striking and we're convinced it helped sell the idea to the Sainsbury's confectionery buyer. He was intrigued by the whole concept and agreed to stock the product on condition that Sainsbury's were our exclusive supermarket customer for a six-month period from the launch.

Taste Sensations

Craig: In our brain there are receptors that capture aroma – they're called vanilloid receptors. As soon as they've recognised a scent they produce an enzyme that dissolves it in order to clear the decks for the next one. It all happens really quickly, and a perfume 'nose' or a wine taster must have the ability to identify those scents before they disappear. However, there is stuff that slows those enzymes down and makes it harder for them to dissolve away a smell – a class of molecules called vanilloids. In flavour terms, this means your brain has a split-second longer to appreciate a flavour. This is long enough for it to recall it from previous experience and hold it in the mind. Nobody can really say when you stop savouring an aroma in its physical form and continue to enjoy it in your memory. Vanilloids include: vanillin, found naturally in vanilla beans but also in oak wood and in cocoa; eugenol, in allspice, bay leaves and cloves; zingerol, in ginger – ginger is a wonderful digestive tonic in its own right, but also improves the flavour of foods to which it is added; and capsaicin, in hot peppers and cinnamon. They all smell different, but have one thing in common: they increase the penetration and potency of other aromas by opening up and holding open our vanilloid receptors, which in turn increases our perception of both taste and flavour. That's why vanilla is almost always added to chocolate; it lengthens and expands its impact. It's also why wine is often kept in oak barrels; the vanillins from the oak lengthen its finish. Capsaicin, though, is the most stubborn of these vanilloids – it has a long molecular 'tail' so it takes longer for enzymes to dissolve it, increasing the length of taste you get from foods containing it. The Aztecs added vanilla and hot peppers to their chocolate drinks. When the Portuguese brought the first chilli peppers from the New World to India they were quickly adopted in Indian cuisine, where complex spice blends benefited from the flavour-enhancing qualities of capsaicin.

Into Maya Gold I squeezed vanilla, ginger, allspice, cloves and cinnamon, along with a variety of different citrus flavours. It produces an accessible, memorable and unique combination with a long finish to its flavour. I created this by following three related guiding principles of product development:

- better blatant than latent
- nothing succeeds like excess
- if something is worth doing, it's probably worth overdoing

The result was a chocolate-based flavour so complex that it has no predecessor in the brain's memory bank. It's a totally new aroma that requires several returns to the source of the taste in order to capture exactly what is going on. Often this can result in the consumption of quite a few bars of Maya Gold while this mnemonic reconfiguration takes its course, engaging with all the odorant receptors that remember the 400 or so different flavours in chocolate, but also with the impact of fragrant spices and fruit extracts that lengthen, deepen and expand its reach. Maya Gold is, in my proudly humble opinion as its creator, Wagnerian in the way it weaves together distinctive motifs and creates an experience that transcends memory and can only be repeated by directly experiencing it again. Sensualists may wish to go all the way: try savouring Maya Gold with a glass of tawny port while listening to the prelude to Act III of *Tristan and Isolde*, cuddled up with a loved one.

In November 1993 Craig set off to meet the TCGA in Belize, accompanied by a Soil Association inspector, Michael Michaud, who was an experienced agronomist. We offered a new deal based on this new product concept – Maya Gold. The proposed contract sought to embody mutually beneficial goals:

1. **Confidence:** A five-year rolling contract, paying BZ$1.25 per pound – after their experience of falling prices the farmers needed to be assured that there would be a minimum guaranteed price. As cacao takes five years to grow only a longer-term contract would encourage more production.

2. **Organic**: Help to gain organic certification. We had been assured that no farmers had used any pesticides or chemical fertilisers on their cacao for years – Michael would be able to confirm this and supply an inspection report to the Soil Association's Certification Committee. Although inspectors are not generally supposed to give advice, the farmers needed to understand clearly what constraints they were committing to and also be aware of the consequences of failing to comply with the Soil Association standards.

3. **Cash**: A US $20,000 cash advance so the farmer members were guaranteed spot cash instead of vouchers to be redeemed at some later date.

4. **Training**: Key co-op members would be trained in management accounting, correct fermentation and quality control to ensure the best quality cocoa. With a high cocoa solids product, the quality of the cacao is absolutely crucial; we wanted the farmers to be in with us for the long term, to steadily improve the fermentation and flavour development that is under their control.

5. **Biodiversity:** An additional 5 cents per pound premium was offered for farmers who planted mahogany, cedar, mamey apple and cohune palm as shade trees. If a farmer planted them then the shade cover essential to organic cacao production would also have economic value. After twenty years a mahogany or a red cedar would be worth a great deal of money. Growing mahogany on cacao plantations would also discourage illegal logging of these trees from the forest reserves stretching up into the Maya Mountains. Mamey apple and cohune produced fruits and nuts that encouraged birds, monkeys, gibnuts (guinea-pig-like rodents) and other forest creatures.

6. **Exclusivity**: We guaranteed that we would use no other cocoa in Maya Gold unless the TCGA were unable to supply our needs. This guarantee, with a five-year termination notice period, offered a great deal more security than the sudden arrival of a large chocolate buyer's agent offering a take-it-or-leave-it price on a day's notice.

This deal was, on paper, pretty attractive: no more expenditure on chemicals and a price that more than compensated for any possible yield reductions. But representatives of the Britain's Overseas Development Administration (ODA – now DfID) and the UN Food and Agriculture Organisation (FAO) urged the farmers at a meeting in the car park of a roadside café on the road to Big Falls *not* to go down the organic route. They had spent years teaching the Maya how to farm rice and citrus in a modern way, using fertilisers and sprays and their initial, if misplaced, fear was that going organic would mean reverting to primitive, inefficient and disease-ridden farming methods.

Nothing was further from the truth. The farmers would be relying on science, but it would be the daily application of their own scientific observation and skill rather than the products of an agrochemical company. The ODA's expert advice was that to 'go organic' would be a disaster, but we were offering the only hope of a way out of the low price/high debt dilemma that the Mayan farmers were facing. The TCGA board members unanimously agreed to sign the contract. It was a difficult judgement for them – nobody had heard of Green & Black's and they were taking a risk to invest many hours of valuable time in cultivating cacao organically.

The next step was to get organic certification. As long as the Soil Association inspector, Michael Michaud, could satisfy himself that no agrochemicals had been used in the previous two years the Soil Association could certify as organic the cacao from TCGA members, so long as certain strict criteria were met in the future. The inspection was inevitably extremely rigorous as it sought to establish compliance in the absence of previous record-keeping. However, because of their innate reluctance to spend money on chemicals and because of the poor cacao prices that had prevailed, the farmers, with few exceptions, were able to satisfy the inspector. Despite poking around in the corners of people's houses and fields, looking for empty pesticide containers or fertiliser sacks, Michael could find no evidence of any chemical use apart from one farmer who poured diesel oil into the nests of leaf-cutter ants. The nests were not on the cacao-orchard land, so that farmer's cacao was approved as well.

On 8 December 1993 the Soil Association Certification Committee granted provisional certification to the TCGA, subject to a further inspection in April 1994 to verify their compliance with various conditions that were specified – mainly to do with record-keeping. All the elements were in place: we had a product that Sainsbury's would stock; a final recipe; a label design; a brand name; a contract with the growers; and a probable green light from the Soil Association. It was all done and dusted.

But there was another element we thought could be added to the mix. Jo had stumbled across the Fairtrade Foundation while watching, of all things, Oracle – the clunky old teletext on-screen news service. (This is an illustration of how, when you're doing the right thing in business, the universe does its level best to support you.) A short news story announced this new charity: an organisation which sought to certify fair-trade claims being made by brands, so that consumers could have the reassurance of knowing that the premium they paid for products really was ending up in the producer's pocket, not just beefing up the manufacturer's profits. But as yet, so the story read, there was a catch: the Fairtrade Foundation hadn't actually got a product to certify. Because Oracle's news items appeared on screen at a snail's pace, Jo had had plenty of time to read the criteria for Fairtrade certification: a higher price should be paid to growers, who should sell their crops through a democratic cooperative. They should have the security of contracts (which would enable them to plan for the future). Products should be grown without the dirty dozen of the world's most toxic agrochemicals. The deal we were trying to set up with the Belizean farmers – our soon to be secondary supply of cocoa – ticked all these boxes effortlessly.

Coincidentally, Craig then met Mike Drury, managing director of the Fairtrade Foundation, at a press conference organised by Café Direct during which a Mexican coffee grower spoke about the benefits of fair trade. Craig told Mike about the project and said how hopeful we were that the Soil Association would approve the TCGA. As he explained the details of the contract, Mike suggested that Green & Black's might qualify for the Fairtrade Mark. As Jo had thought, we appeared to comply with all their requirements. The Fairtrade Foundation had just been through a breakdown of negotiations with Typhoo Tea to produce a Fairtrade-marked line. A higher-profile brand would have been better for the launch of the Mark, but we were willing and able – and ready – to take it to the wider world.

We didn't have to make a single change to fulfil the Fairtrade Foundation's criteria. Quite simply it was how we did business because, ethically, it felt right, but also because, at that stage in the global organic market, relationships with farmers were all-important. We didn't have the luxury of being able to go to a commodity trader to buy cocoa, so we really had to build stable, mutually beneficial relationships with the farmers who supplied our beans. It turned out that because we were paying an organic premium for our cocoa, our price was pretty much at the level that the Fairtrade Foundation had set as a fair one. We actually increased it to BZ$1.75 a pound, which was more than we'd originally agreed. This helped fund the cooperative's operating costs. But a huge benefit for farmers of fair trade is that they know the price they're getting won't plummet

Symbolic Gestures

Jo: Organic symbols and fair-trade marks are a useful short cut which tell you, at a glance, a lot of a product's virtues, but Craig and I think the French chef Alain Passard has the right idea. He has three Michelin stars and grows all the vegetables for his astonishing restaurant in a five-acre walled garden south-west of Paris. The produce is delivered fresh to his restaurant Arpège in the Rue de Varenne every day. It is grown without pesticides, herbicides or artificial fertilisers and the garden uses horses, not machines. Arpège also serves the best butter you could wish to eat, from a St Malo butter-maker called Bordier who refuses to have his produce certified as organic, insisting that it is food grown with chemicals which should be labelled; why should anyone who grows food that is naked as nature intended have to prove what *isn't* in it? Alas, while we wait for sanity to prevail in the food world (we're not holding our breath), proving that you *don't* have chemicals in your product through organic certification is a hoop companies just have to jump through, to create the paper trail that leads from the shelf back to the farm. It does mean, though, that we know the name of every single farmer who grows cacao for Green & Black's.

if the world price sinks as it has, at various points since we started buying beans. It was looking good.

At the beginning of January 1994, Mike Drury, along with Bill Yates from Oxfam, one of the main supporters of the Fairtrade Foundation, flew to Belize to see for themselves. They returned completely satisfied. Drury's words were: 'It embodies everything we were led to expect, and more.'

We were ready to rock and started to develop the final packaging, with the Soil Association and the Fairtrade Mark. If we hadn't had the Fairtrade Mark, we would still have gone ahead with Maya

Gold, but it was good to tell our story under the Fairtrade banner, particularly as it allowed us to join forces with some very influential organisations. The backing to set up the Fairtrade Foundation had come from Oxfam, Christian Aid, CAFOD (the Catholic Fund for Overseas Development), the Women's Institute, the World Development Movement and the Joseph Rowntree Foundation, a philanthropic body which seeks to alleviate poverty, here and abroad. They were all immensely excited, and when it came to finally having a Fairtrade-marked product to promote, they were like greyhounds at the starting gate.

We were confident that the Fairtrade Foundation would make a big splash about this debut Fairtrade-Marked product; it was the culmination of years of hard work and frustration on their part, as so many other potential Fairtrade-Marked products had fallen at various hurdles. One of the stumbling blocks for big companies was the fear that highlighting the fair trade relationships behind one product, was almost tantamount to saying that everything else was produced by slave labour. Not true, of course, but the same kind of thinking also for a long time deterred big brands like Heinz from launching one or two organic lines, alongside those produced by conventional agriculture. Would it be declaring: 'these other products are full of chemicals'?

We didn't have the same problems: trading fairly was a way of life for us, and we knew our story would stand up to scrutiny no matter how deep a journalist might dig. (With all ventures, though, it is way, way easier to be ethical and organic if you're starting from scratch, rather than trying to shift a corporate culture – which can be the business equivalent of trying to turn round a battleship – or convert a recipe, say, which has always been made using E numbers and hydrogenated fat. Although if Marks & Spencer can do it with the whole of a huge and complicated range, then frankly anyone can and there is absolutely no excuse for not trying.)

The Foundation organised a launch, inviting lots of key journalists:

it was a news story, as well as a food story. They even persuaded the BBC to send a film crew, to capture our Maya cacao farmers on camera. The resulting coverage was amazing. On the day of Maya Gold's launch – 9 March 1994 – the chocolate was mentioned on the BBC twice. First Michael Buerk on the evening news announced it and the Fairtrade Mark, with a huge photo of our chocolate behind his head. We switched over to BBC2 for *The Food Programme*, one of UK TV's earliest, ground-breaking foodie shows, to see Michael Barry explain the concept of fair trade, extol its virtues and nibble, on camera, a bar of Maya Gold, heaping praise upon its bittersweet spicyness. A huge picture of the bar was also projected on a screen behind his head. A few days later John Craven's *Newsround* ran a five-minute feature about the Mayan farmers, with recent footage from Belize of them harvesting cacao and their kids eating bars of Maya Gold. This made it onto the evening news, the Welsh-language BBC news and was syndicated worldwide via CNN. If we had spent a million pounds on advertising we could not have raised awareness as effectively as the campaign of which we had become the spearhead. In less than a year we had brought a product from original concept to national distribution and the whole world knew about it. It was the embodiment of a new way of doing business.

We're not saying there weren't some real skin of our teeth moments, however. Launching Maya Gold in less than three months from certification approval was as challenging as a previous effort when Whole Earth had launched Swiss-style muesli for Sainsbury's in a similar time frame – only a small, flexible company could do this sort of thing (most mainstream launches take eighteen months to two years to reach the shelves), but we were pushing right to the limit. We knew precisely when the ship carrying the cocoa beans would arrive at Le Havre and had all the paperwork ready in advance for French customs and the organic certifiers. The Chocolaterie d'Aquitaine factory in Bordeaux was ready to go and all the other ingredients were already in stock. The ship arrived a day early (perhaps the Gulf Stream was a little brisker than usual) so we improved our time margin. Every day helped.

Craig was scheduled to be at the factory as the chocolate came off the line to make sure it was as it should be. His flight was booked for the Tuesday, so he'd be there on Tuesday and Wednesday for the production. The return flight was Wednesday afternoon arriving at Gatwick in time to get the chocolate to the National Hall at Olympia, where the press would be waiting for the unveiling of Maya Gold. The launch was scheduled for 7 p.m. on the Oxfam stand at the BBC Good Food Show, for the press and celebrity preview evening, so it wouldn't be an exaggeration to say that we were cutting things fine.

On Monday Alan, then Green & Black's Managing Director, and Craig headed off to Sainsbury's to see the buyer and finalise the details for the launch, the number of stores that would be carrying the bar and what our plans were to support Maya Gold. They called a minicab from our local All Saints Road company and rattled off towards Sainsbury's HQ in Southwark. At Hyde Park Corner Craig watched in horror as the driver ploughed straight into the side of a London taxi. Alan was absorbed in his notes and hardly noticed. Fortunately, though, they were able to get to the meeting and everything seemed fine.

The next morning, however, when Craig got up to go to the airport he discovered that his neck and shoulders were frozen rigid. He was in excruciating pain, locked in a twisted shape and needed to see an osteopath, quick. There was no way he could fly off to Bordeaux in a few hours, so Alan had the ticket transferred to his name and went instead. On Wednesday evening we were all on tenterhooks – Alan's flight had landed on time at Gatwick and he had cleared customs, with a couple of suitcases full of freshly minted Maya Gold. The Oxfam stand at Olympia was crowded with representatives of all the organisations that had supported the Fairtrade Foundation as well as journalists.

We called Alan on his mobile – he was in a cab and was stuck in traffic on the M25. There was still an hour to go, so as long as the traffic eased, it would all be fine. At 6.50 his cab pulled up outside the entrance to the hall. Craig opened Alan's suitcase, removed a bar, ripped it open, sniffed it, snapped it, tasted it. It was better than we had dared hope – the samples had been made in a lab using different cocoa beans so they could only approximate what the final outcome would be. It could have gone either way, but we could hold our heads high. We left four cases (forty bars) of Maya Gold in the taxi and sent it on to BBC HQ at White City, where the crew from John Craven's *Newsround* were preparing to fly to Belize.

The rest of the suitcases were whisked to the Oxfam stand where Mike Drury and Craig made short speeches, chocolate was sampled to delighted 'Ooohs' and 'Aaahs' – though some people undoubtedly found it a bit too rich and challenging for their taste. It was the first ever Fairtrade-marked product and they were so delighted that their efforts had finally come to fruition that the unfamiliar complexity of high cocoa solids dark chocolate, combined with an overlay of spicy, citrus flavours, wasn't going to deter anyone.

Alan relaxed a bit and told us how the fragrance of Maya Gold as it came off the line had affected the production manager at Chocolaterie d'Aquitaine, who had tasted a bar and rhapsodised: 'This chocolate is amazing, the whole factory smells like a woman; the chocolate smells like a woman . . .' Then, after tasting a few squares: 'It even tastes like a woman.' Many years later, when Craig was playing around with the Maya Gold spice blend trying to create a perfume, for fun, he added in attar of rose, sandalwood, vanilla and ylang-ylang. Jo took one sniff and scuttled off immediately to a cupboard where she keeps ancient bottles of perfume, useful bits and bobs and other unthrowawayable girly stuff and came back with a bottle of Goya 'Aqua Manda' – which she said had been *the* perfume for younger women in the 1970s. It smelled orangy and spicy, and was uncannily like the Maya Gold creation. Perhaps our French colleague had been transported back to some youthful moment of passion by the aroma?

The launch was a great success, but we knew from previous experience that you have to keep the publicity going. For that, we were lucky enough to get help from unusual quarters. Because of the close relationship between Christian Aid and the Third World, Maya Gold got an enormous amount of support from churchgoers, who organised tastings at their coffee mornings, and from vicars, who gave sermons about the virtues of Maya Gold and Fairtrade, urging their congregations to go forth and multiply our sales. A fair few vicars and priests even took it upon themselves, unbidden by us, to call supermarket buyers and lobby them to stock Maya Gold. At the same time, the Young Methodists organisation were planning a run for fair trade round the UK, to raise awareness about the fact that, as shoppers, we actually have huge power to change people's lives through the products we choose to buy. They set out to run from town to town, in some cases carrying flaming torches; their destinations were supermarkets, where they'd summon the manager and lobby him to stock fair-trade products. Twenty thousand Young Methodists running with flaming torches, encouraging supermarkets to stock our product – certainly not the type of activity you can write into any marketing plan.

Christian Aid News, the quarterly newspaper that goes to 400,000 faith-based households, ran Maya Gold as the cover story, under the banner headline: 'CHOCS AWAY!' With a picture of Maya Gold and another of the Fairtrade Mark, it encouraged their Trade for Change supporters to switch to people-friendly products and ask supermarket managers to stock Maya Gold.

Maya Gold captured the imaginations of the British public, and it wasn't long after the launch that we started getting enquiries from travellers who wanted to visit the plantation. As the Prince of Wales says, when it comes to organic agriculture, seeing is believing. We had a story to tell about Maya Gold, and – at a time when shoppers were starting to reconnect with food, and where it came from – we wanted to share it. While we were on a visit to Belize for the annual Toledo Cacao Growers' Association AGM (always accompanied by a hog roast, which was an ethical dilemma for two mostly vegetarians), we met Jo Clarkson, a young Bristol-based travel agent, whose company was called TRIPS, scoping out eco-tourism possibilities in southern Belize. Chet Schmidt of Nature's Way Guest House in Punta Gorda had already told us he'd had several Green & Black's groupies staying there, who'd travelled under their own steam to visit the cacao-growing villages, partly from a sense of adventure and partly out of a deep love of chocolate. So we put our heads together with the other Jo and came up with an idea for a special Maya Gold package, which included a stay at Chet's guest house, and several nights in the mountain villages where the cacao-growing farmers lived.

As per usual, there was no budget to promote this – so we advertised it on the inside of the wrapper. The promotion worked a treat. Jo Clarkson had literally dozens of G & B's tourists organise their visits through TRIPS. For the farmers, it was a welcome extra income: the tourists got to stay in the village guest houses – generously proportioned, straw-roofed huts, with somewhat basic facilities, but comfortable enough. They got to eat with Mayan families: usually tortillas, rice and beans (the typical diet, and delicious). Sometimes, the Maya would put on a dance, or play instruments and sing.

We were particularly pleased about the dancing. Until the arrival of Green & Black's in the south of Belize, the Maya had become increasingly dependent on aid – not trade. In some cases, these aid projects were funded by Christian missionary groups, who encouraged the locals to join their church, wear the (often inappropriate) frumpy clothes that were donated by Midwesterners (polyester is not very jungle-friendly) and to embrace pious ways, abandoning their dances and native costumes. Now, we're not talking bare-breasted natives doing *ayahuasca*-fuelled stomps, here – but beautifully embroidered homespun cotton summer dresses and a little spirited jigging. As the dependence on aid receded, those cultural aspects of Mayan life began to flourish again. It's hard to say 'no' to a missionary when you don't know where your next Belizean dollar is coming from, but when a community starts to have an independent income, they can decide what to wear, what to sing and where to worship. And yes, we are pleased to have played a part in establishing that independence, which is one of the more unexpected bonuses of fair trade.

Spilling the Beans

Jo: It is a simple truth that nobody can sell a product better than the person who founded the company that makes it; you will have a passion for the frock/lipstick/chocolate bar that probably far outstrips anyone who's simply on a salary (or even commission), because you live, breathe and believe in it. Alan Wills, then Green & Black's Managing Director, duly made some appointments for me to see buyers. This is a very scary prospect for someone who flunked maths O Level, because at some point in the discussion, conversation is going to get round to margins, mark-ups, discounts and overriders. (I had come up with a way of dealing with this: I would say, 'I'm afraid I don't do sums', and Alan would whip out his calculator.) Scariest of all was the prospect of seeing Howard Robbins at Tesco. In those days, Tesco buyers then had a reputation for being incredibly tough: sales reps came out of their Cheshunt HQ wincing in pain, having had their margins ruthlessly squeezed (as it were). I was as nervous as I've ever been, dressed in my chocolate-brown Joseph trouser suit, and carrying a Moschino handbag which was – I'd found – a useful talking point with buyers: it was made of cream and brown leather, designed to look as if chocolate was dripping all over the side.

Inside my Moschino bag was a cocoa pod, carefully Sellotaped together. I had discovered something extraordinary: despite the fact they bought chocolate, day in and day out, confectionery buyers really didn't know how it grew. They didn't know that cocoa starts as a flower, a little like a fragrant orchid, which grows out of the trunk of a cacao tree. They didn't know that the flowers ultimately turn into pods, inside which are thirty or so cocoa beans. They didn't know that the beans are cocooned in a fleshy white pulp, delectably fruity in flavour, which is just about the most delicious thing you could ever taste. (Although you never will, unless you visit a cacao farmer, because the pulp is left with the beans and is eaten up by yeasts during the fermentation process.) We happened to have a dried cocoa pod from Belize, and I'd found that most buyers were fascinated to see it.

So I flourished it from my handbag, in front of the all-powerful Mr Robbins

– and promptly showered him with cocoa beans, as the pod flew open. (Later, when I told him this story, Craig roared with laughter; he had once been to see the very same Howard Robbins, who was then buying pasta sauces. Howard had unscrewed the top of the jar of Whole Earth Italiano sauce to taste it – and sauce exploded all over his suit.) As I gathered up the stray cocoa beans and tried to regain my equilibrium, Howard Robbins leaned back in his chair, put his feet on his desk like the quintessential alpha male, and posed the question: 'Now, why should I buy your chocolate? Tastes horrible, dunnit?' At that point it took all my strength not to burst into tears, or scoop up my wayward beans and flounce out going, 'I never wanted you to stock our chocolate anyway.' Instead, I took a deep, calming breath and reached further into the 'chocolate' bag, to pull out a sheaf of press cuttings. 'Actually, I think you'll find that we have scored very high marks in several magazine taste tests, including *Good Housekeeping*,' I replied, and went on to tell him about our plans to launch Maya Gold. At one point, I revealed that the magazine produced by Christian Aid for their many supporters had promised they would be featuring Maya Gold as a cover story. 'Yeah, but that's just a bunch of Christians, innit?' was his dismissive reply. And so it went on . . .

At the end of an hour like this, I collapsed into the seat of my car, ready to drive Alan back to Portobello Road. 'I feel exactly like a mouse who's been played with by a particularly vindictive cat,' I groaned. 'Yes, but we'll get an order for chocolate,' he responded. 'No *way* will we,' I said, opening and promptly consuming an entire bar of milk chocolate, to make up for the stress of the experience. 'You wait.' Alan smiled. 'He wouldn't have kept us there for an hour if he didn't intend to stock it. We'd have been out of the door in ten minutes.' A few weeks afterwards, I got a call from Howard Robbins, who'd been on the receiving end of phone calls from unexpected quarters, lobbying him to stock the chocolate. ''Ere, what's this chocolate all these vicars keep ringing me about?' he wanted to know. And we were into Tesco.

6

New Lines
and False Trails

By 1993 we had been a dark-only chocolate brand for a year. And yet in the market milk chocolate sales dominate, though today our tastes are becoming more sophisticated. In Britain, overall chocolate sales have always been about 95% milk chocolate and only 5% dark, though this is changing as more people discover the pleasure of dark. So naturally, supermarket buyers urged us to create a milk 'sister' product to our dark delight, and we felt it was a great idea, not least because some of our sweeter-toothed friends and family members found our dark – well, just too dark. Because tastes in chocolate are so very different, we didn't feel a milk bar would cannibalise our existing sales, but would bring in a whole new crowd of slightly more sweet-toothed customers. In line with the fact that our original chocolate had loads of cocoa in, though, the milk chocolate had to be more cocoa-rich than other bars out there. So we went out, bought a stack of bars, tasted them – and started squinting at the ingredients lists.

In some milk chocolate bars, not more than a tenth of the recipe is cocoa mass, the rest is milk, fat and sugar. Some, we realised, had so little cocoa they even added caramel colouring to make it look darker. So we worked with the factory in France on recipes, having managed to source a rich, organic spray-dried milk (that's the type used in chocolate), which came from cows that grazed in Alpine pastures. Sample bars arrived from Bordeaux which we'd taste together, running the gamut from 25% all the way to 40% cocoa mass and pretty soon we settled on a bar we were happy with: 34% cocoa solids (as many cocoa solids as a bar of Bournville, at that time), a smooth creaminess, and not quite as sweet as a lot of the sickly-tasting confections out there.

We had a few prototype bars at home when Jo's brother Alastair dropped by Portobello Road, with our niece and nephew Carson and Paris. As a special treat, we gave the kids a few squares of the new milk bar. They disappeared upstairs – then Carson, aged three, came downstairs and declared: 'Auntie Jo, we *need* some more of that stuff.' We actually high-fived each other. What was particularly exciting about the milk chocolate was that it provided a stepping stone to our darker flavours – for many people the actual taste of cocoa took a bit of getting used to, so our darker milk chocolate educated their taste buds gently. We were also pleased to have a product that would appeal to the growing number of organically minded parents, who were raising their children on organic baby foods (either homemade or from new brands like Baby Organix), and didn't feel comfortable weaning them on to non-organic foods. (At what point does Mum say, 'Little Johnny's old enough for his pesticides, now?')

Anyway, our milk chocolate pressed all the right buttons with milk-chocolate lovers, even though we couldn't bang the drum quite so loudly about its low sugar message. (It still has less sugar than almost any other milk chocolate, though.) Craig had a bit more of a tussle with his conscience over this launch than he had with our dark, antioxidant-rich debut product, but pleased comments from happy, organic-lifestyle-living parents helped re-assure him that he was not, in fact, the devil incarnate. And it meant that – with two products – we had the beginnings of a brand, not a one hit wonder.

The following year, 1994, we launched Maya Gold. By then, we had three classic chocolate bars under our belts, but we weren't about to leave it at that. We felt we had the expertise to create organic alternatives to all the classic flavours you might find in a super-market, newsagent or fine chocolate shop: bars with nuts, with mint, with caramel fillings or other 'bits' in. Each success spurred us on to create another potential success. There was another reason to keep introducing new lines: food-lovers like to have their taste buds tantalised by new discoveries, while remaining loyal to the classics in their store cupboard.

It really is a case of innovate or die: having created 70% Dark, Milk and Maya Gold, we had to find a way of keeping the food press excited, too (and through them, the chocolate-lover intrigued). If you don't, there's a risk that other, newer brands and exciting innovations will come along and start to nibble away at your market share, because you've dropped off the media radar and your competitors are putting fresh energies behind new launches. Dark, Milk and Maya Gold were quite established by then, and the chances are they would have kept ticking over nicely, thanks. But each time Green & Black's is mentioned in the context of a new launch, it serves as a valuable reminder when consumers next go shopping about the chocolate varieties they already know and love. And without new launches – whether chocolate, face cream or handbags – there's a risk that a brand begins to stagnate.

We knew, however, that it doesn't pay to be too clever. Have you ever seen Earl Grey, lavender, green tea or even chilli in a top ten of favourite chocolate flavours? We'd watched other upscale brands in the market bring out flavours which (to our mind) were too esoteric or downright wacky for the average palate. So we decided to do normal. Normal – but excellent normal; in other words, no weird flavours, just very good versions of products that historically had pushed lots of chocolate buttons. (As it were.)

Mind the Gap

Jo: Good business ideas fill gaps that nobody else has spotted. But these gaps don't have to be off-the-wall niches: there can be a quality gap. Being first does give a tremendous news advantage, but it's not the only opportunity. Maybe there's already a similar product in the market, but is there a way to do it better, more stylishly, and/or more deliciously, by taking something that someone is already doing and improving on it? Of course it can be disheartening to have your idea nixed, with the put-down: 'Someone's already done that.' Well, maybe they have. But if you honestly feel you can do it better, there's always room for better, especially as markets and consumers become ever more sophisticated.

Maya Gold was perhaps the exception to this rule of 'normal'. Orange-flavoured chocolate was familiar to British kids, but nobody had combined spices and a medley of citrus flavours before. Next came mint: was a dinner party ever complete without a palate-cleansing chocolate to counterbalance the richness of the complicated three course meal? (Not when Jo was growing up in darkest Bromley, certainly, where women sought to out-Cordon Bleu each other.) Developing the mint bar was a departure for us as it was the first one to have a filling, which meant it had to be made at a different factory. The dark chocolate for the mint version of G & B's was made at the same factory as our 70% bars, then shipped to Alsace, where, like many continental chocolate factories, they know a thing or two about runny fillings. We came up with a recipe that had a real hit of Moroccan spearmint, boosted with peppermint oil from wild mint collected in the Sierra Nevada of Andalucia by gypsies who would take bundles of it to Seville to be distilled to make a potent menthol. For research, we sampled lots of after-dinner mints but found they lacked punch (and were too sweet), so our specification to the factory was to turbo-charge the mintiness and avoid any sickliness by not going OTT with sugar in the filling. As we went through the tasting process and bars arrived in the post for us to sample, we realised that wishy-washy flavours simply couldn't compete with the rich intensity of our chocolate. We also noticed how important texture was, and ended up rejecting a lot of samples that dribbled down the chin as you bit into them. We finally got it right – too much sugar and the filling was hard and crystallised, too little and it dribbled. So we added a bit of honey to a harder filling and found the honey's natural enzymes helped keep it at just the right viscosity. This meant our product would exclude vegans, which was a pity as a lot of the early market for our dark chocolate came from people who avoided dairy products for dietary reasons and, because bees make honey, some of our customers would avoid it on animal welfare grounds. It was several years before we discovered that we could use wheat malt extract to achieve the same effect.

Not every new product idea made it to the shelf, though. In 1997, we were almost sidetracked by a brainwave for a women's chocolate bar – a functional food, that would tap into women's magnetic attraction for chocolate, but offer actual health benefits. One of our early US champions was Nan Fuchs, PhD – a prominent American nutritionist, who actually recommended Green & Black's 70% chocolate to her influential group of subscribers to the *Women's Health Letter*. Nan emphasised that chocolate was important to women's well-being: it's the richest natural source of magnesium (a mineral that helps combat PMT), and an abundant source of copper, another important mineral. Nan wrote that eating dark chocolate is the quickest way of increasing dietary copper intake, and benefiting from its anti-inflammatory effects. And non-organic chocolate, she maintained, was out of the question.

Now, you don't need to be a nutritionist to notice women's near-obsession with chocolate, especially at certain times of the month. But having these women-specific facts to hand made us think: what about a bar specially confected to appeal to women? Eureka! The

Mixing Business with Pleasure

Jo: What's it been like to live and work so closely together? There are couples who say that, for them, it would be a recipe for divorce, but we're still pathetically happy after getting on for two decades – and there's no doubt that founding Green & Black's together is a huge bond. Going into business with a partner/wife/husband gives you a big advantage: you trust the other person implicitly. (Or if you don't, why are you together?) That's something that's just not true of anyone else you'll ever launch a business with (except, possibly, a sibling, parent or child. But even then there can be rivalries . . .)

Growing Green & Black's together meant that we were *never* stuck for conversation (or dessert!). But how to stop that spilling over into our free time? Actually, we maintained separate offices – we had the luxury of space. And I had a rule: never discuss business at weekends. From Friday night to Sunday night was sacred. But we did devote a whole hour, every night, to conversationally downloading the day's events, brainstorming, talking through plans and discussing the competition as Lindt launched 70%, or Valrhona sought to capture the high ground by pushing single estate chocolate, along the lines of fine wines . . .

We'd do this while taking a long, ritual walk through our neighbourhood (always punctuated with me worshipping at Cath Kidston's Clarendon Road shop, long before she developed her own global empire). We could bounce ideas off each other while decompressing after the day's stresses, and it was hugely productive: we came up with product names, ideas, concepts, marketing campaigns . . . Craig carried a mini Voice It recorder in his pocket (because according to Buckminster Fuller, you've got a matter of seconds to capture an idea before it flies out of your head again). Craig would play back the ideas when we got home, so we could action them. My technique is somewhat less high tech: I write things on my hand. Not elegant. Not very grown-up. Probably toxic. But it works for me.

Eve bar, as we called it, was conceived. Based on the nutritional benefits of a daily 40g of dark chocolate, we added in 1g of dong quai – or Chinese angelica, also known as women's ginseng because it helps optimise hormonal balance and reduce menstrual and menopausal symptoms. Along with this, we put in a small amount of sea kelp, since iodine is another mineral which most people who don't eat seaweed are lacking. Based on our research, we felt this combination of ingredients, consumed more or less daily, would help a woman to maintain a healthy, well-balanced level of energy.

Jo included a message on the bright pink draft wrapper, designed with an astrological symbol of Venus, representing womanhood, next to the name EVE. It read:

Chocolate cravings are something that most women know all about, stronger at some times of the month than others. With the Eve bar I've kept the sugar-level low, and added cocoa powder to enrich the cocoa content – then I've added my favourite herb, Chinese angelica and a dash of sea kelp. I really enjoy its contribution to my diet, and I hope you do too.

Yours sincerely,
Josephine Fairley

Launching this under the Green & Black's brand would have been a big no-no from a marketing point of view – it was just too off the wall. This left us with one option: launching Eve as a stand-alone brand. Then we discovered that dong quai was also used to speed up uterine contractions in childbirth because of its hormonal activity, and we decided that perhaps we'd better stick to making good chocolate and leave nutrition to someone else. The Eve bar was shelved, with a twinge of regret.

Instead, we focussed on Hazelnut & Currant: a grown-up version of the fruit and nut combination so many of us bought at the school tuck shop, sophisticatedly made with dark chocolate. (It is still one of the unsung heroes of the Green & Black's range, and outsells the milk version created later.) Now, there aren't too many industry standards for creating chocolate bars (other than the need for milk chocolate to contain, yes, milk, and the fact it must contain cocoa). But we instinctively felt it was important never to skimp on the add-ins: the bits you put in the recipe to add texture, bite or additional sweetness (and in the case of our dark chocolate with cherry, actual sourness for a winning sweet 'n' sour combination). It's not rocket science: if you're going to buy a bar with fruit and nut in it, the fruit and the nuts have to play a starring role, and not lurk shyly in the chorus line. Again, samples went to and fro between Portobello Road and the factory, until we felt we had just the right balance of crunchy nut, plump currants and dark 60% chocolate. (The 70% was too bitter a contrast.)

Next up was something for people's inner Milky Bar Kid: white chocolate. As before, we started by tasting the competition – going out and buying every bar of white chocolate we could get our hands on. Eating loads and loads of chocolate doesn't sound too painful, but in this case it really was a tough job. Most of it made us feel nauseous – with the exception of one bar, from Harrods, which tasted crisp and fragrant, rather than cloying and sickly. We scanned the ingredients lists; except for that Harrods bar, all featured vanillin. So we did a little research about vanillin (having already established from the Soil Association that it was an organic no-no). We discovered that actually, it had never been near a vanilla orchid, but instead was chemically synthesised. To get that same vanilla hit in our white chocolate, we'd be using real vanilla pods from the island of Bourbon (now known as Réunion) off Madagascar, where most of the world's top-quality vanilla still comes from, frozen to an extremely low temperature in a process known as cryogenic milling and pulverised. Blended into our white chocolate, it looks like tiny specks of black pepper, but each one bursts on the tongue to give that familiar, comforting hint of custard. Far from being sickly, these real vanilla Green & Black's samples were still sweet – but clean-tasting. Once again, we knew we'd got it. How do we define that eureka moment? It's totally unscientific. There is just a particular sample during the tasting process that makes your taste buds tingle and gets you excited: yes, yes this is it! I want MORE! Then, of course, we'd try it out on friends and colleagues to confirm our view, but democracy isn't always the best path when you're doing something completely original – you have to make a fine judgement at a personal level and then rely on your customers' good judgment to share your perception.

Alas, we can't promise any of chocolate's health benefits with our white chocolate, as the polyphenol antioxidants are found in the dark bits, not the butter. But health benefits can be mental as well as physical. Our white chocolate virtually kept Jo's great-aunt Florrie alive for several years: she would consume a 100g bar every single day, even when poorly, claiming that it gave her something to live for. She finally died at the age of 103.

The best chocolate-eating weather is dry – customers aren't reluctant to go out to the shops – but cold enough for them to feel really hungry and up for a spot of comfort eating. Snow is disastrous for sales, as are blistering hot days which can lead to bloom. Bloom is an occupational hazard with chocolate: if it melts and re-solidifies, the cocoa butter crystallises on the surface. It tastes fine but looks awful as if it's gone mouldy. Quite often it happens if a shop puts it in the window, or if a shopper leaves their shopping bag out in the sun. Whenever we received a complaint about bloom we would always unquestioningly replace the bar. Our philosophy is that our customers are always, always right. Always, always, always. (Even when they're wrong.) We are passionate about customer service. Much as we both hate 'have a nice day' shallowness, as consumers we have expectations of being treated courteously and efficiently, and of having any complaints we might make dealt with swiftly. Even when we couldn't pick up the phone ourselves, we worked hard to make sure that a customer's first interaction with our company was entirely positive. To be honest, we didn't get too many complaints, but we'd always unquestioningly send customers some replacement bars, to help build their loyalty to Green & Black's.

It was at the Hampton Court Flower Show in 1995 that we got our first real insight into the dramatic impact that the weather can have on chocolate sales. Christian Aid – important founding supporters of the Fairtrade Foundation – had ambitiously decided to create a Fairtrade garden. They asked us to take part, and we were more than happy to attend and use the opportunity to pop all-important squares of chocolate into as many people's mouths as possible. The garden itself wasn't quite as bursting with colour as most of the other gardens – Christian Aid had worked with various UK botanic gardens to get some cacao trees and coffee plants (which were returned to their glasshouses when the show packed up) – but it did make visitors think. Each of the exhibitors (Cafédirect and Clipper Tea also took part) had a straw hut to work out of, like a Third World shack, and a gravel path between the tropical planting invited visitors to walk past us, and chat. The first three days were cool and breezy, a mixture of cloud and some sun. Our chocolate samples disappeared in seconds. On day four the weather was almost tropical, and the garden-loving public completely lost interest in our chocolate. Literally thousands of people asked, 'Do you do ice cream?', while politely declining a square of (somewhat softened) chocolate. Which is how we found out what other chocolate companies understand: that above 80 degrees, sales go into free-fall. Even though plenty of bars are still sold in the air-conditioned environment of supermarkets, they languish in the store cupboard back home until the weather cools down again. It was a no-brainer: Green & Black's had to start making ice cream.

The Water Cure

Jo: I had no idea, till we started taking part in shows and exhibitions, that simply talking can dramatically lower the level of the body's water reserves, and I've since learned that the dryness you feel so uncomfortably on your tongue and in your mouth is also happening in the brain, creating stress. My best anti-stress tip – at any time, not just at a trade show – is simply a long, cool glass of water. Frees up the brain instantly. Maybe it's psychological, but it works every time.

But what flavours? Chocolate was an obvious choice, but we had a hunch we should have vanilla, too, since sales of vanilla ice cream far outstrip the fancier flavours. Again, we learned a lot about ice cream on the hoof, partly through our friend Vince Adams, who set up the ice cream deal for us with a small Kent-based factory called Real Ice. It was important to us to make the ice cream in the UK. There were no factories here that could create bean to bar chocolate, but ice cream was a simpler proposition, and Staplehurst felt positively local. Vince and Craig went to the factory, which made high-quality ice cream for customers like Waitrose and Sainsbury's and the managing director, David Alfille, signed an exclusivity agreement that he would only make organic ice cream for us. We were then prepared to share all our sources of organic ingredients and hold their hand while they went through the Soil Association certification process. To do all of that for them and then have seen them use that hard-earned knowledge and skill base to offer organic ice cream to customers who would compete with us was unacceptable and David agreed. We were confident about the other ingredients: actual Green & Black's chocolate (which was melted down and added to the mixture), cocoa, sugar, vanilla and milk powder. But cream was still a rarity and, organically, a luxury, so we needed to have a reliable source.

There was only one person producing organic cream in Britain at that time. So we went to visit the source, a farmer called John Jones based on the borders of Hereford and Wales, near Kington. We checked out his farm and his creamery, tramped across his fields to meet his friendly cows and got him to commit to supply us with enough cream so we could launch the ice cream with the confidence that we wouldn't run out of this crucial ingredient. We learnt a lot about organic dairy farming and the importance of permanent pasture to good milk quality and healthy cows, and meeting people like John and his wife always makes doing business a pleasure.

Ice cream, we found, is one of the only products still sold by volume, not by weight. As a result you can have two identical tubs of ice cream, one that's so full of air it's surprising it doesn't float off the table and another that's so dense you could do some serious damage were you to throw it at something – and yet they'd be considered equivalent. The difference is down to 'overrun' – a euphemism for the quantity of air that's whipped into ice cream during the manufacturing. Inexpensive supermarket ice creams have lots of air in them, so we decided that Green & Black's ice cream should have the minimum amount of air possible. As a result it melts frustratingly slowly – to the point where some people have in desperation actually taken a bread knife to the tub in an attempt to slice it.

Probably because the ice cream had less air – and because it also, of course, contained real Green & Black's dark chocolate – the samples that arrived were dangerously good: fudgy and moreish. So moreish that the night after they were delivered, Craig woke up with the urge to taste them one more time, to reassure himself they were as good as he remembered. The samples were at that moment in a fridge in the locked offices three floors below us, to which he could only gain access by going out onto Portobello Road in his pjs in the pouring rain, unlocking the office door, switching off the burglar alarm – and then reversing the process to return to bed with a tub of ice cream. Which is exactly what 'Mr Macrobiotic' (as Jo teased him) did. That siren call from the deep freeze gave us a pretty good clue that we were on to another winner.

Sure enough, the ice cream was soon a hot seller – and not just in summer. Food writers are usually purists about making their own ice cream, but they seemed to love ours, which tasted as rich and was as creamy as homemade, but with none of the hassle; Nigel Slater was even photographed for the cover of *Observer Food Monthly* seated on his kitchen floor holding a tub of Green & Black's Chocolate Ice Cream in one hand and licking a spoon with a guilty look. When Jo attended a reception for women of achievement at Buckingham Palace, Sharon Osbourne came over to her and said, 'Omigod, *Green & Black's*! Do you know that at 2 a.m. this morning, I got out of bed, padded downstairs, opened the freezer and devoured an entire tub of your chocolate ice cream?' Even though we've received a lot of praise over the years, it's always incredibly thrilling to hear how much people love our products.

Real Ice told us that we had the option to make the ice cream in small tubs, too – perfect, we reasoned, for cinemas (and our own local one, the Gate Cinema in Notting Hill Gate, was an early adopter). The mini-tubs work almost like a paid-for sampling exercise: you buy a small pot in the movies, or at a concert, then pick up a 500ml tub next time you're in Planet Organic or Sainsbury's.

Much more recently, we also used these small tubs – as well as dinky mini-bars of chocolate – in one of our marketing whiz-kid Mark Palmer's many clever ideas. By 2003 (after the private equity injection of cash) we had a bit more of a marketing budget – £700,000 – and we dedicated a huge chunk of it to sponsoring twenty-two Music on a Summer's Evening picnic concerts at stately homes throughout the UK, to which picnickers would flock to listen to everyone from Bryan Ferry to Jools Holland and

A Launch Too Far?

Jo: When you've created a brand, at some point you're probably going to want to extend it. It's an important question: just how far *can* you extend your brand? Craig, famously, expanded Whole Earth Foods into all sorts of sectors – the only common thread being the no added sugar vibe and (in some cases) pioneering organicness – resulting in a ridiculously wide portfolio of products. Soft drinks. Peanut butter. Breakfast cereals. Baked beans. Ketchup. Honey cake. Pickles. (I miss the piccalilli, personally.) Jams. Pot noodles. (Yes, pot noodles; despite being surprisingly delicious, these failed to grip the imagination either of supermarket buyers or wholefood shoppers.) My own favourite – as a cook who can out-lazy Nigella Lawson any day – was a can of ready prepared brown rice, for re-heating (without the hassle of waiting an hour, or scrubbing the pan where it stuck). As had become the pattern, Craig asked me to come up with a name for it, and Ready Rice sprang to mind.

Very, very early on in our courtship, Craig had rung me with the exciting news that he had just bought forty tonnes of organic greengages, to make Whole Earth jam, but was a little worried that the public didn't really 'get' greengages. 'OK, what you've got is forty tonnes of Golden Plum Jam,' I told him. The label was duly designed (by our friend Larry Smart), and Golden Plum Jam flew off the shelves. Coming up with product names was something I'd always fancied – anything the creator of Curly Wurly, Twix or Hobnobs could do, I figured, I could do too – so this was a small dreamette come true. Craig would present me with a product and it was my job to think up something catchy. I remember standing on our stall at the first BioFach organic fair in so glamorous Mannheim (*not!*), where he presented me with the first samples of a grain-based hot drink to which he'd added guarana powder – a truly great-tasting alternative to coffee, without the Java jitters. (So good we have been known to give it to builders and they can't tell it from instant, actually.) Craig handed me a piece of paper and a pen, and I started scribbling.

Reading over my shoulder, he exclaimed 'No!' At the next attempt: 'No again! Keep going!' I felt like the rocking horse winner – the boy in the movie of the same name, being whipped until I collapsed! And then it came to me, in a flash: Wake Cup. (Go on, say it.) And, for its sister product – same delicious coffee flavour, *sans* guarana, it seemed blindingly obvious: not decaf but NoCaf. And yes, as we discovered, the trademarks were available ...

But having such a wide portfolio of products was a management nightmare: so many different factories to deal with, and so many different buyers to see when it came to selling what they produced for us. As a brand, it was probably stretched to breaking point. So when it came to range extensions for Green & Black's, we decided to be more cautious. We talked to a lovely couple who'd relocated to France and created a jam-making company called Tea Together, who were interested in making high-quality jams under the Green & Black's label. We loved their rich marmalade and the juiciness of the seasonal jams – probably the closest thing to homemade jam that you can find, outside a branch of the Women's Institute. But having learned a lesson from Whole Earth, we took the sensible decision to stay focussed – on chocolate (and chocolatey items like ice cream), and so said no to the jams.

Dame Kiri Te Kanawa (not on the same bill!). Countless chocolate and ice-cream samples were handed out; there were even special baker's boy bicycles incorporating a frozen compartment with a smart Green & Black's livery, to carry samples of small tubs of Green & Black's vanilla and chocolate ice cream. By taking out ads in the programmes for the evenings' musical events (which most people seem to keep as souvenirs), and wrapping the mini-bars in a stylishly designed card sleeve – with much more space to tell the message behind Green & Black's than on a bar itself – we reinforced brand awareness (not our natural terminology, but hey), once the chocophiles got home. (A hundred and twenty-five thousand of them, across each three-week summer season. No wonder it was repeated, three years in a row.) 'Tasting is believing' had been our philosophy from day one – and it's been hugely successful through partnerships with Eurostar (where first-class travellers were offered Green & Black's after a meal), and British Airways. Music on a Summer's Evening was a sampling exercise on a grander, statelier scale than we could ever have envisaged.

After the ice cream, there were other launches. hot chocolate; cocoa powder (the other essential ingredient in so many chocolate recipes); and hazelnut and chocolate spread. For product development, we again enlisted the help of our niece Carson – a Nutella-aholic. We really wanted to respond to the postbagful of letters from concerned parents who wanted an organic version of the nutty spread lavishly applied each morning to toast up and down the country, so we had a Dutch factory (we'd found out that they're really great at spreads in Holland) create a Green & Black's version for us. The first version we came up with did not meet with Carson's approval. 'No, it's not as good as Nutella; wouldn't eat it.' We went back to the drawing board. The second got the same negative response from our foodie niece, as did the third. Eventually – with some trepidation, after several months of to-ing and fro-ing with the Dutch factory – we handed her a spoon and the jar of Trial No. 4. Her sky-blue eyes lit up. 'Yes, it's better than Nutella,' she said, almost swooning, and proceeded to polish off a third of the jar. And we knew we had our recipe.

Later on in the evolution of Green & Black's, when investors and then Cadbury's injected some capital into the business, there was the opportunity for more creativity to be unleashed: milk chocolate with almonds, dark with cherries, dark with ginger, many of the recipes perfected (from 2005 onwards) by Micah Carr-Hill, the in-house taster, whose palate (crucially) we trust.

But the process has been more or less the same for each launch: identify a potential product; check out the competition; come up with a brief for the chocolate factory – a rough idea of cocoa percentage, a specification for the size of an addition (like nuts or ginger pieces), or the taste of a particular fruit – sour cherries, for instance, as opposed to sweet, which might make the chocolate too icky. Then the factory – with their years of expertise – create sample bars in their lab and send them to us. The process of assessment then happens. When the first samples of caramel-filled bar came in, for instance, they were really sickly. Remembering the saltiness of the so-successful Reese's peanut butter cups, we suggested upping the salt level – and the result was pure perfection. But the key has always been to go by the opinions of a very small panel (for years, just the two of us), rather than a focus group or a committee. In our experience, developing ideas by committee is the fastest way to create a product which – yes – pleases all of the people, in some way, but is probably rather dull. And chocolate, above all, should inspire real passion.

While building up our series of bars, we felt we had a lot of the old favourites covered, but what was lacking was what is known in the business as a 'count line' – Green & Black's answer to the Mars Bar, the Twix, the Snickers. Something for the grab 'n' go trade, the snack market. Our bars were fine – but they didn't answer everyone's hunger for something sugary and textured (crunchy, wafery, whatever), which is the signature of the count line. Craig starting pulling together ideas for our count line in our own kitchen, and he slaved over a hot double boiler until he came up with what we felt could be a winning recipe. It involved dark chocolate and peanut butter, among other ingredients, and it's fair to say that product development doesn't get much more exciting than that: waiting for a warm bar to cool in the fridge, so you can tuck into it.

Once we'd cracked the recipe, the next step was to come up with a name. The 'Green & Black's Bar' just wasn't snappy enough, and confectionery lines are sub-brands all of their own: Twix, Kit-Kat, Marathon, Revels, Minstrels, Snickers – the list is endless. So we came up with lists of suggestions of our own – something we hoped would be catchily memorable. (If it could have a subliminal eco-message like the green in Green & Black's – then so much the better, but it wasn't essential.) Ideas included the Earth Bar; Planet Bar; Cosmo Bar. Any names we liked we had to check to see if they'd already been trademarked. Even in the mid-1990s, the records hadn't yet been digitised, and we had to employ a (rather expensive) trademark agent, Mr Axe of A. J. Axe and Co. to do the checks. We were amazed at what he discovered: every one of our ideas had already been registered by another company – mostly by Mars and Nestlé – but they hadn't yet got around to making anything using that brand name.

Still stuck for a name, Craig had the idea of eliciting suggestions from our nearest and dearest (and pretty much anyone else whose path we crossed, around that time). We had (yet another) list of our own ideas printed up, with a space for other suggestions and possibilities left at the bottom, which read like this:

Dragon	Gaia
Earth	Terra
Mondo	Globe
Apache	Smiley
Dream	Love
Space	Nutta
Cosmic	Pulse
Karma	Good Times

Samsara	Nirvana
Togo	Boffo
Aloha	Ahimsa
Bar None	Bliss
Chic	Bongo

We gave it to brothers, stepchildren, the Green & Black's team – and Jo's two ninetysomething great-aunts. Great-auntie Doris duly filled in her form, and in spindly writing at the bottom asked: 'Why don't you call it Jojo?' (Which had been Jo's childhood nick-name.) The Jojo Bar. It was catchy, a little bit funky and there was a story we could tell about it. A fantastic name, in fact, which goes to show: no harm in brainstorming with ninety-year-olds.

But to save yet another wild goose chase, Mr Axe, our trade-mark agent, asked whether perhaps someone might already be using it? No way, Jo countered, knowing that if a Jojo bar existed anywhere in the world, she'd have been showered with them, over the years. After a few weeks' wait, Mr Axe wrote to Craig: no go. It was registered to Trebor Bassett – part of Cadbury's, ironically. We decided to make them a small offer, reasoning that if the trade-mark was indeed idling in obscurity they might accept it. UK trademark law allows you to challenge someone's registration if they've had it for more than five years and haven't launched a product using it. A few letters and £500 later, we had the right to the JoJo trademark, and Jo got a certificate, confirming that she actually *owned* her name. Unfortunately, though, while all this had been going on, the yummy peanut bar had bloomed badly because the fat in the filling had migrated to the surface. The recipe, according to our technical director Simon Wright, was a non-starter. We'd so loved the flavour of this bar, though, that anything else we subsequently tried was a let down, and the whole count line project was put on a back burner. It was a great shame, not least because it would have given us the challenge of opening a door into the newsagent/confectionery trade, where at that time we had zero distribution. The resources simply weren't there. But one day, we hope, there will be a Green & Black's count line. Although it's safe to say, it won't be called Jojo; a few years after buying her name, Jo got an offer from a small German liquorice company for it – and, though it hurt to sell, parted with it for £500. Exactly what she'd paid for it.

Dealing with trademark law had been frustrating, and we had discovered first-hand how protective large companies can become when they think that an attempt has been made to infringe on their brands and intellectual property. A landmark on this voyage of discovery came in 1996 when we received a letter from Cadbury's lawyers pointing out that we were using the words 'dairy milk' on the front wrapper of our Green & Black's Milk Chocolate where we declared: 'The creamy richness of dairy milk combines with 34% cocoa solids for a completely authentic organic chocolate with a full, smooth flavour'. As 'Dairy Milk' was Cadbury's registered trade mark they asked us to reword our blurb. We had used those precise words because we wanted to dispel the assumption that, just because the chocolate was labelled 'organic,' it would be made with soya milk or possibly even carob. The popular imagination at the time assumed that anything organic would have to be made from 'health food' ingredients, and milk chocolate just wasn't seen as part of that grouping, even though increased awareness of the benefits of high cocoa solids chocolate had been helping it to shed its naughty image. We had wanted to make sure our customers didn't think that they were getting something worthy but unappetising, so we were keen to get the message across clearly on our wrappers. When the letter came through, though, we remembered how irritated we had become when rival companies came out with new brands called things like 'Inca Gold' after we had been so successful with Maya Gold, so it was easy to see their point and as a result we reworded the text.

They also referred to our use of the colour purple on the wrapper of our milk chocolate. Cadbury had claimed rights and registered the colour purple for chocolate as their intellectual property and a similar shade of purple was their exclusive property so they therefore had a sound legal basis for taking issue with the design of our milk chocolate wrappers, which were a solid violet colour. Cadbury's rights to the colour purple enabled them to protect this distinctive aspect of their intellectual property from would-be imitators. To see a similar shade of the colour purple on a bar of milk chocolate the same size and shape as a Cadbury Dairy Milk bar might not have engendered that much confusion with an organic milk chocolate selling at a much higher price, but if allowed to stand could have opened the door to imitators with a very similar product.

The letter marked the beginning of discussions between our two companies. We were all keen to talk through the issues; while we could see Cadbury's point on both the items they raised, we knew we had meant no harm and we were not out to copy them or hijack their intellectual property in any way, so we sought an outcome that would be satisfactory for both of us. Nobody likes to go to court, with all the cost and unpleasantness that can entail, so we worked hard to come up with an out of court solution that offered certainty and avoided unpredictable costs.

The interesting outcome of the dispute was that we met with Cadbury's people and got to know them, albeit initially in a somewhat tense environment. They were actually nice and reasonable, we discovered. We pointed out that our entire range was based on a sequence of colours (brown for 70% dark, orange for Maya Gold, green for mint chocolate, deep blue for hazelnut and currant and, of course, violet for milk chocolate). We would have to rethink the range and probably redesign it so that it remained coherent once we had changed the look of the milk chocolate to move away from the colour purple and the lyrical descriptive text on the front wrapper. As we undertook those changes we would have the burden of all the design costs of updating our range, originating new packaging artwork, changing over to the new look and reflecting this change in all our promotional materials and the write-off costs of unusable packaging. Frankly, it would have been financially challenging. By this time Cadbury's had realised that we were innocent of any malice, had not intended to rip them off and worked with us in redesigning the range. A more aggressive company might have given us short shrift with our appeal for friendly compromise, but we were pleased that Cadbury's showed understanding and heart in bringing the matter to a mutually satisfactory conclusion. Violet became a gorgeous shade of sky blue, and we never got a single word of feedback from Green & Black's lovers that anybody missed the colour purple.

Developing Recipes

Jo: One of the most effective ideas we had for promoting Green & Black's was to focus on the cooks who were using it in recipes. Before Green & Black's, there was no such thing as 70% dark chocolate. By 1994, every TV and glossy magazine chef worth his Maldon salt was declaring 70% to be the benchmark of excellence for any recipe that used chocolate, and were increasingly mentioning Green & Black's by name. (High point: Jamie Oliver thwacking Green & Black's, on his cult cooking show.) Why not produce a recipe leaflet, then? It was a perfect way of targeting a key market: cooks and chefs. So I wrote to absolutely every restaurateur friend and food writer I could think of. Hugh Fearnley-Whittingstall gave us his recipe for Maya Gold mousse (long before River Cottage was a twinkle in his eye). Launceston Place – then a deeply groovy Kensington watering-hole – shared with readers the secret of their chocolate berry torte. Alastair Little – whose Soho restaurant had been a mecca for foodies since the 1980s – gave us his recipe for fudge sauce. The Groucho Club willingly offered their chocolate cake recipe. (We threw in some recipes from friends, too: my god-daughter Haley Foxen's choc-dipped fruit, and some brilliant confections created by Hilary Meth, a vegan recipe developer, to cater to the happy vegans who could guiltlessly enjoy our dark 70%.)

We had met Linda McCartney a little while previously at a Soil Association do at Highgrove – one of the very first organic soirées to be generously hosted by HRH The Prince of Wales, to tell the great and the good some more about the charity's work. Linda discovered we lived very near each other, and a few days after the event, she called us up to invite us round for Sunday breakfast: a fry-up around the kitchen table with Stella, Mary, James, Heather (the original Heather McCartney, Linda's daughter), rabbits, cats, dogs and a guitar-strumming Paul. Linda was a completely fabulous woman. You couldn't help but fall in love with her. She was totally down to earth – an earth mother, in fact, and a very hip chick indeed. She welcomed family, friends – and us – into the bosom of the McCartney household, and was rarely more than two steps away from the frying pan, loving to feed us all with her veggie sausages, burgers and eggs laid on the McCartney's organic 1,200-acre farm. She was also surgically attached to her camera at all times. I remember sitting at the table one day, when Linda leaped up and started snapping: on the curve of the rail at the bottom of the banisters was a tiny, banister-coloured field mouse. Talk usually turned to food, and specifically to organics; Paul and Linda would have loved to make the Linda McCartney range organic, but the existing recipes were packed with hydrogenated fat (an organic no-no), and Ross Foods – who they'd licensed the brand to – just weren't interested.

One day, Linda asked for Craig's help on another culinary challenge. 'I've always tried to make my family brownie recipe in this country, but it uses unsweetened chocolate, which I can't get in the UK,' drawled native New Yorker Linda. Back home, he got out the calculator and experimented with her recipe, using our 70% dark chocolate, until he had created the perfect Linda McCartney brownie. We took them over for a tasting, and Linda was over the moon. So were we: we could now bake the perfect brownie at home: rich, fudgey, crumbly on the top – and with just the right balance of salt to sweetness.

I wrote to Linda: could we possibly use her brownie recipe, in our leaflet? She told us she was more than happy. Here it is.

Brownies

115g Green & Black's 70% Dark Chocolate (or use the 72% baking chocolate)
115g butter
2 large eggs, at room temperature
170g granulated sugar
5ml/1 tsp vanilla essence
55g self-raising flour
55g pecan nuts or walnuts, broken

Preheat the oven to 350°F/180°C/gas mark 4. Lightly grease and flour a 25cm or 30cm square tin. (The smaller tin makes a thicker brownie.) Melt the chocolate in a double boiler or bain marie (or a Pyrex bowl suspended over a pan of boiling water); stir the butter into the melted chocolate and remove from the heat. Allow to cool.

Whisk the eggs in a large mixing bowl, add the sugar and vanilla and beat until thick. Stir in the melted chocolate. Sift the flour into this mixture and add the nuts, stirring very well. Pour into the prepared tin. Bake for 20–30 minutes, until just set. Cool in the pan. Cut into 12 squares. The brownies should be moist and sticky and should be served when cool (if you can wait).

Our friendship with Linda blossomed, mostly over those veggie fry-ups at their farmhouse a few miles away. (I remember a teenage Stella once coming in with an armful of trophies: a pile of vintage clothing she'd picked up in the Rye branch of Oxfam, showing early signs of the style consciousness which has made her one of the world's leading fashion designers today). The McCartneys came to visit us at home (Linda arrived once having forgotten to bring wine, and sent the driver back 15 miles to fetch it. A very fine bottle of red it was, too.) More often, we'd go to their farm, which was ringed by the security you'd expect for someone whose band mate was shot dead by a psycho. One Sunday night, I turned on the TV to see a paparazzi photo of Paul and Linda driving away from the hospital where she'd been diagnosed with breast cancer. Linda wasn't about to give up. She opened the door next time we visited with, 'Breast cancer – bummer, eh?', and proceeded to feed us, yet again, having breezily broken the taboo about her illness. Tragically and famously, Linda lost her fight. After the memorial service in St Martin-in-the-Fields, celebrating her life – in a church garlanded almost from floor to rafters with lilies and other white flowers – we were all handed a bunch of lily of the valley, wrapped in white tissue, as a memento. When we got them home to put them in water, we found the plants still had roots on, so we planted them in our garden in Hastings, where they still bloom. And every time we eat a brownie made with Green & Black's, we remember Linda.

Part Three

GROWING PAINS

7

Organic Goes Mainstream

The organic market was booming by the late 1990s. In 1974, when the total market size was £3 million, organic was growing at 30% a year. Normally, you'd expect this rate to level off as the market expands, but in 1992 it was *still* growing at 30% per annum and was worth nearly £100 million. (By 2007 it had continued at 30% to reach £2 billion.) By then, you could have a fully organic diet without making too many sacrifices. Organic crumpets were available in Sainsbury's; you could see that times had changed!

By 1990 at Whole Earth we had organic beans for our tinned baked beans and soon had organic tomato purée and organic vinegar. But there was still no organic sugar, no organic solid fats and only small amounts of very expensive organic butter. Over the years various businessmen had been interested in investing in the Whole Earth operation, but it was always a dead giveaway when they'd adjust their suits, lean forward and ask anxiously: 'How long do you think this organic fad is going to last?' Craig used to say this was the point at which he would truly despair that organic food was just seen as the latest fashion, like hula hoops or ra-ra skirts. It seemed obvious to us that organic food was a long-term trend carrying a certain amount of historical inevitability about it; that in fact the real 'fad' was the aberrant belief that you could industrialise nature, both on the farm and in the human digestive system. We knew it was transfats, additives and agrochemicals whose days were numbered – not organics.

The key organisation that has worked towards laying the foundation for organic food and farming is the Soil Association, which was founded in 1946 by Lady Eve Balfour, an organic farmer from Suffolk, and Dr Innes Pearce, who ran the Peckham Experiment at the Pioneer Health Centre in South London during the 1930s. This ground-breaking experiment was set up to teach ordinary working-class families about healthy eating and domestic hygiene. The results were impressive: they were ill less often, their children did better at school, their marriages were more stable and employment levels improved. Eve Balfour and Innes Pearce nurtured a vision for a post-war Britain where healthy eating and organic farming would prevail. This vision was worked into William Beveridge's early plans for the National Health Service, and it was because he foresaw a general improvement in the nation's health that he budgeted for a fall in expenditure in the NHS by the 1950s. In fact, by 1948, after energetic lobbying from the powerful pharmaceutical and chemical industries, preventive medicine and sustainable agriculture had been marginalised by policies that subsidised, and so encouraged, drugs, surgery and the use of chemicals in agriculture. Far from the budgeted fall in healthcare costs, the NHS is now Europe's biggest employer, with massive budgets rising with increasing rates of diet-related illness.

The Soil Association spent the 1940s and 50s keeping the flame of sustainability alive before the tide began to turn with the emergence of the alternative culture in the late 1960s. In 1972 Craig's brother Gregory sat on the Soil Association committee that set out the very first comprehensive organic standards which became the blueprint for organic standards worldwide. The farming standards exclude chemical fertilisers, pesticides, routine drug or hormone use and require soil conservation and animal welfare protection. Those for processing food prohibit the use of chemicals, artificial additives and unnatural foods such as hydrogenated fat (which is liquid fat made solid as plastic by the addition of hydrogen atoms). By 1989 the Soil Association was having some influence over the supermarkets – Waitrose and Safeway in particular stocked a few organic fruits and vegetables and even some organic milk.

When, in 1990, Charlotte Mitchell, a Scottish wholefood pioneer (and our good friend) was elected as chair of the Soil Association's council of trustees, she asked Craig to stand for election in the hope that he would replace her as treasurer. He didn't get elected but they co-opted him on to the council anyway to fill a vacant seat. Together they set about putting the charity's finances in order, which at that stage were in a terrible state. Charlotte worked unpaid as general manager of the charity for several years until the Soil Association could finally afford to employ someone in that role. As she lived in Edinburgh this involved a long commute to Bristol and prolonged absences from her family, but she soldiered on until a few substantial legacies and a growing membership helped put the charity on a sound enough footing for full-time management staff to be employed.

At Whole Earth and Green & Black's we did everything we could to help raise the profile of the Soil Association. Whole Earth packaging always carried a green ribbon with an image of a red wax seal in the centre of which was the Soil Association logo. When we launched Green & Black's in 1991 we used the same design, modified to look more upmarket. The great thing about both these designs was that the Soil Association logo was, for the first time ever, prominently displayed as part of a company's branding. Conventional marketing wisdom says that you should not compromise your own brand identity with anyone else's, but we felt the Soil Association logo, situated a few millimetres to the right of the word 'organic' on the front of our labels, acted as an independent and trusted authentication. As our sales grew, customer exposure to the sight of the logo grew. We also printed a Soil Association membership offer on the inside of our chocolate wrappers and this offer became the charity's biggest source of membership recruitment. People were discovering that organic food could be fun and, as they delved more deeply into the principles underlying the organic way, they became natural supporters of the charity that was leading the organic movement.

One of the Soil Association's great challenges was over the issue of genetic modification (GM), which blew up in 1996. With no warning, US exporters of soybeans announced that 4% of the US soya crop was genetically modified and that the GM beans would be mixed in with all other soybeans because it would be impossible to segregate them. Greenpeace sent inflatable boats up the Mississippi to block the grain elevators but the US exporters, mainly ADM and Cargill, were determined to push this measure through.

All sorts of extravagant claims were made for GM crops: they would give up to double the yields of conventional crops; they would reduce the use of herbicides and insecticides and this would consequently benefit the environment (hollow words from the same people who had, until a year previously, been stoutly denying that these noxious chemicals did any harm at all); they would reduce soil erosion; they would enable farmers to get crops from dried-out salinated land (most of which had been ruined by overuse of chemical fertilisers); they would make farmers rich and would eventually be able to fix nitrogen from the air, eliminating the need for chemical fertilisers.

Yet all these claims were unproven, and they seemed to raise as many questions as they answered. What if introducing new genes into crops created a new allergen, like the one people who are allergic to nuts react to? And how about the effects on our immune systems? How could we be sure that no damage was going to be done? Even allowing for the distant possibility that eventually scientists could engineer a crop that would solve the world's problems, it was simply the case that in 1996 not enough research had been done. In fact, many scientists in the field of genetic modification in medical research were horrified by the sudden rolling out of GM crops in that year. They operated strict laboratory protocols to prevent any genetically modified material escaping into the environment and here was GM soya and maize being planted out on farmland with all the risks of cross-pollination and irreversible genetic contamination they had been so careful to avoid.

Two UK-based molecular biologists, Dr Michael Antoniou and Dr Ricarda Steinbrecher, gave lectures and wrote articles to warn the public of the risks, both to the environment and to human health. They had the scientific knowledge to point out convincingly that there was no scientific basis for most of the pro-GM claims and that in fact most of them were just wishful thinking. There had been no proper feeding trials to ensure there were no health risks from consuming GM foods – the Food and Drug Administration (FDA) declared them 'substantially equivalent' to non-GM foods, thereby eliminating any requirement to test for safety.

The move to GM was led by Monsanto, an agricultural and chemical company that had bought up most of America's independent seed companies in the early 1990s. As a result they more or less controlled the distribution of seeds to US farmers and were promoting their GM corn and soybean seeds. Monsanto are the same folks who brought us Agent Orange, the herbicide that had poisoned so much of Vietnam and so many of the GIs who served there. They bought G. D. Searle, whose CEO Donald Rumsfeld successfully lobbied for government approval of Nutrasweet, even though there were serious objections from the FDA. In 2002 Monsanto was found guilty of 'outrageous behavior' in Alabama when it was proven they had polluted a community's water supplies with deadly PCBs (chemicals used for industrial coolants). Under Alabama law, the rare claim of outrage typically requires conduct 'so outrageous in character and extreme in degree as to go beyond all possible bounds of decency so as to be regarded as atrocious and utterly intolerable in civilized society'. We were a tad suspicious of their miraculous claims for genetic engineering.

At the Soil Association there was a vigorous debate about GM – some people considered a technology that could insert pest resistance into plants was the organic farmer's dream come true. No need for pesticides: our dream of wholesome clean food realised! Others were more sceptical, and felt that the case had yet to be proven that these advances were possible. Yet others felt that this move was part of a more sinister agenda: the final industrialisation of our food supply and its control by a handful of monopolistic chemical and pharmaceutical companies. Neil Harl, a professor at Iowa State University, had written in 1995 that companies like Monsanto and Dow Chemical were paying three to four times the market value to acquire seed companies. He judged that this was because they aimed to reach a point were there was nothing to stop them from raising the cost of seed and obtaining a monopoly stranglehold over the basics of the nation's food supply.

After a long and sometimes heated debate in the summer of 1997 at Badminton House, the Soil Association Council decided that GM had no place in organic food or animal feeds and they would rigorously enforce the EU standard that prohibited GM ingredients in organic products. In addition, they concluded that any GM crops released into the environment could be dangerous and so they also opposed GM crops in non-organic farming. In doing this, the council created the first standards that didn't just ban GM but set down rules that would prevent cross-contamination of organic food and farmland. These standards were adopted round the world and formed a global bulwark against unwelcome GM damage.

At Green & Black's it was vital we keep our organic status, and for us the GM threat came from soya beans. Soya was the source of the lecithin we used in chocolate, at half of 1%, to help ensure smooth texture and good snap in our bars. Our suppliers told us

'Hello, Green & Black's . . .'

Jo: For eight years, I answered the Green & Black's phone myself. Call me a control freak, I don't care. I still maintain it's one of the best ways to keep your finger on the pulse of everything that's happening in your business. It was through answering the phone that I first twigged how important the issue of genetic modification was to our customers. In just one week, I fielded over 200 calls from concerned customers who had started to hear about GM crops on the radio, or read about them in newspapers. They had scanned the ingredients list on the back of our bars, and wanted to be sure that the soya lecithin we used was organic. I hated telling them that we couldn't guarantee it. Not only that – if we didn't fix the lecithin problem the chocolate would lose its organic status. And if the chocolate lost its organic status . . . well, we wouldn't have a business. Aaaaaaaargh. Luckily at Green and Black's we were used to finding solutions to tricky problems.

they could no longer ensure GM-free lecithin because US exporters had decided that there would be 5–10% GM soy in all soya exports. It seemed as though they were trying to present Europe with a fait accompli to crush any attempt to resist genetically engineered foods.

It was definitely time for the trade to take action and Richard Auston, of Rainbow Wholefoods in Norwich, rose to the challenge. He recruited Lindsay Keenan and brought together a grass roots campaign. Lindsay's employers, Green City Wholefoods in Glasgow, offered a desk and a telephone and Richard and Lindsay got to work. They formed Wholefood Wholesalers Against GM (WWAGM). Whole Earth, Green & Black's and several other wholefood processors and wholesalers chipped in £200 each to fund the campaign. The UK wholefood wholesalers gathered in a former squat behind King's Cross station and mapped out a plan. They would all (Green City, Community, Rainbow, Essential, Harvest, Infinity, Suma, Highland and Goodness) begin by writing to British Arkady Soy Products, the main supplier of TVP (Textured Vegetable Protein), to ask them for an assurance that this popular vegetarian alternative to meat, which came in chunks, ground bits, chicken shapes and other meat-like formats, would be GM-free. British Arkady was a wholly owned subsidiary of ADM (Archer Daniels Midland) who happened to be Monsanto's marketing partners and the major US trader of many of the US and the world's agricultural commodities. ADM's chairman, Dwayne Andreas, famously once said, 'The competitor is our friend and the customer is our enemy.' Their response to our request was a curt 'No'. Soya with GM mixed in was a reality, they claimed, get over it. It would be too expensive to segregate what was then only a small percentage of the US soya supply from the remainder.

The WWAGM group wrote back advising British Arkady they would no longer have them as customers for their soya protein unless they could provide guarantees of segregated soya. We wrote as one group but there had been internal disputes that got a bit ugly. Suma, a workers' collective, had calculated they would have to reduce their numbers by one member if they destocked TVP, because of the impact of the dip in sales on their business. They were not prepared to do this as their primary loyalty was to the members of their collective, regardless of the pros and cons of GM, so they continued to stock TVP but discovered their sales went down anyway, even though they were the only wholesaler stocking it, thanks to retailer and consumer awareness. They discontinued stocking TVP after just a few months. By now the message had got through to the large agricultural-commodities traders and British Arkady announced they could provide GM-free TVP from identity preserved soybeans. The WWAGM got their guarantees and this led to ongoing segregation of GM soya which continues to this day.

However, for lecithin it was not so easy. One thousand tonnes of soybeans will produce less than 1 tonne of soya lecithin. Lecithin is a tiny part of a soybean and Green & Black's was a tiny part of the market for lecithin. We couldn't get a guarantee out of anyone who processed soybeans in Europe or the US. We were stumped and had to try other options. We looked for sources of lecithin from Brazil, where GM soybeans had not been permitted. No luck there, either. The soya might have been GM-free, but the Brazilian processors also used Argentine soybeans, where GM was permitted.

We liaised with Hercules, a Danish supplier of a wide range of food ingredients including lecithin. They had many other customers who were beside themselves with anxiety over how they would resolve this issue, so they were working to develop a source, using our combined demand as a means of getting someone to help.

Another possible solution was the genetic ID testing system that had been developed by a molecular biologist called John Fagan, but it wouldn't work on lecithin as the offending DNA was in the protein of the soybeans, not the lecithin residue itself. There was only one way to have verification: there had to be an unbroken trail of trace-ability all the way to the farm where the soybeans were grown. The people at Hercules were moving as fast as they could, under relentless pressure from companies like ours who'd made solemn and binding commitments to their GM-averse customers that they would never allow GM ingredients in their products. Now we were faced with a real problem in keeping our promise.

Having encountered these huge difficulties trying to ensure a GM-free supply, we tried making chocolate without lecithin – but to get the right mouthfeel and snap we'd have had to increase the cocoa-butter content and doing so would have reduced the intensity of flavour that was our signature and the key factor in our success. Belgian chocolate is high in cocoa butter and has a rich, almost greasy texture as a result. Green & Black's characteristic texture was less oily, almost (but not quite) chalky.

We tried sunflower lecithin from Romania. It worked a dream – as far as the factory were concerned. But it imparted a just perceptible dusty-musty taste to the chocolate – not something many of our customers might have noticed. However, we could tell it was there and we didn't like it. But we'd run out of options and for about six months we carried on with sunflower lecithin, while we continued to push hard for GM-free soya.

Meanwhile Friends of the Earth and Greenpeace realised this was an issue that could galvanise their members. They both came out in support of organic food as it represented the only safe haven from GM. This gave organic food a great boost and encouraged the environmental movement to support a solution rather than just oppose or try to delay a problem. Non-government organisations (NGOs) have a tendency to be competitive, but for this one golden moment they all pulled together on a unified campaign. A rally organised by the anti-GM movement gathered at the National Farmers Union (NFU) headquarters in Shaftesbury Avenue. Craig went along with Patrick Holden, director of the Soil Association, to join the campaigners and present a petition to Ben Gill, the deputy president of the National Farmers Union at that time, calling for a ban on GM until the risks were fully assessed. They then marched through Trafalgar Square and down Whitehall to the Ministry of Agriculture's offices, holding placards with slogans such as 'NO TO FRANKENFOODS' and 'KEEP BRITAIN GM FREE' and attempted to hand in a similar petition there. Nobody at the door would accept it, so Patrick used his mobile to call John Byng, a senior civil servant with responsibility for organic food regulations, who then came out, took the petition and went back inside, promising to deliver it to the minister. In the end 'clean' lecithin came through from Hercules Ingredients, who had developed identity-preserved soybeans from Brazil. We were back on track. Getting key ingredients such as lecithin, soya protein, corn starch and other raw materials from non-GM sources helped to create an important secondary and premium-priced market for non-GM foods. It gave a huge boost to Brazil's soybean industry and gave smaller processors and traders of food ingredients a niche to compete against the monolithic corporations such as Cargill and ADM who had such strong links to the USDA and Monsanto.

On 9 September 1999 Patrick Holden and Craig were invited to a meeting with Monsanto's top brass at the Grosvenor House Hotel in Park Lane by the Environment Council, a group which sought to build bridges of understanding over environmental issues. They went along and met Hendrik Verfaille, the CEO, Hugh Grant, his deputy and successor and Kate Fish, their communications director. Monsanto wanted to see who these troublesome people were that had so upset their plans. Of course, our collective efforts didn't stop GM in its tracks, but it gave the world time to pause and think about its food supply and what industrialisation was doing to society and to human health. It was the breather from GM that we needed while the organic revolution gathered momentum.

It was a very interesting time – one where you could see organic concerns, which had previously been quite niche, breaking out in the mainstream. A large body of public opinion, with support from newspapers like the *Daily Mail* and the *Independent*, was deeply concerned about GM foods and people were looking for an alternative. Customers wrote to food companies and supermarkets urging them to keep GM food out of the supply chain and to guarantee their range of products would remain GM-free. The only honest response supermarkets could give to these requests was to say they offered organic food and that this would always be GM-free. As a result, across the board, from natural food stores to supermarkets, the demand for organic products, particularly where soya or maize or vegetable oils were concerned, was escalating.

In 1997, Safeway were still the market leaders in organic food. However a McKinsey report they'd commissioned a few years earlier had misguidedly placed them on the track of low-value cheap foods and they were losing their organic customers to Sainsbury's and Waitrose. In October, Craig was at the Soil Association's Lady Eve Balfour Memorial Lecture when he ran into Steven Esom and Chris Dawson, two top executives from Waitrose. Chris asked after Whole Earth's sales, which were going very well at that time. For eight years, Safeway had stocked Whole Earth's organic baked beans in ninety of their stores, but they had just rolled out the line to all of their 300 or so shops. This was an unmistakeable indication that sales, with no promotional activity from us, had broken through to levels where extending the range to all the shops made economic sense. Steve and Chris glanced at each other – they were looking for confirmation that their instincts about what was bubbling under with organic food were right.

That evening Steven Esom sat next to Charlotte Mitchell, who was just about to stand down as chair of the Soil Association, and asked her if she'd be interested in a consultancy to help them develop a serious organic food offering. Their target launch date was spring 1998.

Sainsbury's were also aware that things were happening. Their computer analysis of sales trends was getting more sophisticated and they could see that organic products were delivering faster rates of growth and higher margins. However, they were also still victims of the conventional wisdom that organic food was a fad the public would get over once they found a new fad to obsess over. Simon Wright, the invaluable and brilliant technical director at Whole Earth and Green & Black's, had recently moved to a freelance basis and Sainsbury's snapped him up in a role similar to Charlotte's at

Waitrose: holding their hand as they delved more deeply into the weird (to them) and wonderful world of organic food and farming.

A race was on. Both supermarket chains had set their sights on achieving a range of about 300 organic products, from basics like bread, butter and chocolate to more exotic foods such as olive oil, dried fruit, sauces and dressings. At this sort of level they could advertise and invest in promoting their organic offerings. This would be good news for everyone in the organic movement as we moved from the margins to the mainstream. We were thrilled that the supermarkets were finally getting on board.

When Whole Earth was set up, it was hard to get appointments with supermarket buyers. It's always the same for small companies. When you finally manage to schedule a meeting, you tend to get the sense that they're thinking more about how they could get one of their existing suppliers to give them what you're offering, rather than burdening their ordering and logistics departments with yet another new supplier who would have to be ordered from and paid separately. Supermarkets love to rationalise and cut costs, so adding a new supplier goes against the grain. One thing that really impresses supermarket buyers is marketing spend; if you're putting a million pounds or so behind a product then you can be pretty confident you'll get a listing covering all the stores, from the largest to the smallest, in a supermarket chain. If you're just bringing a worthy product with little or no marketing support, if you are lucky you get listed for the supermarket's largest store category, where they have lots of products already and enough shelf space to add yours without having to remove someone else's.

A major selling point so far as supermarket buyers were concerned was the fact that at least 10% of a supermarket's customers are regular customers at a natural food or health food store. This meant that when a supermarket listed a product from Whole Earth or Green & Black's it would immediately be recognised by 10% of their customers. Not only that, those customers would also be

And the Winner Is . . .

Jo: When we didn't have a lot of money to spend on advertising, entering awards was a great way to raise Green & Black's profile; awards are news, and third-party endorsements of your product are always far more credible than simply raving about it yourself. In 1992 we were the first winners of the Ethical Consumer Association's Ethical Product award. Another of our early awards was from Worldaware, an independent UK charity (their patron is the Queen), which was set up to encourage sustainable social and economic progress in developing countries in Latin America, Africa and Asia – in short, to give people in the Third World a helping hand, not through large dollops of cash (which invariably runs out after a while), but through education and help in building sustainable trading relationships. We were invited to enter, and come up with a few hundred words about our business and its impact on the Third World farmers we bought cocoa from. A couple of months later, a letter landed on my desk: we had been awarded the Booker Tate Award for Small Businesses, to be given at a ceremony by the then Chancellor of the Exchequer Kenneth Clarke MP.

There was a certain irony in this as I couldn't resist pointing out in the first line of my acceptance speech. 'I'd like to thank Mr Clarke – the man who, through VAT on chocolate, makes more out of every bar of Maya Gold than Green & Black's and the Maya put together . . .' (17.5% of retail sales – then and now!) Deathly silence – then a big Ken grin – and the room laughed, more with relief than from amusement at my wit.

In 1996, we were the first IFOAM (International Federation of Organic Agriculture Movements) Organic World Exhibition Award winner – cue more celebrations. But perhaps the most astonishing win had been a Caroline Walker Award in 1994. The Caroline Walker Trust, set up in memory of a distinguished nutritionist, writer and campaigner, gave out an annual Industry Award 'for the improvement of public health by means of good food'. Surely the first – and maybe last – time that a chocolate brand has received a prize for nutrition. But our sugar warning on those early wrappers had deeply impressed the distinguished judges. And the 'gong' that made us smile most of all? The *Good Housekeeping* Award in 2008 for Favourite Comfort Food, voted by *Good Housekeeping* readers, beating Dairy Milk and Heinz Tomato Soup. (Who also voted us as winners of the Best Organic Range and Best Fairtrade Product. And it means a huge amount when real people, who buy our products, nominate and vote for them.)

Some awards, like the Worldaware Award, the Good Housekeeping Awards and the Caroline Walker Award are given out of the blue. Others, like the Organic Food Awards (which we won in 1993, 1995 and 1996), you have to enter, which means lots of paperwork and working out the logistics of getting your product to a judging session. (This wasn't such an issue with chocolate. It's harder now I have a bakery, but I'm just as ambitious to win awards as I ever was, even if it means getting up at 4 a.m. to carefully wrap still-warm loaves and croissants in tissue paper, before transporting them by a five-hour train journey to a judging session halfway across the country.) Our feeling about awards is that it is always worth entering, because if you win, the publicity potential is tremendous. My mother used to have a saying about life: 'If you don't buy a ticket, you can't win the lottery.' This was odd, as it was years before the National Lottery, but it could certainly apply equally to awards.

more likely to buy it because they respected its integrity from having already seen it in the natural food shop. An advertising campaign is considered a great success if it can achieve a 10% level of recognition, so we were able to offer the same level of awareness without waving big ad spends under the buyers' noses. This was persuasive, but we usually had to climb our way slowly up the ladder, starting in the biggest shops of a chain and gradually, as the sales figures came through, getting rolled out to the rest.

By the late 1990s we had developed a really credible offering of organic chocolate with Dark, Milk, Maya Gold, Hazelnut and Currant, Mint and White, as well as hot chocolate and cocoa. And at Whole Earth, the organic menu included peanut butter, pure fruit spreads, baked beans, cornflakes, ketchup and fizzy drinks such as lemonade, cola and orange soda. We had no intention of passing up the opportunity to be part of Sainsbury's and Waitrose's big organic launches. With two people, Charlotte Mitchell and Simon Wright, working at a strategic level with the supermarkets, both 'organic insiders' who (with their backgrounds at the Soil Association and Whole Earth respectively) understood and respected the integrity and authenticity of our range – we were ideal candidates to supply this new demand from supermarkets for organic grocery lines.

Our working relationship with Duerr's in Manchester – our warehousing and distribution partner – enabled us to offer just-in-time deliveries to the supermarket depots that were also cost effective for us, so we had the logistical ability to deal with supermarket expectations. There were few companies who were as up to speed in this respect as we were. We could take orders electronically, pick them quickly and, if the customer wanted the delivery at 2.20 on Monday afternoon, the truck was there at 2.15, ready to unload. Many of our competitors, such as Meridian Foods, suffered huge cost burdens in trying to achieve the same service levels.

Selling organic food was, for once, like pushing at an open door – we just needed a dedicated somebody to get out there and go round all the supermarkets. Alan Wills, our Managing Director, was a brilliant salesman and the original plan had been that he would focus almost entirely on selling our products to supermarkets and the natural food stores. But in practice, you can't run a business,

Get it in Writing

Craig: Many a shopkeeper will promise you anything, but once they've signed an order form they're committed to squeezing you onto their precious shelf space. Plenty of shops were jealous of the lower prices that supermarkets could offer and their customers lost no time in making it known that they could buy our chocolate for 20p less at Sainsbury's or Waitrose. To counter this we gave the independent retailers special offers to balance out promotions in the supermarkets. Just giving them a price reduction didn't work – the saving didn't get passed on because the retailer would stock up on product while it was cheap, and take the risk that they would be selling ageing stock for months afterwards, at a higher than usual margin. So we printed special price-marked packs of chocolate with a bold '99p' in the top corner to make sure the savings actually got passed on. Some retailers saw this as coercive and didn't like it, but the ones that bought price-marked stock enjoyed a boost to sales, built goodwill and blunted their customers' concerns about supermarkets' lower prices. It was those customers who would be the ones that stocked up on chocolate – and this meant that they rarely found themselves with an empty kitchen cupboard; there was always a good stash of chocolate lurking there to satisfy a craving whenever it hit.

covering the finances, the logistics and the commercial side of things and get out there and sell, too. Selling involves making lots of phone calls, writing letters, following up leads and spending as much time as possible *out* of the office – which is, after all, where the customers are. So we recruited a full-time sales person, a chirpy and hungry young guy called Steve Rudkin, who multi-tasked working both on Green & Black's and Whole Earth. Alan took Steve out on his first calls to teach him the ropes and introduce him to the buyers he would be dealing with.

Sales started to accelerate and we were on a roll. In August

1997 when Alan went to Sainsbury's to show Whole Earth corn-flakes to the cereal buyer, he was asked if we had any other cereals, as the feeling was that one line would look lonely on the shelves. So Craig came up with a Swiss-style muesli that fitted the bill. With tight control over packaging design and the creative process, Whole Earth had a recipe accepted within a week along with a rough pack design. By October the product was on their shelves – just three months later. Big companies couldn't begin to respond and deliver within such a narrow time frame – we were building respect. For the buyers, organic food was something that repre-sented a lot of hassle for little return on the performance meas-ures on which their bonuses were assessed. So if we could help simplify things, we got the listings. The categories were too small to allow for two of the same organic product which meant that once we bagged a slot on the shelf, there was no room for our competitors. As yet we didn't have many, but we knew more were coming.

By December 1997 we were firing on all cylinders and the Big Bang of organic food was coming down the line quickly – Waitrose had tentatively set a date of May 1998 for their big organic push and Sainsbury's were one month behind, aiming for June.

Waitrose's launch went off perfectly. They had an O logo and little shelf-wobblers (the O logo on stalks) which stuck out from the edge of the shelf so a customer who was looking for organic products had little trouble finding them. They didn't advertise much, but the major publicity advantage from being first was effective in drawing in customers looking for organic food. A year earlier Marks & Spencer's had called a press conference to announce they thought the steam had gone out of organic food and they were discontinuing it. It had been a big news story and was, for the organic movement, momentarily demoralising. Getting it so wrong was symptomatic of deeper problems at M & S and this mistaken policy practically shovelled their customers in the direction of Waitrose, who appealed to the same higher income and age demographic: a little cooler, a little more affluent, and definitely foodie.

Just a few weeks later, Sainsbury's launched with national advertising based on a jolly scarecrow in a field to symbolise the earthiness of organics and its non-dependence on chemical pest controls. It was a powerful campaign and stole a march on Tesco. Because customers now expected to find organic products in every branch of Waitrose and Sainsbury's our ranges were no longer just in the larger branches but in every single supermarket in the chain. Some products that were initially only in ninety Sainsbury's were rolled out to all 450 shops. Waitrose's 120 branches had generous displays of chocolate and sales responded accordingly. Friends and acquaintances started to tell us how they now saw our product everywhere. The fuse had been lit and sales were taking off like a rocket.

Beware of Pirates

Craig: One of the things that always irritates people who create valuable stuff is that once they've done the hard part (sourcing, creating, financing, launching, marketing) other people come along and snaffle the result. A pertinent Caribbean example is the progression of gold from the Maya, who accumulated it, to the Aztecs, who invaded and stole it, to the Spanish who invaded and shipped it off to Spain, to the English privateers such as Captain Morgan who captured the Spanish treasure ships and diverted the wealth to England (and himself).

At one point, it looked as though a rival might just swoop and make off with the cocoa which went into Maya Gold, a product we had so painstakingly sourced, created, financed, launched and marketed. We perhaps shouldn't have been surprised at this development. Chocolate is really a modern form of gold, with a similar progression: the Maya developed it and traded it; the Aztecs invaded and forced the Maya to supply them with it; the Spanish enslaved the population to grow cocoa to ship to Spain; the Portuguese took cocoa beans to Africa and got slaves to grow it there. Through our nurturing of one of the first organic cacao-growing projects, we faced a similar risk. In the spring of 1997 the Toledo Cacao Growers' Association (TCGA) had an unexpected visitor, Joe Whinney.

Joe Whinney had a company called the Organic Commodities Project (OCP). This company imported organic cocoa from growers in Panama and the Dominican Republic and sold it to ADM Cocoa, the world's second largest cocoa-processing company and the suppliers of chocolate to Paul Newman's brand of chocolate, Newman's Own. This brand, operated by Newman's daughter Nell, was easily the bestselling brand of organic chocolate in the USA, way ahead of Rapunzel (which had a molasses flavour because of the spray-dried cane sugar they used) and Green & Black's. We were just establishing a toehold in the US market but were, of course, storming in the UK. We didn't really see Newman's Own as a rival: it wasn't a premium chocolate;

basically, it was an organic version of a Hershey bar, but at that stage in the evolution of American connoisseurship of chocolate, that Hersheyness was a familiar taste to US chocolate-lovers, who hadn't really experienced the flavour of premium chocolate. We admired Newman's Own: all their products, from canned drinks to pasta sauces and salad dressing, as well as the chocolate, gave all profits after tax to Paul Newman's own charities for children (over $200 million and counting). We liked Nell, who we'd see at trade shows, where she wasn't above putting in long days breaking up squares of the chocolate bars on which her face – alongside her famous dad's – were emblazoned. (Craig is always threatening to strike back at food marketing box office idols like Paul Newman and Terence Stamp by becoming a movie star; he has an idea that people should stick to what they do best.)

Joe Whinney was down in Toledo province visiting his friend Mark Cohen, who ran an organisation called BARC (Belize Agroforestry Research Council). Mark had set up BARC with support from people back in his hometown in Ohio and he had a bunkhouse where supporters could come down, stay, help out on the farm and pay for the privilege of learning about tropical agroforestry. BARC tried valiantly to develop ways to help save the rainforest by making it economically competitive with agricultural systems that depended on removing the forest and exhausting the fertility of the soil below. Set in the foothills of Lubaantun, close to the village of San Pedro Columbia, it had a beautiful frontage on the Columbia river. They had planted a few cacao trees and were experimenting with growing ginger in the spaces between them, alongside other ways to generate more income from forestry crops.

When Joe met up with the TCGA, he told them they were being underpaid by Green & Black's, even though they were getting US $1,925 a tonne when the world market price was US $1,000. They said they were happy with the relationship, but Joe offered US $2,200 a tonne. The guys at the TCGA gave this some thought but realised that Green & Black's was a bird in the hand and the security of our relationship was worth more than Joe's OCP bird in the bush. They were polite but unwilling to deal.

Undeterred, Joe ended up talking to some of the cacao growers in the San Pedro area, who he persuaded of the benefits of dealing with him.

Those farmers were convinced and set up their own 'shadow' cooperative. Joe went back to the States and this breakaway cooperative held back their supply of cocoa to the TCGA, in anticipation of getting the higher price from Joe. They even got a local aid worker to help them put together an application for a grant to build a storage depot for the cocoa they were planning to sell to Joe, which they submitted to various funders. Without this important source of cocoa, the TCGA went short, and it took that much longer to fill up a container to ship to our factory.

Meanwhile, back in the States, Joe found that sales of Newman's Own were beginning to feel the impact of Green & Black's, as organic chocolate-lovers made the switch. Rather than needing more supplies of organic cocoa, he was looking at a warehouse full of the stuff that he'd purchased in anticipation of growing sales of Newman's Own which now looked like they'd be slowing down.

The farmers in San Pedro didn't hear from him again – he was busy dealing with his cash flow. In fact the next time we heard anything about Joe was when a cooperative of organic cacao farmers from Panama who he had been buying from at US$2,200 per tonne, got in touch with Green & Black's. He was no longer buying their cocoa, they told us. In fact the OCP had gone bust under the US Chapter 17 rules, so there was nothing at all to help clear the debts. They hadn't been paid for their most recent shipments. Would we be interested in buying their cocoa in future? We got some samples of their beans. The fermentation levels were well below what we could accept. For a Hershey's-style chocolate they didn't make much difference but for a 70% solids dark chocolate it would have alienated our loyal customers because of the astringent and smoky off-tastes it contained. With great regret we declined their offer.

Joe went on to become a successful artisan chocolate maker and a colleague of his told us that he always found him to be extremely conscientious, insistent on verification about any cocoa that he purchases. There had been no malice in Joe's actions: he probably thought he really was doing the farmers a favour, but dealing with a company like ADM is fraught with difficulties. In addition, his expectations for the upward growth of the Newman's Own brand were based on historic growth which had all taken place in a competitive vacuum. With Green & Black's and some very good non-organic-quality brands nipping at their heels, Newman's Own sales were beginning to falter. Joe was caught in the middle: he couldn't honour his commitments to his existing suppliers, and his new targets were soon forgotten.

Nowadays the TCGA get several visits a year from many different people who are keen to purchase their cocoa. It's the best, so you'd expect that to happen. Although our contract with them has a five-year notice period, there is nothing to stop their members resigning and forming a new co-operative so that they can sell to someone else. But there have been no such initiatives so far and the TCGA membership total is now over 1,000, and everyone sells to Green & Black's. Loyalty cuts both ways, and our loyalty to the farmers through hurricanes and price fluctuations has been rewarded with their loyalty to us.

In the twenty-first century, there's another type of piracy on the horizon: bio-piracy. The International Cocoa Gene Bank of Trinidad has established an invaluable collection of over 2,500 different types of cocoa on a 33-hectare farm in Trinidad. Trinitario cocoa beans are all hybrids that have been derived from this extraordinary gene bank – a common resource to protect diversity and maintain genetic traits that can help disease resistance. It is supported by donations, and exists for the benefit of cacao growers worldwide. Similar seed banks, in fact, exist for most of the world's food crops.

But that genetic material is now in some cases being bought up by multi-national companies, who want to control it – and the world's food supply – for themselves. We have seen how genetically diverse varieties of maize that were developed by Mexican farmers over thousands of years were then taken by American seed companies, hybridised and patented. In turn, these companies were then taken over by genetic-engineering companies such as Monsanto, who injected them with proprietary Roundup-resistant genes (so that fields could be sprayed with heavy doses of Roundup herbicide, without killing the crops). Because they identified and modified the genetic material, these varieties became the private property of Monsanto. Under US and Canadian law, if a farmer's own crop is contaminated with these genes – even if some of the patented seed falls off a truck and starts to grow on that farmer's land – the farmer must pay a penalty fee (usually about $10,000) to the owner of the patent. This is why American and Canadian farmers have warned European farmers to resist strongly the inflow of genetically modified seed.

The Indian government has supported lawsuits against some of these nefarious activities and has successfully protected heritage plants such as basmati rice and neem trees from having their genes hijacked, but it seems wrong that you should have to spend a fortune in legal fees to protect what your ancestors cultivated and bred for the common good.

It would be a tragedy if the same thing happened to the wonderful and amazingly diverse collection of cacao stock that exists in Trinidad. The TCGA have reported several cases where a mystery visitor, usually accompanied by a government official, turns up and disappears into the high forest with a guide to seek out wild or feral cacao varieties. These are then taken away and nobody really knows where they've gone or why. Some years ago the 'gee whiz' genetic engineering buffs were enthusing over how they could make cocoa butter by putting the right genes into soya beans (a potential catastrophe for cacao farmers), so who knows what the high-tech future holds, as they get their hands on rare cacao varieties? It seems there are still pirates in the Caribbean, and frankly we find them a lot scarier than Long John Silver or Captain Jack Sparrow.

8

The Black Hole

Most businesses look good on paper. If you do a lot of business, you make a lot of money; if things are slow you reduce staff and overheads, and keep going. Unless you're very careless about pricing, you should be able to operate at a profit. But cash flow is the real key to survival. If you can't pay your bills, it doesn't matter how much you're owed or how much stock you've got in your warehouse; the people you owe money to won't give you any more stock or services and eventually they'll close you down. In the bad old days the grocery trade was full of horror stories of perfectly viable businesses that went under because a major supermarket took ninety days to pay invoices that were based on agreed terms of forty-five. The big supermarkets are more aware of their responsibilities now and lenders are better at buying debt, through factoring or invoice discounting, so the poor supplier can get 80% of his cash when he shows the bank the invoice, and then pay the bank the difference when the customer pays up. With factoring, the customer pays direct to your bank, which is a bit embarrassing as it's in effect telling your customer that you're weak in the cash department. But it sure beats going bust.

We had always tried to keep costs down at Green & Black's, and some of the fastest ways to fritter money away while you're building a business are swanky offices, and over-staffing. We had funky offices, not swanky offices: Whole Earth and Green & Black's lurked

In Small Businesses, Cash Is King

Craig: In 1982 Whole Earth Foods had been on the ropes. Our account-ants, KPMG, told us to call in the receivers. Our shareholders didn't want to put up any more money. We called the bank manager but he was too busy to see us and it was the end of May bank holiday, so we booked in to see him on Tuesday to ask him to call in the receivers. Over the weekend I realised something: we weren't really in that much trouble at all – we were healthy, but too big. The real problem was that we were carrying too much stock and the cost of warehousing and financing it was tying up our cash and eating up our profits. By Tuesday I had a plan to cut the business down to a profitable size – I called it a balance sheet projection, which was really a fancy name for a crude cash-flow forecast. The bank manager didn't want to close us down (this was in an era when bank managers were still allowed to use their own judgement) and he saw the merit of my grubby piece of paper, full of erased pencilled numbers. Over the next few months I paid off a £95,000 bank loan, repaid our share-holders £200,000 and was making profit. I'd finally understood and applied the miracle of cash flow. Maybe I should have paid more attention at Wharton.

behind a faux window display of cereal boxes and jam jars in the centre of Portobello Market, and both the front door and the fascia were painted to look like a pink button-back sofa.

Ours was the second most famous front door in Notting Hill, after 'the blue door' (to which, after the Hugh Grant/Julia Roberts film *Notting Hill* we got asked directions every single time we stepped outside). Nikon once used our front door for the back-ground in a photo shoot. One day we even got a call from Stanley Kubrick's office, asking if he could shoot Tom Cruise and Nicole Kidman coming out of our front door, for *Eyes Wide Shut*, in a night shoot for which we'd get £1,000 and a night in a hotel. Sadly, because we were quite excited about a night in a hotel, not to mention seeing 269 Portobello Road in Panavision, they pulled out, unable to get the correct angle for shooting (every shot also captured the somewhat less glamorous TV-repair shop next door).

Craig's office was on the first floor, with an AstroTurfed roof deck outside, where – whenever the sun emerged – he'd disappear to think (and tan). Downstairs was Barbara, Craig's high-octane PA, Philip (accounts), Simon (technical director), Alan (MD, before he left), and the stockroom (known as 'Uncle Craig's free shop' by our niece and nephew). Jo's office was in a rented flat next door; in the morning she went out through our front door up the stairs next door and manned the Green & Black's phones in a room into which we could have knocked through a doorway from our bedroom. It allowed her the discipline of feeling as though she was going to work, so that she wasn't distracted by domestic comings and goings, but was still very convenient for meetings, brainstorming or (sometimes) lunch.

Keeping the costs down in-house allowed us to make the most of sales revenue, and a few months after the organic range launches at Waitrose and Sainsbury's, the monthly sales figures were steadily rising and our cash flow was healthy. But there was an unexpected problem on the money front: we had suffered severe setbacks to our accounting systems when the London Electricity Board lost power in May 1997 just as we were backing up our accounts on our old Apple II computers.

We called in a special team from our auditors who painstakingly recreated the accounts as best they could, working with our bookkeeper Philip, and under the supervision of Alan Wills. Things were beginning to make sense and we had transferred our accounts to slightly less archaic PCs when another spate of power cuts hit and we lost everything again. Every Wednesday afternoon for weeks, the lights would start to flicker in our offices, the computer screen would go black and moments later, we'd be plunged into darkness. We have no idea why it was always a Wednesday, but it soon started happening like clockwork. The butcher's a few doors away would have to close. The Market Bar would be silenced. Ellis Black's refurbished TV shop next door at 267, would shut: no point trying to sell tellies without enough juice to turn them on. A Blitz spirit set in; we joked with each other about reading books by candlelight and enjoying the respite from computers. Either that or we were on the phone screaming at the electricity board who always, miraculously, managed to restore the supply just a few minutes before they would have been liable for compensating us for the loss of more than four hours' electricity.

Philip and Alan did their best to restore the situation after the power cuts but there was a gap in the trail of information and data that had been otherwise unbroken for the previous twenty years. Our auditors really struggled to make sense of it all. However, as long as we had money in the bank, rising sales and were paying all our creditors on time, we weren't losing too much sleep over it. There'd have to be some deft judgement when we filed our annual tax returns, but the overall picture was rosy.

Philip left us and we recruited a replacement bookkeeper, Pardeep Bahanda, who had been at the New Covent Garden Soup Company and came with excellent references from the finance director there, Nick Beart. Nick and the soup company's MD, William Kendall, were selling their business to a listed company and Pardeep's job was going to go as part of the takeover. (We had no idea then just how well we'd get to know William and Nick in years to come.)

On 7 December 1997 Alan nipped up to Craig's office for 'an update on developments'. Without our knowledge, Alan had been working with Charles Byrne, an entrepreneur who had collaborated with scientists at Cork University on a high-tech project for 'ambient ice cream' and Alan saw this as his key to financial freedom. The product seemed pretty clever: you put a vanilla or chocolate mousse into a tub and sterilised it so it could be stored without refrigeration. Then it could be sold in shops on the regular shelves and, at home when dessert was needed (or a craving struck), you just put the tub in the freezer for half an hour and, hey presto!, it turned into ice cream, ready to eat.

Alan reckoned this would cut the legs off the freezer- and energy-dependent traditional ice-cream makers, and had cooked up a deal with Duerr's. They'd invested £250,000 in start-up money and Alan was all set to go. He'd come in to the office to give notice of his intention to leave. We were surprised that just as things were going so well with Green & Black's he should up sticks and quit but could see he saw this as a once in a lifetime opportunity to get seriously rich. Craig was very disappointed that Duerr's, his long-trusted allies who he'd introduced to the pure fruit spread and peanut butter business (which in turn had helped them transform their own stagnant hundred-year-old family business) had been secretly planning this with our trusted chief executive. Some might call it treason. Others might just say 'That's business – get over it'. Our accounts showed that Whole Earth, in particular, had made a good profit for the year so Alan asked for and received a profit-share bonus of £32,000. We were sorry to see him go, but didn't regret paying the cheque as it was just a fraction of the profit we'd made.

We set about recruiting a successor, but quickly concluded that the obvious choice was staring us in the face: Cliff Moss. Cliff had worked for Whole Earth as operations director from 1989 to 1991 and had then moved on to buy a soft drink brand called Free. He had also worked with Nigel Phipps, who ran a consultancy and sales agency that helped companies (including ours) to deal with the health food trade wholesalers and retailers, doing the legwork of visiting independent shops, which was very manpower-intensive, and something we didn't have the resources to do ourselves. When Nigel died after a long illness, Cliff offered to buy the business from his widow, but she sold the agency to someone else. The guy she sold to was on our blacklist: he'd never paid us for stock some years earlier so we didn't want to work with him again. Cliff then created his own company called Healthy Sales and Marketing, to fulfil the same role as Nigel's consultancy, and we had been his first clients. He knew our products, we knew and trusted him and he was happy to take the job as the new MD as long as he could maintain his other interests. He joined the company in early 1998 and Alan handed over the reins to him.

In March 1998, Craig had planned a trip to Belize to meet the new chairman of the Toledo Cacao Growers Association. He was going on this mixing-business-with-pleasure trip with Hugh Raven, a Soil Association trustee, and his wife Jane Stuart-Smith, a lawyer at Farrers (the Queen's solicitors) who specialised in employment rights law. On the morning of our departure Cliff came into Craig's office, looking grim. 'Craig, I hesitated about whether I should bring this up or not just before you go away, but thought you should know we might have a problem. I got a phone call from André Deberdt (Green & Black's French chocolate supplier) – he's chasing up some payments. He says that £175,000 is due this week and there's more in the pipeline – we have no record of these invoices being due. In fact we have no record of these invoices at all . . .'

It's hard to describe the horrific sinking feeling in your guts when you realise your whole business has gone in just a few seconds from being a thriving enterprise to a shipwrecked hulk. £175,000 is a lot of money to find at short notice. We were having a good year, but our cash flow would be severely damaged by having to pay out such a large sum in one go. Even though Alan had left by that point, Craig urged Cliff to get in touch with him and find out what he knew. We were sure it must have been an accounting problem

Lunch Hour? What's a Lunch Hour?

Jo: One of the most important lessons most entrepreneurs learn is that to be successful, you pretty much have to give up any notion of schedules, and regular work times – or lunch breaks. You do what needs to be done, when it needs to be done, whether that's at 5.30 a.m. (me) or 11.30 p.m. (Craig). Very often, it is only those hours outside the regular working day when you manage to get anything done at all – before the world wakes up, or when it's watching evening telly. Life is one long interruption, one long round of fire-fighting, and you'd better be prepared to put up with that and be flexible enough to deal with it. I always thank my lucky stars if I get a five-minute straight run at any particular task; I've trained myself to rein in my thoughts rapidly after each interruption, and focus again fast on what I was doing before the phone rang/someone knocked on my door, rather than taking a few minutes to settle down again. I'm always impressed by interviews with 'superwomen' who manage religiously to leave the office at 6 p.m. to go home to their families, but I'll bet they're on their 'crackberries' again the second the kids are snoring gently. We had one big advantage, in that department: Green & Black's is our baby. If Craig had been working that late for anyone else, I'd have read him the riot act. But when you're doing it for yourself, for your children/grandchildren, not to mention hundreds of Third World farmers whose security is dependent on your success, you don't give it a second thought, frankly.

– after all we had just had our most successful and profitable year in a decade, so the money had to be there to sort this out – somewhere.

Even though Craig found it hard to leave when there was such a big question mark hanging over the business, the visit to Belize was worth every minute. It was the first time he'd had the opportunity to enjoy the beautiful Toledo District in the south of the country, and having Hugh and Jane there turned it into a real holiday. The area has so much to offer (as many Green & Black's customers, who've made the pilgrimage to Belize, have discovered). Craig, Jane and Hugh went snorkelling, fly-fishing and swimming at Sapodilla Caye, 15 miles out to sea from Punta Gorda, spending time at Punta Negra village, a small Garifuna village situated on a sand spit north of Punta Gorda and tombstoning off a rocky ledge into the cool waters below a waterfall on the Columbia river near the village of Santa Cruz. As she was climbing up the rocks there Jane reached out to grab a branch for a handhold which slithered away – a biting but non-poisonous green snake. She earned the moniker 'Jungle Jane' for her total cool in this situation. It was a great escapist time and Craig almost forgot the situation – actually, a growing nightmare – that was unfolding at home. At a touching ceremony at the TCGA headquarters, Ines Coc, the vice-chairlady of the cooperative, presented Craig with a hand-woven shoulder bag and made a short speech on behalf of the Mayan growers, thanking Green & Black's for being their partner in cacao. Jane was so moved that she wept as she watched. But inwardly, Craig couldn't help trembling at the thought that the TCGA would lose everything we had built over the years if the problems back home weren't sorted out.

While there Craig recruited a young and computer-literate American called Chris Nesbitt, who was a friend of his daughter Rima, to help the Maya with the administration of their compliance with organic certification. The Soil Association were happy with the way the Maya farmed, but unhappy with weaknesses in their paperwork: many of the farmers were illiterate and record-keeping procedures were not always observed to the letter. John Myers, the inspector who had most recently visited, said he was completely confident that the cocoa was organic, but suggested that Chris, who had driven him out to the villages on his inspection visit, might be a help in computerising the records and helping Cayetano Ico, the chair of the cooperative, to bring the admin side up to scratch.

When Craig got back to the UK, Hugh and Jane invited him round to a dinner party at their house in nearby Notting Dale. By one of fate's serendipitous coincidences one of the guests was William Kendall, formerly of the New Covent Garden Soup Company. After the sale of 'Soup' (as William called it), he had fallen out with his buyers over the terms of his post-deal employment; Jane had successfully acted on his behalf in the resulting legal tussle. 'Ah, *you're* the person who was responsible for "the best holiday ever"' he commented to Craig when they met.

While Craig had been away, Cliff had got word that Peter Beckwith, an entrepreneur who he had helped with the marketing of some soft drinks, was interested in investing in Whole Earth and Green & Black's. Even though at that stage we were still not sure our financial problems were really that severe, we thought it would be worth considering his offer and had met him over lunch in Wimbledon, near his home. Craig thought William's would be a good brain to pick about how to sell a business successfully, and offered to buy him lunch. Craig and William went out for a meal, and William's initial advice was: 'Remember, Craig, if you just sell one share in your business, it's not yours any more.' It was a sobering thought.

By the end of the meal, however, William was clearly intrigued by the situation; he asked if he could return the lunch and bring along his financial manager, Nick Beart. At a meeting a few weeks later at the Groucho Club, Craig frankly set out the unfolding problems that were besetting the company. Nick had a vague idea about it anyway as Pardeep (his former right-hand man at the soup company) was still in touch. They were both interested in further discussions and Craig agreed to let Nick take a closer look at the finances of the business, as they seemed genuinely interested in investing. The investors who had backed them at

New Covent Garden Soup were very happy with the result – a £2-million company had been turned into a £22-million a year company in just a few years, under Nick and William's management – and were keen to reinvest the proceeds in another tax-efficient scheme. We were an ideal prospect for them.

Opening up this avenue with Nick and William seemed exciting, but we knew we were going to have to get to the bottom of these missing invoices if we were going to stand any chance of moving forward. Unfortunately, Cliff had drawn a blank in his discussions with Alan Wills, who said that as far as he was concerned there shouldn't be any problems and that he was too busy with his ice-cream project to come in and investigate the situation. It's hard to know what was going on in Cliff's mind, but he stayed the course at a time when a lesser man would have thrown his hands in the air and said, 'Nobody told me what I was getting into here, I'm getting out!' We're eternally grateful for his commitment to the project, despite the fact that things were not at all as he'd been told.

We were racking our brains over the situation when Jo suddenly brightened up and exclaimed: 'Cousin Bob!'

'Cousin who?'

'My cousin Bob Williamson is an accountant – he's been working in the Gulf for the past few years but now he's back in Devon and is semi-retired. I think he's standing for his local council in the next elections. He's married to my cousin Jenny, who I grew up with in Bromley.' Jo thought he would be the ideal person to unmacramé our complicated financial situation.

We called Bob, who came up to London for a visit. He was the most charming man imaginable. He had courted Jenny at the Croydon swimming baths, which was one of the few places in England in the 1950s where you could hang out with women and actually see their legs and arms. They were both enthusiastic competitive swimmers and still have the strong-limbed physique of athletes. We got on really well and, as we explained the situation,

As Long as the Job Gets Done . . .

Jo: We have, of course, had help from some fantastic people who've worked with me over the years. In most cases, people have stayed with me (and/or Craig) for five, six, seven years or even much, much longer. Recruiting and retaining good staff is key to success, and saves endlessly having to train new people. Personally, I have three golden rules of employment.

1. Work should be fun for people, or why bother? This means outings, laughs, celebrations: these will go a long way towards keeping morale up when money's tight or everyone's stressed. I used to work for Carlton, a wonderful publishing company where they'd give us flowers on the first day of spring, arrange trips to the races, and presents of Waterford Crystal glasses on the magazine's 'birthday'. Small gestures, which were rewarded with amazing devotion. I tried to learn from that.

2. The working environment should be attractive; you spend far more waking hours there than at home, so have flowers, nice pictures on the wall, lovely mugs, nice filing boxes, etc. None of these cost a fortune, but they all help create a place where you want to go to work.

3. In an office, if people get the job done, I don't care when they do it. Clock-watching is absolutely OUT. If someone wants to come in early and go home early, or the opposite, then fine. If they want to skip lunch so they can pick their kids up from school, that's fine, too. Nine to five breeds a nine to five mentality. Cluny and Gail, fantastic PAs who worked for me while Green & Black's was growing, were both single, working mothers with young children who occasionally got sick or who needed to go to carol concerts. My flexibility in understanding those tugs on their time was repaid ten times over by their loyalty. The same applies if people want

to get a job done at home; yes, you need face-to-face contact in an office occasionally, but 'tele-working' saves on office rent and, in my experience of over twenty years of working for myself, I know it's often easier to get a job done at home without inter-ruptions. If the project's completed on time, does it matter if it's done at the office, at home, or even at Starbucks, logged onto their free Wi-Fi?

he had a remarkably calming effect on us all. If there is an account-ing equivalent to a doctor's bedside manner Bob had it in spades. Cliff brought him up to speed with the situation so far and Bob prepared a long list of questions for Craig, Cliff, André and, of course, Alan.

Our cash flow for the past year had been extremely healthy (which also made us question how we could not have been profitable), so paying André what we owed was actually possible. Once we'd veri-fied that the outstanding invoices were valid, we reluctantly settled them, but this brought us up against a much tighter cash situation than we had been in before.

The foundation of our cash flow at Whole Earth and Green & Black's was our close relationships with Community Foods and Duerr's. Community Foods is a health food wholesaler that had been set up to sell brown rice and other macrobiotic and natural foods in the early 1970s, mopping up a lot of the business Harmony Foods had left behind as it morphed into Whole Earth. Duerr's, established in 1881, is a family company that manufactures jams. In 1988 Craig had set them up to manufacture peanut butter, selling them an entire production line from the Whole Earth factory. As part of the deal they agreed not to make no added sugar jam or peanut butter for anyone else. As well as being Whole Earth's jam and peanut-butter supplier, they were our warehousing and distribution partner, so we were almost joined at the hip. Community Foods helped us to purchase the chocolate from André Deberdt in France and Duerr's helped us to ship it out. Because both companies had such a long-standing relationship with us, they were happy to extend decent credit terms that really helped with our cash flow. As long as we were trading profitably they didn't have anything to worry about: they knew they'd get their money in due course. Unfortunately, though, the bills from André had made a huge hole in our profits.

But how could this have happened? If the Portobello power cuts hadn't destroyed our records, we might have been able to figure things out sooner, but as it was Cousin Bob had a lot of unravelling to do. He had several meetings with Andy Collinson, the finance director at Duerr's, and with the chief accountant at Community. Things were beginning to become clearer, but Alan was still too busy and too dismissive of the problem to help us clarify what had happened. His memory of events could have helped fill in the gaps because he had been in control at the time.

In desperation, Craig wrote to Tony Duerr, the chairman of Duerr's, urging him to insist that Alan cooperate. Eventually, under pressure from Tony, Alan came to the office, while Cousin Bob was up from Devon (and billeted in our spare room). They sat down and Alan repeated all the points he had made over the previous few months, but they all proved hollow. We recognised that Bob's forensic analysis of our situation was correct: we were in a deep hole and it was time to stop digging.

What Bob had discovered was that someone had been putting André's invoices in a folder instead of booking them into our accounts system. In total we were missing £350,000: money that had gone out of the system somewhere, somehow. We believed we'd had a successful year and our accounts had been audited and approved, but our profitability was an illusion. What was especially galling was that we had paid Alan a £32,000 profit-share bonus – money we now realised we had been ill able to afford.

Poor old Pardeep Bahanda had jumped out of the New Covent Garden Soup Company frying pan into an unexpectedly hot fire with us. Nick Beart was taking an interest as a potential investor and examining the figures for the business going forward, but the pressing problems of the here and now were something we were going to have to tackle ourselves before we could expect anyone to buy shares in the business.

Bob had also discovered that not *all* the missing money was simply due to unrecorded invoices. Our agreement with Community was that we would keep 'their' chocolate in contract refrigerated storage at Salveson's in Yorkshire. Whenever we sent chocolate out we would notify Community and they would invoice us. We hadn't been giving them stock updates, but they trusted us. In fact, in the latter part of the previous year, stock had been sold direct to customers without Community being notified. When we found out we had no choice but to tell them, and this led to more than £100,000 of additional loss, added to the £175,000 of Deberdt's invoices that had been mislaid.

How is it that this all this could have happened without our knowledge? Hmmm. How is it that a rogue trader at Société Générale can lose the bank over $7.2 billion? Being out of touch with the nuts and bolts of invoices coming in and stock or cash going out isn't unusual for senior managers. Figureheads are frequently focussed on the big picture: the outward-facing roles, such as marketing, PR, sourcing, product development. But as Martha Stewart points out in her excellent book *The Martha Rules: 10 Essentials to Achieving Success as You Start, Grow or Manage a Business*, it helps to have not just a telescope for the big picture, but also a microscope, when looking at your company. We had taken the monthly figures at face value, not realising they didn't show the whole picture.

By now Community was getting very restless: they, too, were waiting for a payment. Together with Cliff, we went up to their warehouse in north London for a summit meeting. Bill Henry, their

MD, was furious we'd sold their stock and was threatening to cut us adrift and take us to court. Tim Powell, their sales director, was less aggressive and was more open to the idea that we might be able to figure something out. Craig had known Community for ever; they were whole food pioneers together. Not only that, we were also 'health food show' compatriots, hanging out in the bar together drinking those oh-so-welcome lagers at the end of foot-weary days. The Green & Black's team had taken part in Community's five-a-side industry football tournament. Before Notting Hill became the country's organic heartland, with several organic outposts (and one of London's earliest farmer's markets), we bought our organic staples at Community's cash and carry, filling the boot of Jo's car with cases of soya milk, tahini and brown rice. But, despite our history, this meeting had the feeling of a showdown. The crunch.

A couple of years beforehand, we had bought a small house in Hastings. There'd been no point buying a house in London; the company rented the Whole Earth office building, we had a small, somewhat eccentric flat upstairs and even in the early 1990s, Notting Hill prices were beyond us. But we'd wanted a toe-hold on the property ladder. Weekends had been spent in Bath, Dorset, Kent and Suffolk looking at the tumbledown cottages and poky town-houses that were within our very modest budget. Jo's family had Hastings roots: her great-grandparents and great-aunts had lived there, and it had become a place associated with sunny skies, lazy days and good times.

In Hastings, we could afford a three-bedroom Victorian terraced house in the Old Town, just a few minutes' walk from both the beach and the country park, and it had become our sanity, our retreat from the increasing madness of Portobello Road. Somehow, we could keep going like Duracell bunnies all week, working from dawn till way, way beyond dusk so long as we had the carrot of a weekend in Hastings dangling ahead of us. The second the taxi turned into our quiet seaside street on a Friday evening, our blood pressure would plummet. Home and family is very, very important to both of us, and we had worked hard to protect our haven. But now Community Foods wanted our home as security for bailing us out.

We hadn't expected this. We already had a mortgage (so the bank had first dibs on any proceeds from a house sale), but the cash payment towards the house had come from the money Jo had made selling her flat before our marriage. The same money she'd used to bankroll those first few consignments of Green & Black's. And now Community Foods wanted to get their hands on it, if Green & Black's wobbled, at some point in the future.

Jo couldn't help it, she burst into tears and fled the room. 'It's just not FAIR!' she shouted, terrified and unhappy. It wasn't a tactic; Jo was genuinely heart-broken at the thought of losing our home (and everything else we had worked for). It had a very unexpected effect. Those genuine tears melted Tim and Bill's hearts, and when she dried her eyes and went back into the room, feeling both less than professional and emotionally battered, they had retracted the request to put the house up as security for any future deal.

We were out of the woods with Community, but by that point the bank had smelled trouble and realised their branch manager was out of his depth. They had a special division in Pall Mall that dealt with companies having problems and they sent in a guy who was a sort of pre-receivership receiver. His job was to see if there was any way to save the company, see if there were potential buyers for the assets and most importantly, to make sure that our creditors couldn't sue Barclays for allowing this fiasco to happen. He was very helpful, we got along well, but we all knew it was time to put the full story to Duerr's, who were still unaware of the implications of our situation to their balance sheet. If they had to pay Community for chocolate we couldn't pay them for, they would face a loss of at least £350,000.

What Goes Up . . .

Jo: I learned a very important lesson that day in North London. Like those financial-service ads tell us, what goes up may go down. 'You can lose your shirt, and everything else, and you'd better be prepared for that (which I wasn't). But when you've been faced with the prospect of downshifting into a rented bedsit *à deux* – well, let me tell you: any future success tastes much sweeter. We can all joke about it, now: Bill and Tim have done very nicely, thank you, selling Community Foods to the pension fund of Milk Marque, while continuing at the helm. (They're still handing out dried figs and cashew nuts at trade fairs, and will probably go on doing so for ever.)

So Cliff created a Powerpoint slide show that set out, step by step, a clear exposition of the entire situation. Craig and Cliff went up to Duerr's in Manchester with a computer screen and a laptop and Cliff talked them through to the final slide, where the full cost to Duerr's was there, in black and white. Andy Collinson, the finance director, was ashen-faced and Mark Duerr, the MD, looked at Andy with barely concealed horror and fury. They then retired to their meeting room to discuss possible solutions.

In the middle of the meeting the phone rang – it was Nick Beart. He had talked his way past the telephonist, insisting that this was an urgent matter and he had to be put through to Craig immediately. With urgency in his voice he said, 'Craig, don't agree anything with Duerr's – we can do a much better deal for you if you keep your distance from them. Don't make any concessions.'

'OK, Nick, thanks for the call. We're not at that stage anyway,' replied Craig, distinctly intrigued.

At that point, we still really wanted to fix things with Duerr's – better the devil you know, after all – and so we discussed various rescue options, mostly revolving around Duerr's giving us a loan and financing all our stock. Craig and Cliff then set off back to London, feeling a bit more positive about the situation. It was November, Christmas and the holidays were coming, and it was a great time of year for chocolate, second only to Easter in sales potential. Cash was still flowing but the bank was pressing hard for a resolution. Duerr's had by now fallen out with Alan Wills – the ice-cream project had swallowed £250,000 of their initial investment with nothing to show for it and they were pulling the plug, disillusioned with the project and with Alan.

We decided to take Alan to court, and eventually got a court order requiring him to repay the £32,000 profit share we had given him in good faith. He fought it to the bitter end, but by that point we could make depositions in court that made a ruling in our favour inevitable. We talked to Duerr's on the phone and on 6 December 1998 we took the train to Manchester and hammered out a final rescue plan with them. The first step was that they would take over all our stock and finance it completely. They would also invoice and collect the debts on our behalf and bank the money in a Whole Earth Foods bank account. But before they deposited any money, they would deduct payment for the stock. The cost of their managing this would be a 1% handling fee together with interest at 2% over bank rate. Finally, they offered us a loan of £600,000 to cover our previous losses at 2% over bank rate.

They knew better than anyone else that we were a sound company with underlying healthy profitability. And we were anticipating an improvement in our profitability because our relationship with André Deberdt was nearly at an end. By that point André, who'd had so many business problems of his own, had been virtually taken over by Cantalou, the giant French chocolate company who made an own-label organic chocolate that André sold to Carrefour, the largest chain of French supermarkets. If

In it Together

Craig: If we had gone under, we would certainly not have been the only losers. Business is all about interconnectedness and interdependency. Community would have had a fight on their hands to get their money out of Duerr's. Duerr's would have lost the value of our jam and peanut-butter business and the help in defraying their own distribution costs. ICAM would have lost a valuable customer at a time when they were struggling to make any profit as their main business was supplying own-label chocolate at low prices to Italian supermarket chains. The cacao growers in Belize and the Dominican Republic would have lost a dream customer for their organic production. Barclays Bank would have lost a good business customer who put a lot of valuable interest-bearing transactions through them and had great growth potential. They might also have been exposed to claims from our creditors on the basis that they should never have allowed our position to deteriorate so badly. In a situation like that there were an awful lot of people who had a vested interest in our survival and continuation. So remember: when the roof is caving in, don't feel like the house is falling down, because there are always a lot of people who have more of an interest in keeping you going than seeing you go under.

Cantalou swallowed André's company, we didn't want to be next in their sights, but our financial crisis made us vulnerable.

For some time, our chocolate had been made by an Italian company called ICAM, and then shipped to Cantalou to mould into bars – an arrangement André set up, and something that happened a lot in the chocolate world. We knew that ICAM made terrific bar chocolate – we'd had samples – and so it seemed to make sense to get ICAM to do the whole thing in their factory on the shores of Lake Como. (As gorgeous a setting for any factory as you can imagine, surrounded by mountains rising out of the deep lake. Business trips to see ICAM were never a hardship.)

Craig flew down and did a deal with them agreeing that we could buy the chocolate direct. This deal was a brilliant one for the future of Green & Black's, increasing our margins on chocolate by more than 20%. The future profitability picture was very, very healthy. Duerr's didn't want to lose the £2.5 million turnover that came from selling us jam and peanut butter and this deal secured it for them for the foreseeable future.

So we agreed the key factors of the new deal with Duerr's and agreed to instruct lawyers. Boarding the train at Manchester Piccadilly, Cliff and Craig were unable to stop grinning: the nightmare was over. They upgraded to first class, ordered a bottle of champagne and travelled back to London Euston as two of the happiest, or at least the most relieved, men in Britain.

We never did find out where or how the money had disappeared, but we had a super deal that would set us on course to realising the value of the brands, pay off the accumulated losses and allow us to focus on sales and marketing, which was our strength. Duerr's would take care of the back-office stuff and we could capitalise on all the hard work and creativity that had gone into creating the two leading organic food brands in Britain. Cliff had proved himself an extremely competent, loyal and reliable chief executive under the most testing of conditions. Christmas was coming and things were looking up.

Networking Works

Jo: Networking isn't something that comes naturally to British people, but seems to be in Americans' DNA. (Although Craig isn't a natural networker, and he was born in Nebraska.) Anita Roddick told us about a group called Social Venture Network (SVN) and encouraged us to join. Founded by an American called Josh Mailman, a shy, quiet man who had inherited money and was committed to giving most of it away, SVN organised conferences where those of us who wanted to do good, as well as do business, could meet once or twice a year. (I first met Josh when he flew out to see Anita in Texas and Mexico, when we were visiting her aloe farmers.) These were the very early days of ethical business, and few of us imagined that corporate social responsibility (CSR) would, a few years into the twenty-first century, be a major concern of every company in the world (CSR efforts are today even acknowledged in most annual reports).

The SVN mob – Anita, Gordon, Stonyfield Farms' Gary Hirshberg, Ben & Jerry (of ice-cream fame), PR dynamo Lynne Franks and 100 or so others – met in hotels in Boston and up Swiss and Italian mountains, to talk about our efforts and share our experiences. This sharing may be a very American way of doing things (group hugging was occasionally involved), but it was hugely inspiring at a time when if you talked about giving back, in a corporate context, it was mostly met with blank stares. For a few days, we felt like fish swimming as part of a shoal – instead of lone salmon, fighting to get upstream.

For that reason, networking is invaluable. It isn't just about making contacts (we never really got anything, business-wise, out of SVN, for instance, other than an appointment to see a supermarket buyer from the French chain Auchan, which came to *rien*). It's about being inspired, fired up, rekindling your passion for what you do, so that when you look at those big, fat red minus signs on the bank statement, you've got the gumption to go on. We listened to talks by CEOs who gave their staff paid time off to go and paint hostels for homeless people, we heard Anita rant about the plight of Amazonian Indians and how buying Brazil-nut butter could help save them, we were intrigued by Ben (or was it Jerry?) sharing the story of two crazy ice-cream makers who went on to become household names. Basically, for two or three days, we didn't feel like weirdos. (Or if we were weirdos, we were in good company.) Our guru was a charismatic American hippy turned spiritual teacher called Ram Dass, who led yoga classes and taught those of us who weren't still sleeping off a hangover how to tackle our stress and find clarity of thought through meditation. (Yoga and meditation both work wonders for me, to this day. Can't recommend them highly enough for those moments when the treacle you are wading through at work threatens to turn to toffee.)

Another opportunity to network positively was a weekend in 1996 at Glen House, the ancestral home of Lord Glenconner in the Borders, where green venture capitalist Tessa Tennant gathered (with Smith & Hawken founder and environmental campaigner Paul Hawken as the star guest), to throw ideas around about the 'triple bottom line' – a phrase coined by one of the weekend's other guests, SustainAbility's John Elkington, to describe the idea that companies now have to factor social and environmental responsibility into their business plans, as well as financial turnover. John and Julia Hailes, his co-author and (then) SustainAbility business partner had also helped give Green & Black's a little boost, at the dawn of the brand, with their book *The Green Consumer Guide*, which was originally published in 1988 and regularly updated to feature the greener products, from household cleaners to energy-saving light bulbs, which you otherwise had to be like Sherlock Holmes to track down, then. By the end of the weekend, any feeling of hopelessness at the task ahead had evaporated and we all returned to London on the GNER train restored, revived and with our loins girded (as it were) for the challenges ahead.

9

Under New Management

The Duerr's deal was a dream come true – but we dropped a line to William Kendall anyway, advising him of progress and thanking him for his interest. We both felt it was a pity they hadn't come up with a tangible, on the table offer, but imagined they were reluctant to climb aboard what they might have seen as a sinking ship. We'd opened up our accounts to them, and they knew our situation was precarious. If Green & Black's had gone pear-shaped, they could have picked up the pieces cheaply without taking on our heavy liabilities. The letter advising them we had a rescue plan up our sleeve with Duerr's quickly concentrated their minds.

On 27 December 1998 Nick Beart got in touch. He advised us strongly against the Duerr's deal and said, 'We'll pay two million pounds for a share in the business and inject enough capital to really build it up on the sales and marketing front.' This was the first time he had offered a specific cash amount. We were both intrigued and excited. Over the next couple of days, when we should have been sitting with our lawyers finalising the Duerr's deal we were thinking over this new offer, talking it through with everyone we knew.

'Don't be stupid. You've struggled enough. Take the money and let *them* worry about the business,' was the pretty universal advice. Everyone had seen how stressful things had been, and we weren't the only ones who had been on tenterhooks. For Craig's children,

Rima and Karim the future of their health food energy drink Gusto, which was distributed by Whole Earth, lay in the balance. William and Nick's deal would give them £50,000 each and an ongoing stake in the future of the business. Craig's brother Gregory had cashed in on his VegeBurger business many years previously and counselled breaking free with some cash. We each had a small mountain of personal debt and a mortgage on a house in Hastings, so the idea of having cash was hugely attractive. It was a tough decision – did we really want to hand over power to a couple of ex-public school boys who seemed pretty clever but were not entirely on our wavelength? Then again, perhaps the business needed a more 'straight' approach. After all, at that point it was turning over £4 million a year and growing fast. Would we be able to sort that out for ourselves, now the cash-flow problems were resolved? On the other hand, if they bought us out, solved the cash-flow problems and injected still more money into the business to pump up the sales and marketing side, wouldn't that help the brand take off and be able to repel the competition that was popping up everywhere? These were just some of the dilemmas that kept us tossing and turning at night, while we tried to make up our minds.

The Duerr's deal would fund our organic growth (excuse the pun). It would allow us to continue on the trajectory we had established, but that was about it. William and Nick's offer would fund the growth, give us a reasonable pile of money and inject financial adrenaline into the sales and marketing process. Attractive, yes, but the downside was that they were in for the short term: their plan, as with Soup, was to pump up the brands and then sell them off, either to a larger company or to float them on the stock market. We'd had endless letters from customers who wanted to invest in Green & Black's – perhaps their auntie had just left them some money and they wanted to spend it on shares in a company they loved. Such devotion boded well for an eventual flotation. We could imagine it being so successful that we could sit back and live on the dividends.

Not only was it tricky to decide what to do, it was also difficult to explore the new offer without putting the first one in jeopardy. Once we'd burned our bridges with Duerr's there would be little hope of rebuilding them, and if William and Nick reneged on what were still only offers, albeit in writing but hedged with 'subject to contract' and other legal verbiage, we would be very exposed.

We decided to go for the adrenaline approach and stalled the Duerr's lawyers while we hammered out the outlines of a deal with William and Nick. We both had very real reservations about selling to the 'dynamic duo'. Jo, in particular, wanted to know if there would be a role for her, and they were cagey about it. But if we did strike a deal along the lines of what they were offering, there'd be no more bursting into tears in Community's office, or fears of losing the roof over our heads. After the past year we had come to understand the importance of capital. Being an entrepreneur/juggler was all very well, but sleeping at night was also an attractive prospect. Capital was the key to a good night's slumber and helped you concentrate on driving the business forward without being constantly diverted by fire-fighting problems of cash shortages.

We wanted them to invest in the business, but also wanted to sell as few shares as possible because we knew we would be losing out on its future value. *They* wanted *us* to have less than 30% so that we couldn't exercise any difficult rights under UK company law. In the end it was agreed that we would retain 25% and the price for the shares was adjusted upwards accordingly. They sold off blocks of shares to other individuals in modules of £50,000 each and most of their former investors picked up two or three blocks. Nick and William also got 10% each for putting the deal together. That part of the deal would instantly dilute our 25% down to 20%.

The money for the shares was great: we paid off our debts and our mortgage and had cash in the bank. It was a new experience for both of us.

We knew we'd made the right decision in selling to them because of their track record. The New Covent Garden Soup Company was similar to Green & Black's in so many ways: first of its kind, championed by the press, widely available yet loved by foodies who still retained that sense of discovery that is so important in luxury food purchases. People really felt that New Covent Garden Soup was 'their' soup, just as so many of our customers felt that Green & Black's was 'their' chocolate. But even though we knew they were the right people to be looking after our company, it was incredibly hard to let go. We were both used to dealing with things as they arose without consulting with anyone else, rarely even each other; we both trusted the other to make the right decision. We were experiencing a phenomenon that has a name: 'vendor remorse'. When you sell something you get the money in return but then realise it's not yours any more. This moment of realisation is painful; it tarnishes the beautiful moment of getting a big dollop of cash and, for some people, the pain of separation never completely heals. But we felt our baby was in good hands and there was money and talent to drive it forward. We were both unsure of our future roles in the business, though. William would be the CEO, but his background was in marketing so he would want to have a handle on the brands. He had already indicated that he would drop some products, and that he didn't like some of the packaging, particularly Whole Earth's, so there were changes in the offing.

Nick came into the offices like a white tornado. Every filing cabinet was stripped down to the barest legal minimum of what had to be retained. Old packaging, signage, leaflets, memorabilia, were pushed towards a skip that stood outside the door. Lorna, our cleaner, filtered out items that she thought would be of interest and brought them upstairs. We accumulated a large store of memorabilia, old labels and even old products in their original packaging. If there's ever a Green & Black's or Whole Earth museum we'll be able to supply it with lots of unique treasures.

Photographic Memories

Jo: If there's one thing I wish we'd done when building the business, it's that we'd taken more photographs. You're so busy, head down, bum up that it's hard to imagine that one day, you may want a complete photographic record of launches, parties, rainforest expeditions, of packaging, factory visits and so on. There are precious few pictures of us during the years when we were growing the business. They're useful for press purposes, for sentimental reasons and, you never know, one day, a publisher might want them for the story of your brand! With digital cameras, it costs virtually nothing to take hundreds of pictures which are then at your fingertips for use in mailshots, on websites, to give to picture editors on magazines or newspapers who may want to write about what you're doing. If you haven't got a budget for photography, enlist the help of a keen amateur friend to take good portraits, still-life shots or reportage-type photos, whenever appropriate. Chances are there's something you make or do you can barter for some of their time.

William proposed that Craig take on the role of president – a role that acknowledged his stature without giving him any executive responsibility. Jo's anticipation of a marketing role was unfulfilled, though. It was felt that to take Green & Black's to the next level a full-time marketing person would be needed and Jo had writing commitments. They had just the person in mind: Caroline Jeremy, who had worked with them at the soup company in recipe development and later in marketing. They decided Green & Black's also needed a public relations agency, and gave the account to Phipps PR, a company that already successfully managed several leading food accounts such as Jordan's and had been founded by William's wife Miranda. This left Jo somewhat on the margins of the company twiddling her thumbs, as marketing and PR had been her main roles.

Losing Control

Jo: I am flattered that business colleagues often ask my advice, when they're thinking of selling their own companies. I always reply that it's a bit like choosing adoptive parents for your baby (because your business *is* your baby, and your feelings for it run almost as deep). If you don't like what the new owners do to your brand, or your shop – well, I can only imagine that watching your baby being mistreated by its new parents must feel the same. Happily, we were spared that heartache with the sale of Green & Black's – but for me, it still presented plenty of challenges. There's a real period of adjustment, once the ink is dry on the deal – and I didn't like it at all.

When Nick and William bought into Green & Black's, we had various products in the pipeline that were cancelled, and I had to fight tooth and nail for our Chocolate Hazelnut Spread to make it to the shelves. It was due to have a sister product: a swirly concoction of white and hazelnut-rich milk chocolate, stripey in the jar and ridiculously sinful on the tongue. (Not to mention the waistline.) It was dismissed as 'too down-market', even though we had the factory lined up to make it, the packaging designed, and a few supermarket buyers sniffing round at it. The Chocolate Hazelnut Spread was green-lighted, but the swirly stuff was nixed. I was really upset, because I felt it would get lots of press coverage: journalists had always been happy to write about Green & Black's – some of its earlier champions almost felt they had a stake in its success story – but it's important to keep feeding news through to them. We'd been launching bar after bar, albeit with different flavours, and I sensed 'slab fatigue'. When our planned launch was axed, I ranted and raved to Craig.

Now, my husband is a very wise soul. He seemed perfectly sanguine about the sale. (Craig is more of a Henry Kissinger than me, great on committees and boards.) One night, as I sobbed myself to sleep for the umpteenth time, he turned to me and said, 'Jo, you can either have the money *or* the control. Not both.' There had been a moment when we almost lost our house, because of Green & Black's cash-flow problems and growing pains. We had both lain awake at night, fretting in the wee small hours, worrying about the company's future and whether we'd be bankrupted by it. That simple comment put everything into sharp focus: yes, it would be nice to retain control, but I was ready for some decent sleep. I dried my tears and never shed another, remembering Craig's sage words whenever frustrations surfaced. And they did.

To add to her frustration, the new marketing team recruited Cluny Brown, who'd been her trusted PA for six years. Cluny dithered, but did what was right for her career with Jo's blessing. But it left Jo without a right hand for a while: someone who (in Cluny's case) could almost psychically know what Jo would do in any given situation, and make it happen. (Everyone needs someone like that.)

Jo could see everything that went on, though, because like us, Nick and William never really believed in ritzy offices. They just moved into the rabbit warren on Portobello. As the company rapidly grew, they made a takeover bid for our living space and we agreed. The small spare bedroom where we used to have visiting friends to stay became whizzy sales director Neil Turpin's and William's office. Our living room became the boardroom, to the point where if we wanted to have friends to lunch or dinner, we had to book it on a time sheet. Jo would come home from work next door, reheat some Ready Rice in the open-plan kitchen while a marketing meeting took place round the dining table, and eat it in the bedroom. For several years, we were essentially living in a bedsit, until eventually Green & Black's burst at the seams, moved to fourth-floor (no lift) offices in Southwark, and we got our front room back. But not a penny that could be spent on marketing, advertising or design had been wasted on unnecessary overheads, while they squatted at our place.

Under this new regime, Green & Black's was working rather well, so it was Whole Earth that William really wanted to focus on. With its roots in the 1960s, and a diverse shopping basket of products that spanned everything from peanut butter and baked beans to breakfast cereals and soft drinks, William felt it was too 'hippy dippy' and this was the first thing they wanted to address. The packaging was really quirky: bright, bold, eye-catching and splashy; many of the cereal boxes and the jam jars featured specially commissioned work by Larry Smart, a magical realist artist Craig had known since the 1960s. It was designed on the principle that it should stand out on the shelf and catch the shopper's eye – after all, rivals were products like Cheerios and Frosties – and have interesting written information to keep the shopper intrigued, or to digest over the breakfast table. The name had to be readable from 10 yards away. But Caroline and William were convinced the range needed to be drastically streamlined, re-designed and toned down. They organised a 'focus group' (which is something we'd never done for Green & Black's, believing that it's nigh-on impossible to get a genuinely unique idea out of a committee). The focus group report agreed with the facilitator's opinion that something more modern and chic was needed. The new look that resulted severed nearly all connection with what had gone before, and we couldn't help thinking that was a bad idea.

At Green & Black's, we'd always made sure to evolve the design of our packaging rather than create a whole new look. Early on, we'd had a lightbulb moment and started to use the inside of the wrapper to tell the story of Green & Black's. Nobody had ever done anything like that before, but it seemed so obvious to us: 48 square inches of blank paper, just crying out to be used to tell the story of Green & Black's. A brand *is* its story, and its relationship with customers – simple as that. What we did with Green & Black's, through telling the story of our product on the inside of the wrapper, was to forge that link with our chocolate-lovers; it helped establish a relationship.

By 1994 we felt something had to be done to sex-up our packaging. We were acutely aware of how important eye-catching packaging can be. There was a lot of packaging on health food shelves at the time G & B's launched which looked as lentil-ish or muesli-ish as the contents, and that little flourish of gold – gold, in a health food store! – helped us stand out from the crowd. But design stakes are being raised all the time in fashion, retail and in the home. Packaging needs to be refreshed, almost constantly, and ours was becoming a little tired-looking. One afternoon, Jo fielded a call from a newly established design agency called Pearlfisher based just down the road from our Portobello offices in Holland Park. 'We love your chocolate and we eat it all the time,' Karen Welman, MD of the company, said, 'but we'd really like to get our hands on the packaging.' Jo went for a meeting with them and they talked her through their design portfolio, which included commissions for Absolut Vodka and Waitrose. Very impressive, but with growing sales, and cash flow being squeezed all the time we didn't have a penny in the budget for a re-design. 'Don't worry,' said Karen. 'We'll do a design for free, if you give us some chocolate to work on. If you like what we do, *then* we can talk.'

Pearlfisher summoned us again a couple of weeks later, to show us what they'd come up with. They had produced not one, not two but ten possible re-designs. They were all stunning, and shown to us in pairs – mauve versions for milk chocolate, brown for dark. There were Aubrey Beardsley swirls. Designs with cocoa pods. There was one look that was evolutionary rather than revolutionary – simply a much more sophisticated, but still 100% recognisable, version of our existing packaging: gold lettering, a ribbon and seal, the (now) famous ampersand. On the flipside of the wrapper, was a beautiful drawing of a Maya-esque woman, and our message stood out against a subtle background of cocoa pods. It all looked fabulous. It would, we knew, put us in another league. We recognised from that moment on our current bar design would for ever look dated and clunky in comparison to these more elegant options. We

Get the Files

Jo: When we did the deal with Pearlfisher they agreed to give us the Quark Express files they created for each label so we could tweak any of the typeset copy on the wrappers, such as the ingredients list, ourselves. This was an important consideration, as we were adding in lots of different markets like Scandinavia and needed foreign-language translations. Having to pay for tiny changes to packaging on an ongoing basis, can be a real 'ouch' factor, and the right to make those niggly changes yourself, on computer in the office, isn't always automatic. It's worth making sure they're included in the deal.

thrashed out a deal with Pearlfisher that was definitely more than we really had to spend, but probably less than they deserved. We would manage it, somehow.

We are personally thrilled that Pearlfisher (deservedly) have gone on to become one of the UK's leading brand design agencies, with an outpost in New York. If we hadn't made that investment in their graphic talent, would we be writing this now? Maybe not. On the other hand, if they hadn't had Green & Black's to their credit, would Pearlfisher be working out of a stunning Georgian building in Brook Green, with brands like Innocent, Fortnum & Mason (nice ampersand!) and Coca-Cola beating a path to their door? Maybe not, either. It seemed like kismet when, in February 2007, we were standing in a room at Soho House, in New York's meat-packing district, launching Green & Black's Ice Cream to the US press and Karen Welman poked her nose inside the door. She was staying at Soho House, had heard familiar voices as she stepped out of the lift en route to her room and was happy to join our celebration of this momentous event in Green & Black's history. We raised a glass of champagne. It was a long way from Notting Hill, in every way.

The Pearlfisher re-design felt completely right because it kept the links with the past. The route Caroline decided to go down for Whole Earth's new look couldn't have been more different. The new packaging was unrecognisable. The thinking, so Caroline explained, had been to use National Trust colours: basically a subtle palette of brown, cream and a splash of burgundy. Jo couldn't help pointing out that the National Trust colours were chosen so that the real treasures in our country houses – the silverware, the paintings, the statues – stood out in sharp relief. On a supermarket shelf it was your product that had to stand out. Craig was underwhelmed – these muted earthy tones had been the style of natural foods packaging in the 1970s and Whole Earth had, to some controversy at the time, adopted a more colourful approach as part of its move into the mainstream.

One Saturday morning, having festered about this for twenty-four hours, Jo fired off an e-mail to William and Caroline (ignoring Craig's sage advice to allow a cooling-off period before hitting the 'send' button). 'Nobody wants to eat beige food out of a beige packet,' she observed. She was genuinely worried about the future of the brand, remembering a conversation about re-designs she'd once had in Melbourne with a chocolate buyer for Coles, the Aussie supermarket chain, during which he had said, 'If I had a dollar for every brand that dramatically changed its look and dropped off the shelf I'd be a rich man.' Jo added in the e-mail, 'I hope you're going to have a focus group about this packaging before it's green-lighted.' There was a plan to have a review, but deadlines were tight and so the revamped range hit the shelves.

Certainly, for a while – till they got used to the new look – friends were ringing us asking why our muesli had been discontinued. It hadn't been, but the new beige 'make-under' had made it less visible on the shelves. Nevertheless, over the next few years, Whole Earth's sales climbed rather than declined, before (to William's relief) the brand was ultimately sold on to Kallo Foods in 2002. The first thing they did was to revamp the packaging again, but they still didn't get it right. In 2007 they relaunched Whole Earth with packaging that echoed the bright colours and landscapes showing the provenance of the ingredients that had typified the original packaging. The range is doing very well and is now one of Britain's top five most recognised organic brands.

The Strange Tale of Long Wolf and Maya Gold

Craig: There was once a series of greetings cards with sayings from noted Indian chiefs, such as Chief Seattle's statement: 'When the last tree is cut, the last river poisoned, and the last fish dead, we will discover that we can't eat money.' I gave one to my mother and she burst into tears. The Winnebago Sioux had originated from the Fox River area of Wisconsin, where her great grandfather Lars Dugstad had settled on their prairie. They still wandered around the area between Emerson and Homer (I often wonder what poetry enthusiast named those two towns), often popping in to a farmhouse to ask for a drink of water. The white settlers didn't like the way they casually crossed their land. More and more virgin prairie was ploughed up, planted and fenced with barbed wire. The Winnebago confined themselves to what was left of their reservation, were clinically depressed and drank heavily, for understandable reasons. My mother, like all her generation, understood their sorrow, knew they were the cause of it, but couldn't do anything to help.

My cousin Julia Ronnfeldt, a computer engineer, became involved with a Sioux on the Pine Ridge Reservation, over the border in South Dakota. He was a member of the American Indian Movement (AIM), and some of the younger guys, remembering the humiliation and betrayal of Wounded Knee (where the US cavalry massacred hundreds of unarmed men, women and children after promising them they would be unharmed) were very radical and militant. The FBI clamped down hard and many are still in jail doing life sentences. To get a university education at Pine Ridge a student has to travel between various different towns – the government still doesn't trust them to congregate in one place. Pine Ridge is the poorest county in terms of per capita income in the entire United States. Bearing in mind that it is below freezing for much of the winter, life for the Sioux is very harsh.

The 1868 Fort Laramie agreement was the first treaty signed between the Sioux and the US government and it promised a settlement and an end to war. One of the Sioux signatories was Chief Long Wolf. However, the relentless movement westwards of settlers, including my great-grandparents Ole and Olina Doxtad, forced the government to break its promises, renegotiate, then break its promises again. Long Wolf, dispossessed and humiliated, joined up with Buffalo Bill (William Cody) and toured the eastern United States and many European capitals with the Buffalo Bill Wild West show. He was treated with respect and dignity that was absent from his encounters with white people in the USA and even met Queen Victoria. However, in the cold London climate he contracted pneumonia and died, pleading to be buried on his native soil. Buffalo Bill arranged a funeral and Long Wolf was buried in a cemetery near Earl's Court. To help identify his grave, an elongated wolf was carved into the top of the headstone. However, nobody ever came to transfer his remains and he was forgotten.

In the 1980s an English author referred to an interesting gravestone in Brompton Cemetery and news of it reached one of Long Wolf's granddaughters in Pine Ridge: Jessie Black Feather. Jessie decided to bring her grandpa home. With Julia's help she organised bake sales, cookie sales, raffles and other events to raise the money to bring his remains back. They flew over to England to exhume Long Wolf assisted by an English chap who published an American Indian newsletter and who promised to return the headstone separately.

A month later I got a phone call from Julia. The man was behaving strangely and said he wouldn't be able to send back the headstone. Julia offered her American Express card to pay for it but he said it would cost £4,000. She became suspicious and asked me to intervene. I got in touch with the guy and it was pretty clear that he wanted to keep this valuable artefact, a direct and durable link with the era of cowboys and Indians that fascinated him. I took charge and sent a van round to collect the headstone. Then we took it to the Essex depot of the shipping agents for our US importer, Belgravia Imports. We had a shipment of Maya Gold going to the US and so we simply put the headstone on a wooden pallet, stacked chocolate on top and sent it off to Boston on the next ship. When it got there, Belgravia's Ronnie Dick dealt with the rather bemused US Customs and put it in his warehouse. Ronnie then arranged transport to Pine Ridge, delivered free of charge. Jessie was delighted. They had to leave the stone for a couple of months because the ground was frozen solid and there was no way to erect it over Long Wolf's new grave. Once the ground thawed there was a great ceremony with tribal elders and chiefs in full ceremonial dress.

In some small way I hope that gesture helped cancel out some of my ancestral karmic debt to the Sioux Indians, whose begrudging abandonment of their land to my farming ancestors made my existence possible. The Indian Law Center has also been of great assistance in enabling the Maya to fight off the 'land grab' of their forest reserve by loggers, so the Sioux and other North American tribes who supported it had indirectly helped the Maya, whose chocolate had helped smooth the return of a venerable Sioux chief and his headstone to his homeland.

10

Hurricane Iris

In September 2001 we were storming. The injection of capital from our investors meant that we could sell as hard as we wanted, spend a bit of money on advertising and really go for maximum growth without being held back by the state of our finances. The growers who supplied us were getting the message, too: 'Grow more cacao and plant more cacao – we're going to be needing it.' If there was anything likely to hold us back it was the time lag between planting cacao and harvesting the first crop: it takes about five years for trees to mature.

So we were doing our best to encourage expansion at the rainforest end. The Toledo Cacao Growers' Association in Belize were increasing their output and had sent us a record amount of cocoa in the January–June season of 2001: getting on for 60 tonnes, with a lot more in the pipeline as the impact of pruning and orchard management started to pay off. Larger farmers were beginning to take us seriously and didn't want to be left behind. In the Dominican Republic we had become the biggest purchaser of organic cocoa and many of the 9,000 members of the Conocado cooperative there were converting to organic production in anticipation of our needs.

News headlines at that time were mostly concerned with the whereabouts of Osama Bin Laden and the proposed invasion of Afghanistan, so few people in the panicky West noticed the tropical depression that was brewing off the coast of Puerto Rico. It suddenly gathered momentum and became a small but intense hurricane named Iris. It had a narrow eye and winds of huge velocity, and it crossed the Caribbean, heading towards Belize City. Then it turned south-west and smashed into the Belize coast at Monkey River Town, north of Punta Gorda, with a ferocious impact that didn't weaken until it hit the Maya Mountain highlands on the Guatemala border, 30 miles inland.

The impact in the cacao-growing villages was horrendous. San Pedro Columbia, a village with 250 houses, saw more than half of them reduced to matchsticks. The shade trees on the cacao plantations were also blown down, smashing onto and obliterating many of the cacao trees below. Farmers had already harvested their corn and beans so they had food, thank heavens. But more than three quarters of the cocoa-production capacity of Belize was lost in a few turbulent minutes. In fact, the prospect for the growers' future was unremittingly bleak.

We needed to take a long hard look at the TCGA project and decide how best to secure its future. Even without Iris punishing Belize, the TCGA had been falling behind our demand – sales of Maya Gold had been booming while production of cocoa was struggling to keep up. Happily, new initiatives had been started in response to this and more trees had been planted in the previous couple of years but, post-hurricane, most of this capacity, new and old, had been destroyed. Aid workers loaned the farmers chainsaws to help them clear the fallen trees, but nobody would be harvesting much cacao for a while. In the course of the clear up, though, the farmers noticed something interesting: their local trees (*criollo* in Spanish) had survived the hurricane far better than the hybrids introduced in the 1980s by the aid workers and Hershey. Flexibility had probably been bred into the trees in this geographical zone where hurricanes have always been a threat, over millennia, by their Mayan ancestors. Most of the modern hybrids came from

Brazilian stock and Brazil doesn't experience hurricanes, so the Amazon cacao trees are likely to be less resilient.

The buying season for cocoa starts in January and carries through to June. In 2002 it was predictably dismal. Output was down dramatically to the lowest levels since Green & Black's came on the scene in 1993: barely 6 tonnes. It was too early to say how much of the shortfall in production came from hurricane damage and how much was the result of farmers abandoning their cacao and concentrating on more urgent tasks like rebuilding their houses and clearing away the debris of the storm.

Things were looking bleak but as often happens, just when you think things can't get any worse, a bolt from the blue comes along that deepens the depression:

'Hi, this is the Tesco chocolate buyer, can I speak to someone in sales?'

'Yes, speaking.'

'Look, I'm pretty hacked off, have you got a minute?'

'Er, yes, of course.' (When a Tesco buyer is hacked off you stand up straight and tall and think furiously what you've done wrong.)

'I've just had someone in here trying to sell me some chocolate called Divine and I didn't like their attitude.'

'Oh? Why are you calling us?'

'They want me to stock their Fairtrade milk chocolate and I told them I already have one that's organic, but they want me to take your milk chocolate off our shelves and replace it with theirs. When I said I didn't see the point, they told me they had a £300,000 marketing grant from the UK government they would be spending in support of their brand, and that the resulting demand for their product would justify me taking yours off the shelf. I told them in no uncertain terms where they could go with their chocolate, but I thought you should know. I don't like it when the government starts supporting one supplier against another and gives them money for advertising.'

'Well, of course, neither do we. Thanks for letting us know.'
'No problem. Good luck to you.'

As soon as he heard this, Craig rang up the Department for International Development (DfID – often pronounced Diffid on the news) and got through to Rosemary Stevenson, who oversaw the grant to Divine at the Business Linkages Challenge Fund. The Labour government had changed the department's name; previously, it had been the Overseas Development Administration (ODA). And although it said pretty much the same thing, the name-change signalled a change in attitude.

The (new) New Labour approach to aid was designed to help emerging economies help themselves, and Divine's project was exactly the sort of thing they'd been looking for. Divine worked with the Kuapa Kokoo cooperative, which had been established (with help from Cadbury's, ironically) in 1993. Divine offered the cooperative a deal: a 33% shareholding in their brand. This concept pushed all the right buttons at DfID so they gave Divine £300,000 towards marketing the chocolate in the UK as a way of helping the Kuapa Kokoo people. Fair enough – this was a nicer way of helping farmers to help themselves than just giving them free medicine and other charitable stuff.

However, it looked a bit unfair to the equally poor growers who depended on Green & Black's success in the marketplace. DfID was, in effect, taking sides with non-organic growers in Ghana against the organic growers in Belize and the Dominican Republic who had been working with Green & Black's for years. So we asked for equal treatment on their behalf. DfID suggested we put in a grant application.

The application for support wasn't just a question of getting some money from the government. We needed to be sure we could justify making the effort, which meant securing the commitment of the Toledo Cacao Growers' Association and their farmer members before we plunged in and started endless form-filling.

Our application to DfID's Business Linkages Challenge Fund focussed on three key points:

1. Hurricane Iris had demolished a very promising initiative, and farmers in the former British colony of Belize needed help to rebuild their cacao orchards.
2. The growth of sales of Maya Gold meant the farmers were falling behind on our demand. As our contract guaranteed to purchase as much cocoa as they could produce at a premium price for our sales of Maya Gold, they were missing out on an opportunity. They needed to increase their production capacity. This meant planting a million new trees. This would cost £250,000 over a three-year period.
3. A larger production capacity for cocoa would enable the farmers' cooperative to become more professional, hire good management and reduce its reliance on volunteer members.

DfID saw the merits of our proposal. They gave it the green light, subject to two conditions:

1. Green & Black's would take responsibility for ensuring that the £250,000 requested was dispensed responsibly, and would provide the accounting and technical expertise necessary to make the project work.
2. Green & Black's had to commit to spend a matching amount of £250,000 on marketing Maya Gold to ensure there was a market for the new cacao when it came to fruition.

Well, it certainly wasn't a juicy £300,000 grant to cover the cost of advertising and celebrity endorsement, but it was a genuine offer of value to the TCGA and we decided to go with it, subject to satisfying ourselves that we hadn't bitten off more than we could chew.

We got some extra help with our grant application from Cadbury's. In 2001 we had stumbled into negotiations with them that had led to them buying a 5% share in Green & Black's. We hadn't planned to sell to anyone; the original scheme had been to build up Whole Earth, Gusto and Green & Black's and then see whether we could sell or float them by around 2004. But, in early 2000 something happened to focus Nick and William's minds: Craig was approached by Gene Kahn, who had just sold his company, Small Planet Foods, to General Mills. Gene was keen to expand into Europe and saw Whole Earth as the ideal brand to work with, as his own brands – Cascadian, Small Planet and Muir Glen – had very little recognition among Europeans. He didn't want Green & Black's, though, just Whole Earth. If we wanted to get a good price, it wasn't smart to negotiate with only one potential buyer; we needed to engender a bit of healthy competition. So we retained Stamford Partners, a specialist investment bank that deals in food business mergers and acquisitions. They shopped around to make sure we were getting the best price for Whole Earth, and word soon got out that we were selling part of the business. In the end, Small Planet dropped out and we sold Whole Earth and Gusto to Kallo Foods, a subsidiary of a Dutch multinational called Wessanen. But in the process Cadbury Schweppes had become interested. Whole Earth wasn't what they had their eye on, though: they made a very generous offer for a 5% shareholding in Green & Black's.

When we told Cadbury's about our DfID grant application they were very interested and supportive of what we were planning to do. They offered us, as a token of good will and at no charge, the services of the man who is probably the world's foremost expert on cocoa, Tony Lass, who had recently retired from his full-time role as their technical director. Tony was the co-author of *Cocoa*, the authoritative reference book that is an essential on the bookshelf of anyone with a commercial interest in it. Unlike a chocolate book by Nigella Lawson or Nigel Slater, it may not set your

The Brand that Boomeranged Back

Craig: If you bought a Rolls Royce would you put a Volkswagen engine in it and slap a Vauxhall badge on the front? That's what people do with brands, for reasons I can't quite understand. If it ain't broke, why fix it? In 1990 my daughter, Rima, decided to go into business with a new energy drink, called Gusto. It contained a good amount of guarana (the Amazon stimulant that has a slower, more relaxed uplift than the caffeine in coffee), a 300mg shot of ginseng and a 350mg shot of Siberian ginseng. Topping it off was 170ml of a Chinese herb blend enchantingly called Free and Easy Wanderer (or Jiawei Xiaoyao San) that had been originally cooked up by a Taoist monk in the late twelfth century and was aimed to lift the heart energy up to the mind. Gusto was, and is, the best energy drink ever made. Most of them are just caffeine (white crystalline powder extracted from coffee during the decaffeination process) with a few vitamins or taurine, and they create a need for repeated doses to keep going. One bottle of Gusto is all you need. (Which is why Jo and I, and countless Gusto fans, rely on it when we have a deadline, or need to stay awake for a late party, or for jet lag.)

When we sold our brands to our investors in 1999 they decided to reformulate Gusto and remove all the ingredients except guarana and give it a lemon-grass flavouring. It tasted different, the packaging looked different (it went into a can, which was more practical, but with a total redesign); in fact it bore no relation to the original product – but it got a listing in Waitrose. Sales were poor, but we managed to sell Gusto, along with the Whole Earth brand, to Kallo Foods in 2002, with its valuation as part of that sale of £100,000. Not long afterwards Gusto was delisted by Waitrose. Kallo didn't really know what to do with it; Gusto was basically in limbo. I made a somewhat bold offer of £2,000 to Kallo for the Gusto brand. (Jo bet me, and lost, that they wouldn't accept the offer.) My son, Karim, relaunched it in 2005 with the original powerfully effective recipe and the original packaging. Sales are steadily increasing and it is back on track: the world's best energy drink and (for now) the only organic one. I don't think we'd sell again unless the purchaser signs (in blood preferably) that they won't tamper with the recipe.

taste buds drooling, but it describes everything you could possibly want to know about cocoa: where it's grown, the different varieties, its history, its processing, the diseases it suffers, fermentation, drying. Everything. We couldn't have hoped for a better, more experienced or more knowledgeable person to help us ensure success. Tony Lass joined Green & Black's commercial director John Kennedy and our technical manager Neil LaCroix on a fact-finding mission to Belize in June 2003.

Tony, John and Neil visited farms in the region and met the TCGA executive. It was a crucial meeting. The TCGA had to decide whether they were prepared to work with us to expand their capacity to a minimum of 200 tonnes, the level where they could be a viable commercial organisation rather than being dependent on volunteers. On the next buying day every member of the TCGA executive stood up in front of the membership and publicly voiced their commitment to support the project. We had lift-off.

Over a three-year period nurseries were established, the best and most resilient varieties of cacao were selected and a lot of land was converted to its production. There were two ways this came about. Either a farmer would venture onto overgrown former plantations or other unused land and thin out the bush, leaving some shade trees, and then prune any existing cacao trees and plant new ones. Alternatively, rice-growing land was converted. Rice requires fertiliser and herbicides, is responsible for a lot of soil erosion and doesn't make any money as the government sets the price at barely more than the cost of production. So its conversion to cacao production has economic, social and environmental benefits.

The Maya Gold Project, as it was called, was a striking example of how a little bit of help from us and DfID could in turn help the TCGA and the Mayan growers to help themselves. A stonking one million trees were planted between 2003 and 2006. They represent increased income of US$300,000 per year once they reach maturity, hurricanes permitting. (In the chocolate business, the Caribbean weather forecast takes on a whole different significance.) This money would transform the economics of the TCGA and bring more money, via the farmers, into the local economy. What's more, even when the aid money ran out there would still be nurseries going full tilt, producing superb young cacao trees, and there were plenty of farmers prepared to purchase these and plant them out.

The contribution from Tony Lass was of inestimable value. His experience in establishing nurseries, identifying and propagating the best stock and in anticipating the problems that could arise helped to make the project a great success. What was also gratifying was to see how his attitude towards organic growing of cacao developed from polite scepticism to a much greater understanding of organic principles and how they could apply to cocoa production elsewhere.

For Cadbury's, the fact that their most respected technical expert was, if not a convert, at least no longer a sceptic about organic production, made an enormous difference. When we eventually sold the entire business to Cadbury's, our experience with Tony helped reassure us that it was going into the right hands. And the growers – whose only exposure to their future trading partner had been Tony – were quietly pleased that a valuable trading relationship had just become a lot more secure.

People often ask us if fair trade really makes a difference to the people who grow cacao, or bananas, or tea, or coffee – or any of the other commodities that go into products which are now emblazoned with the Fairtrade logo. Having seen first-hand how the lives of our cacao farmers have been transformed since we launched Maya Gold in 1994, we can put our hands on our hearts and say, 'Yes, totally.'

People were so cynical, when we first launched, about the impact it would have on the farmers: would they just take the cash and buy TVs and Coca-Cola? But at the very first opportunity, the growers used the extra income from Green & Black's to send their children to secondary school. Until we began trading with the Maya, there was no secondary education for the children from the cacao-growing villages in the rainforest hills. Roads in Belize are terrible – we once drove our four-wheel drive off the edge of a road which simply collapsed under us, and it's a wonder that nobody was killed. The nearest secondary school (in Punta Gorda) was up to 30 miles or so away from San José, Laguna Village, Otoxha and Dolores, villages which at the time were served only by a bi-weekly bus service.

But the parents weren't deterred; they knew their children deserved a proper education. So they paid to board them with willing families in the sleepy southern Belizean port of Punta Gorda and enrolled them in the school. The Green & Black's money enabled the parents to pay for board and lodging, and to buy the books their children needed. Within a couple of years, the bus company realised there'd be a market for a daily bus service to PG (as it's known), which meant the children could live at home and commute to school. Several of those children have gone to university, and will bring their skills back to their villages.

Cayetano Ico, head of the TCGA – has this message for our customers: 'Tell them that every time they buy a bar of chocolate, they send a child to school.' And really, it's that simple. Today, many members of the TCGA are computer-literate. They've built concrete floors for their homes, which makes for hugely improved health and well-being, because the children, and their parents, aren't ankle-deep in mud any longer if the roof leaks during the rainy season (there is only so much that cohune palm thatch can do to keep the rain out). Because good protein sources are rare in this neck of the rainforest (with the possible exception of roast gibnut, a giant guinea-pig-like rodent once served up to the queen on a royal visit, prompting a QUEEN EATS RAT headline in the *Sun*), the women spend some of the money on tinned sardines from the village shops, a rich source of essential fatty acids, to help them through their pregnancies and boost the children's brainpower. When a company buys cocoa, or oranges, or cotton from a cooperative, you can't place conditions on what they spend it on, so it's hugely rewarding that our farmers have done just what we would have hoped with their extra income.

The relationship with Green & Black's has had an effect on the cacao-growing community in other ways, too. When we first began trading with them, the Maya – whose civilisation had once ruled over Belize, their homeland – were considered very much third-class citizens in Belizean society. No getting away from it; the Brits had been in charge for years (it was a colonial outpost, until 1981) and the next layer of Belizean society were the Garifuna tribe, descended from a shipload of Africans who had escaped slavery and come to Belize and become the merchant class. The Maya were a forgotten class (which can also be seen as a blessing; it meant nobody had tried to put a highway through the forest). Happily, that's all changed. Now, when the TCGA have their annual general meeting, the minister of agriculture flies down. When logging companies threaten the wilderness, the Maya have the ear of government: logging would imperil their livelihood, and all the Green & Black's chocolate-lovers would rise up in protest. Politicians in Belize have become aware that through Maya Gold, the profile of this tiny group of indigenous Maya has been dramatically raised. In a small way, we have helped to give the people of this forgotten corner of Central America a voice.

Given how important fair trade is to the ethos of Green & Black's, we're also not surprised when people ask us 'Why don't all the bars carry the Fairtrade Mark?'

Over the years we have tussled with this issue long and hard, blowing hot and cold. It's not that Green & Black's has got anything to hide. We are transparent about our relationship with our farmers, we believe they should be fairly rewarded and given security. The fact that we still deal with the same people we dealt with in the early 1990s testifies to the durability of our trading relationships. We pay fairtrade prices for all our cocoa and often pay organic premiums well above the level set by the Fairtrade Labelling Organisation. So why not put the symbol on more of the packs?

Like many relationships, our relationship with the Fairtrade Foundation is pretty complicated, and has had its ups and downs. The Foundation operates differently to the Soil Association, who charge a modest 0.3% fee on a product's turnover, that goes lower as turnover increases. From the start, the Fairtrade Foundation charged Green & Black's 2% of the price of every bar we sold, a cost we had to pass on to chocolate-lovers and which necessarily made Maya Gold a more expensive option than our existing chocolate. They also had a rule that the higher your sales went the higher the commission they charged, to a top level of 5%. As that was more than our net profit on each bar, we argued that such a high percentage was unsustainable. Eventually they realised we were right and scrapped that policy, and now sometimes do deals with new symbol-holders that are below the 2% we've always paid.

Incredibly, in the early days, having the Fairtrade Mark on our packaging actually threatened our sales in Europe. Green & Black's has always sold internationally, particularly in Scandinavia, Holland and Germany. Each of those countries had its own fair trade mark (Max Havelaar, Transfair) and at that time, they behaved quite territorially. Because of our success in their markets, the different fair trade certification bodies in those countries complained to the UK-based Fairtrade Foundation, saying they either wanted us to refrain from selling on their territory, or pay them a commission on our sales to compensate them for the lost income from brands developed in those countries that our sales displaced. We offered to use stickers with their marks, but they were reluctant about this and wanted us to print separate packaging. (A logistical nightmare, which would have required us to keep stocks of chocolate for different countries, which would sell at different rates and potentially leave us out of stock, at least occasionally, of chocolate for Germany or Holland. In other words, just not do-able.)

Then in October 1994 Martin Kunz of Transfair in Germany told the Fairtrade Foundation they were unwilling to have the Transfair mark on Maya Gold at *all* as the sugar wasn't fair trade. There was only one source of organic sugar at that time from Slovakia, not a Third World country so not eligible for fair trade approval. So in order to be Transfair-approved we would have had to drop our organic status by including non-organic Fairtrade sugar – which clearly wasn't an option for a brand built on organic principles. Unwittingly, Green & Black's found itself at the centre of a complicated internal dispute between different fair trade certifying bodies. It was eventually resolved when they all came under the unifying umbrella of FLO (Fairtrade Labelling Organisation). But it was another factor that made us wary of extending the Fairtrade Mark to any of our other products, while these differences of opinion simmered away.

And then, as if that wasn't enough to make us wary, they threatened to take away our Fairtrade certification completely – yikes! It came to nothing, but it certainly upped our stress levels for a while. In March 1998, a Fairtrade Foundation report on that year's inspection in Belize reported that farmers expected a considerably lower yield of cocoa than in 1997. The report went to FLO's head office in Bonn, where Heini Conrad, one of their executives, got into a lather over the farmers' gloomy forecasts of falling production, which he said was the exact opposite of what fair trade was meant to be about. He called for the Toledo Cacao Growers' Association to be removed from the Fair Trade Register – the official listing of all authorised fair trade producers. Frankly, with such poor communications (at that time, a weekly phone call to the TCGA office was our main point of contact), we were unsure of the facts ourselves. So it wasn't until September, when all that season's crop of cocoa had been shipped to us, that we saw that in fact production had gone up by nearly 20%. Why and how? Well, anyone who knows farmers understands that when you ask them how their crops are doing, they will always seriously underestimate or talk down their prospects. Whether it's superstition or just a canny way of understating supply in order to keep prices high, it's typical of farmers around the world. But for us it was another warning sign that Fairtrade certification carried with it uncertainty that we did not want to risk imposing on the rest of our range.

They also were worried about markets growing too quickly. The Belize farmers belong to a cooperative that juices their oranges, bottles the juice and then freezes it. It's the best tasting orange juice we've ever tried and it's great that the value is added in the country of origin. We wanted to certify the bottles as a Fairtrade product but were told that because it would compete with another fair trade orange juice project that was based in Brazil we couldn't get approval. Our view was that certifying bodies should stick to certifying and let the markets in Europe and elsewhere take care of themselves.

We were also disappointed to discover that companies that were Alternative Trade Organisations (ATO) such as Traidcraft, Divine and Cafédirect only had to pay a 1% licence fee, because it was considered they were putting something back to the communities who supplied them. As we were putting a great deal back into the communities we traded with too, we felt it best to continue to support our growers directly rather than via the FLO, who might send funds raised from us to orange juice producers in Brazil, or coffee growers in Colombia – all of whom deserve support, yes, but we'd have no say in whether or not the dedicated and hard-working Mayan cacao farmers saw a (cocoa) bean of the FLO money.

Belize, of course, isn't our only source of cocoa. There's no way this tiny country could supply all our needs. Working there has been a hugely gratifying experience, because we came into a situation that was in decline, converted every cacao grower in the entire country to organic and Fairtrade production, and had a real impact on farmers' incomes, biodiversity, education and social cohesion. Every cacao tree in Belize is now certified by the Soil Association, giving an opportunity to see what a difference being totally organic can make.

In the Dominican Republic (DR) – our principal source of cocoa – the situation's more complex. The DR produces a lot of low-quality, often unfermented cocoa beans which are mainly sold (quite cheaply) to the US, where they're used to make cocoa, chocolate milk for the US school milk programme and mass-market chocolate.

Encouragingly, though, there is a growing number of organic producers, and a widespread adoption of good fermentation techniques to enable farmers to get premium prices for their cocoa. As a result, the Dominican Republic has become the world's largest producer of fair trade and organic cocoa beans.

Green & Black's efforts in DR have focussed on encouraging non-organic farmers to go through the conversion period in order to become fully organic, and training them in the fermentation methods that are the foundation of the production of premium-quality chocolate like ours. Because of the larger scale of production in the Dominican Republic, we've helped to fund fermentation and drying facilities that can accommodate higher levels of output.

In 2007 Green & Black's invested $510,000 in fermentation and drying equipment, which has enabled farmers to ferment another 3,000 tonnes of organic cacao every year, greatly increasing their ability to sell premium-priced cocoa beans. As fermented beans command a $200 per tonne premium and organic beans command a further $1,500 premium, this adds up to a chunky $1,700 a tonne, which means the farmers will benefit from this investment to the tune of $5 million a year – money they can put towards better housing, schools and healthcare for their families – just as we've seen happen in Belize. The investment should pay dividends in other ways: by setting an example to the extensive network of cooperatives in the Dominican Republic, it will hopefully encourage them, in turn, to invest in equipment and training that can generate a swift return. Their banks are likely to lend for further investment, because they see there's a secure market with us. And what do we get out of it? Access, we hope, to a supply of good-quality cocoa beans – Green & Black's life-blood. We have to accept, though, that other organic chocolate companies will probably benefit from our investment in this community of growers, too, and will probably end up competing with us in the marketplace with chocolate made from the same supply of high-quality cocoa beans that we helped to create. But that's business. It's impossible to handcuff the farmers to us, and there'd be nothing fair about that.

It has been our passionate belief, from the day we first put an organic symbol on our packaging, that one day all organic food would be fairly traded and that one single symbol would not only signify no agrochemicals had been used by the farmers, but that they were being fairly rewarded. It's taken longer than we ever imagined to get to that point, but with the development of their Ethical Trade Mark, the Soil Association's now come up with a standard that combines organic with fair trade principles. Companies that want to use the Ethical Trade Mark will have to show they comply with the rigorous standards necessary to obtain this 'double-certification'. So there will now be a version of the famous three-legged symbol that announces that yes, all the ingredients in this product were all ethically sourced *and* are organic, to boot. Few companies would find it easy to comply, but we hope to pioneer the use of that mark, eventually across the whole Green & Black's range, displaying this prestigious seal of quality on every label.

Land Rights

Craig: One of the problems that disempowers indigenous people is doubt over land tenure. The Maya are no exception.

Their insecurity over their land rights has been a major deterrent to the planting of high-value shade trees. We always wanted to encourage a long-term view, so we offered a 5 cents a pound premium price for cocoa grown in orchards where the shade trees included mahogany and red cedar. Sadly, this part of our plan was thwarted. Soon after the tree premium was agreed in 1993, Neil Bird, Britain's Overseas Development Administration (ODA – now DfID) advisor to the Belize Department of Natural Resources, heard about our offer and told the farmers that any mahogany they planted would be the eventual property of the government.

No farmer wants a government tree-extraction contractor coming on to his land, damaging his cacao trees and taking out a hardwood tree he's nurtured for years, so no mahogany trees were planted. Farmers planted short-lived, low-value shade trees instead. (If just two mahogany trees had been planted on each of the 900 acres of cacao in the region by 2008 the value would have been, at $4,000 for a fifteen-year-old tree, about $7 million in all.)

In 1996 I got an anxious call from my daughter Rima, who was living in Belize in a jungle clearing on the Columbia River, 10 miles inland from Punta Gorda. The minister at the Department of Natural Resources had granted an extraction licence to an Asian logging company called Atlantic Industries, with the approval of Neil Bird. The company were offering sawmill and logging jobs to Kekchi Maya in a blatant attempt to divide the community. Some villages in the area were Mopan Maya, some Kekchi Maya, some were mixed. The Toledo Maya Cultural Council (TMCC) had been established under the leadership of Julian Cho in the early 1990s to bridge the gap and unify the two communities. The TCGA also united the Mopan and Kekchi because they had a single shared interest: to sell as much organic cocoa as possible to Green & Black's.

When details of the logging deal emerged it was shocking. In 1952 the Columbia River Forest Reserve had been established on 100,000 acres to protect large stands of virgin mahogany-rich forest. The Mayan villagers had agreed to respect the boundaries of this forest and to keep it as a natural biodiversity reserve, so they were horrified to learn that a logging concession on this land had been issued to an Asian corporation. The Asian logging firm had already begun to bulldoze roads through the reserve to make way for their heavy equipment.

The TCGA and the TMCC worked closely together to block this and were supported by the political opposition, the People's United Party. There were huge street protests in Punta Gorda televised nationwide and the campaign attracted international interest. At Green & Black's we wrote to UK and Belizean government ministers urging them to hold back as the logging would damage the livelihoods of the farmers.

In March 1998, Hugh Raven and I visited Charles Wright OBE, an old hand from the days of the Colonial Office, which had administered Belize when it was the colony of British Honduras. He had retired in Punta Gorda. He had done the original surveys of the Columbia River Forest Reserve that led to it being protected. He didn't mince his words. 'Neil Bird was hopeless,' he said. 'He never properly visited the forest, got lost when he did, rarely strayed out of sight of his Land Rover. The forest should remain untouched.'

Then, a whiff of scandal. It was suggested that money had gone into the offshore account of a government official. The 1998 election was won by the opposition People's United Party. They suspended the logging, pending further review. The TCGA and the TMCC had shown that with solidarity and determination it was possible to stop the process that has destroyed so many indigenous communities in other parts of the world. A few months later Julian Cho, who played so central a role in rallying the Maya to protest against the logging, was found at his home, dead from a blow to the back of his head. The police eventually decided it was an accident.

The biggest problem for farmers in much of the developing world is the question of land tenure. Even if you have been on your land for a thousand years there is an ever-present risk that your national government will take away your environmental resources and sell them to foreign bidders. If farmers are insecure in their ownership of their land, they will invest the minimum necessary in improving it and extract the maximum from it in a short-termist way. Land-tenure reform is seen as an effective key to poverty eradication and sustainable development, especially in Latin America and Africa. The alternative is short-sighted farming, soil erosion and environmental degradation.

So what does the future hold for the Maya, whose tenure has been so fragile – from a legal perspective – even though they have farmed there for thousands of years? Happily, it looks bright. On 18 October 2007 the chief justice of the supreme court of Belize ruled in favour of a claim for land rights by the inhabitants of two Mayan villages, Santa Cruz and Conejo. The Department of Natural Resources opposed their lawsuit, but the chief justice ordered the government to issue title to the land to the villagers and abstain from any further grants, leases or logging concessions to the land or its resources to outsiders.

This judgement sets a precedent for more than thirty-eight other Mayan villages who will be able to assert their rights to their land. The result is that there are already mahogany nurseries up and running on a small scale, and they'll flourish in the wake of this judgement, with really positive consequences for the long-term income of cacao farmers. We are thrilled that our contribution to Mayan community solidarity may have played a part in arriving at an outcome that will provide security and prosperity for the cacao farmers who have been so important to our success.

Part Four

THE FINAL CHUNK

Part Four

THE FINAL CHUNK

11

Selling On or Selling Out?

'Last month, as you can see from the report, we lost £300,000 which is great news: we were budgeted to lose £350,000,' Green & Black's finance director Nick Beart proudly announced at a board meeting in 2004. Those kinds of losses weren't keeping us awake any more, because they were budgeted for as part of 'the bigger picture'. Sales, in fact, were going even better than expected and the small fortune we were pouring into marketing (as per the budget) was generating an even larger return from our customers. Of course, nobody can lose money like that every month (or not for long), but you have to risk it sometimes. The way the company was going, we knew we would soon be in a great position to sell.

When Cadbury's bought 5% of the company in 2003 there was a strong likelihood that they would ultimately scoop up the remainder, but we had included what are called 'put and call' options under the terms of that purchase, which meant we had the power to hold them off until we were ready to sell. The option for both parties to walk away was there, too, but by 2005 we were getting on extremely well and Cadbury's were the obvious candidate to take our business forward. There were three real issues for us. Would they understand the essence of the brand? Would they remain committed to organic and fair trade through thick and thin? Would they put enough money into supporting the brand to defend it against the inevitable competition that was looming on the horizon?

Choc Horror?

Jo: If you had asked me on day one who I'd have liked to sell the company to, I would have said Cadbury's. Other confectionery companies were interested in us, and there were some other companies we'd have been glad to sell to and others I was hugely relieved we didn't sell to, in the end. Having long supported the Nestlé baby milk boycott, for instance, as a protest against their promotion in the Third World of costly formula milk for babies, which has to be made up with water: a precious and often contaminated commodity, I might have had to become a hermit, move to Tasmania or just change names if Nick, William and the Green & Black's board had decided to sell 'the baby' to them. But Cadbury's has a special place in millions of hearts. Like most British children, I was raised on Cadbury's chocolate. I always preferred Bournville, but I have a fondness for the glass and a half imagery that was Cadbury's Dairy Milk. The trouble is, once you have handed over control of the majority of your company, you no longer have any real say in the outcome; no matter how loud you plead, it's down to shareholder votes. All you can do is pray, keep your fingers crossed, chant – whatever works for you. It's an uncomfortable place to be, in a world that is becoming ever more ethically aware. A lot of my friends buy fair trade, shop organically, boycott sweat-shop clothes, and so on, and I knew we were going to have to face them over the dinner table after the sale of our business. We were lucky to find such great buyers because quite often, sadly, all venture capitalists or investors are interested in is maximum return, not a sale that comes with a feel-good factor by way of a bonus.

Cadbury's 5% shareholding also got them a seat on the board of the company and our board meetings were certainly enlivened by the presence of Mark Reckitt, from the main board of Cadbury Schweppes. We could tell from Mark's input that there was never any question about maintaining the commitment to organic and fair trade. Why buy a brand and then change its fundamentals? What we did know was that they had the financial muscle to ensure that our organic suppliers got a good price and that the idealistic terms we had offered them could be honoured with a confidence that, in our shakier moments, we certainly could not always have guaranteed. And, as for funding the brand, they had plans to take it to a level we had only been able to dream of. It was great to see in their first budgets a commitment to a level of advertising and promotion spend that we knew would make a real difference to our brand's reach.

As for understanding the essence of Green & Black's, well, it's always hard to judge such things, but we both knew that Cadbury's track record in terms of what is now called corporate social responsibility (CSR in business-speak) was terrific. As a young journalist in 1977, Jo had visited their factory in Bournville in Birmingham. This was long before Cadbury's World – the fantastic factory tour that allows anyone to see behind the chocolatey scenes – was a twinkle in a savvy marketing person's eye. But while she was there they gave a presentation about how Cadbury's had always taken care of its workers (in a patrician way), and she thought: Actually, these guys are good eggs. (Creme Eggs, of course!)

The more we found out about them, the happier we were with the outcome. Before the sale was announced (we had to take a vow of silence), we were invited to a gala dinner by Simon Baldry, the head of the Cadbury Trebor Bassett confectionery division (and the same company Jo had bought her Jojo name from).

Held at the Carlton Tower Hotel, it was a company dinner to raise funds for the Ghana Wells Appeal, one of their pet charities, which pays for wells to be dug in cacao-growing villages. This means that instead of walking for hours each day to fetch water for their working parents and the rest of the family, children can go to school. Everyone at Cadbury Trebor Bassett can get involved with this and so far, over 375 wells have been dug, each serving a community of 150 people, supplying over 50,000 cacao farmers and their families with clean, safe, readily accessible water for drinking, cooking and washing. A study by Water Aid showed that each well saves the average Ghanaian family seven and a half hours a day. To those of us who take for granted that we can turn on a tap and water gushes out, it's unimaginable. (For Jo, the other real thrill of the night, which caused real whoops of delight, was when she opened the mini-bar and discovered that the Carlton Tower – which definitely out-swanks our usual hotel choices – stocked just one chocolate bar. It began with a 'G' and a 'B'.)

At dinner, the MD Simon Baldry told Jo about another Cadbury's project, which is even more low-key: their support of Business Action on Homelessness, specifically their Ready for Work and Job Coaching programmes. Ready for Work finds two-week (sometimes longer) placements for people affected by homelessness. Job Coaching is the next stage: Cadbury's employees are matched with a homeless person who has completed a work-experience placement at the company, and they go on to try to help them find – and keep – a permanent job.

In 2005, for instance, fifty-one homeless people completed work placements at Cadbury Trebor Bassett, and 60% of those went on to be given permanent jobs. In fact, the company's commitment to helping homelessness runs even deeper. For the past few years, they've allowed homeless vendors to sell copies of the *Big Issue* in the foyer of their Bournville factory, out of the rain and cold, and it's many of those vendors who have gone on to find work at Cadbury's. Most recently, Cadbury's initiated a Vendor Award Scheme, the first of its kind, which recognises a specific *Big Issue* vendor, not once but four times a year. As John Bird, the *Big Issue* founder and editor in chief put it, 'Instead of keeping the problem at arm's length, Cadbury's have brought people in and got them

working. It is historic and heroic. Cadbury's have brought themselves so close to us that we can get homeless people out of the
ghetto and socially mobile.' It's not an exaggeration to say that
Cadbury's are leading the way by getting into bed (sleeping bag?)
with a charity in this way. It's a shame more businesses don't do it.
For one thing, we've no doubt that the Cadbury's team gets as much
out of their involvement as the homeless do.

The final decision to sell to Cadbury's was taken in early 2005.
We had a good deal based on a formula that combined sales and
profitability and we knew the company was going to be in safe
hands, so we were ready to move on to the next stage. Cadbury's
wanted Craig to stay on as president – he and William both
continued as board members and directors. This was a terrific
outcome, but one we hadn't even considered at the dawn of our
business, when we weren't really thinking more than a few months
ahead. At that time, the idea of a national – let alone global –
brand just wasn't a consideration. We've seen a lot of changes in
our time in business, and a lot of takeovers: L'Oréal scooped up
the Body Shop, Aveda was sold to Estée Lauder and designer Stella
McCartney now belongs to Gucci. Those kinds of buyouts of
organic or artisanal companies by multinationals were unheard
of when we started Green & Black's, so we were never for a
moment distracted from the early day to day frenzy of building
a business by dreams of an exit strategy, however far off. We
weren't even sure exactly what an exit strategy was. Jo has always
been perplexed by the entrepreneurs who start with the idea of
ultimately selling out to someone huge for a big wodge of cash.
It may be naive, but it doesn't quite feel right for entrepreneurs
to go into business with that in mind. It could even be the kiss
of death. You've got to enjoy and be inspired by the journey, not
be fixated on the destination.

It's the passion and drive that entrepreneurs pour into their
businesses that make them grow. Large companies know that no

What Does a President Do?

Craig: As president of Green & Black's I continue my link with the brand Jo and I founded. It's a non-executive role (in the US a president has executive power) but still involves me in key areas. We have a board meeting every two months. Three Cadbury's directors sit on the board and work with us to develop Green & Black's role as one of their major worldwide brands.

When key new people join the company, particularly in sales and marketing, I meet them for a couple of hours to infuse them with the story of the brand, its ethos, anecdotes and interesting stories. This helps them get out of normal corporate-box thinking and appreciate how we operate, so they continue to reflect the way we've evolved. It's quite liberating for some of them, and it's good to see them 'get' it without abandoning the rigorous professionalism that got them the job. The brand essence is thus protected from dilution.

I've done press tours in the US and in Canada, talking to journalists, doing TV shows, getting our message across. In both countries I've also done presentations in conjunction with wine experts where I've told the story of how flavour develops in well-fermented organic cocoa and then presided over tastings of chocolate with selected wines, port and even rum. When we launched in Germany in 2008 I went over to meet the team at the Biofach show in Nuremberg, where I was giving a lecture on fair trade best practice at an IFOAM (International Federation of Organic Agriculture Movements) seminar.

The Cadbury ethical sourcing team were established in 2005 to help bring the same values that inspire Green & Black's into their mainstream business. I've spent time with them and they've learned from our experience. The real test will be as results emerge among the supplier producers in the years ahead.

The rest is pretty straightforward – whenever an idea comes into my or Jo's head, we pass it on to the relevant person at Green & Black's.

> We don't have the power any more to just stamp our little authoritarian feet and say 'Do it!' but, once it's been considered and discussed in the way that happens in democratic corporate hierarchies, it gets done, unless there are good reasons not to.

matter how many focus groups they hold, how much market research they invest in, how large the spend is for new-product-development initiatives and advertising, the failure rate for new food products just eighteen months after launch runs at more than 90%. This is a terrible waste of money and resources by companies too far from the sharp end of things to sniff out and capitalise on emerging trends. Far better for them to sit back and wait to see who emerges from the confusing melée in the marketplace and then offer an attractive price for handing it over. Green & Black's could never have been created within Cadbury's – they were committed to non-organic producers and mainstream popular taste. It was that very commitment that created the vacuum that we rushed in to fill. At first Cadbury's and the other big chocolate companies ignored us. Then, by the time we were big enough to actually show up on their market analysis reports, they realised it would be far easier to buy a good brand than to try to create a competitive one from scratch.

People ask us if we still feel any connection with Green & Black's now it belongs to Cadbury's. This is exactly like asking parents, 'Do you still feel any connection to your child, now he or she has grown up and gone away to university?' A business *is* like a baby. We will never, for instance, get over the thrill of seeing our chocolate bars in cool and groovy venues like the Standard in Miami or Dean and DeLuca in New York. It's the business equivalent of having your kid get an A+ for a project.

We consider ourselves extremely lucky that our baby's foster parents – William Kendall and Nick Beart – helped nurture Green

& Black's through its adolescence and that, ultimately, the baby has ended up with a very good home. But you do have to choose wisely, or (if you no longer have control) pray the new owners will 'get' your brand and respect it. Otherwise it's going to be like a dagger in the heart, every day. That emotional thread will always be there, and it will hurt like hell if you see something you don't like. Jo went through quite a few painful years, seeing what she felt were small mistakes made by the team who originally took over from us. But we are very happy to know that Cadbury's – who know so much about good chocolate, great gifts and good deeds – have given a home to Green & Black's.

Since we sold to Cadbury's, Hershey bought the organic brand Dagoba as well as the artisanal brand Scharffenberger. Mars has launched a range of dark organic chocolate bars and Nestlé look like they're headed in that direction as well. We really have the sense that we got out just in time – with big fish like that thrashing around in what is still a smallish pond, the best place for little fish like us is somewhere less turbulent and more secure. Most of Craig's unique, original and innovative products – organic brown rice, organic wholemeal bread, no sugar added jams, natural peanut butter, organic soft drinks and all those macrobiotic specialties from Japan – were commoditised and taken over by bigger companies. We have seen our chocolate prevail and go on to greater things than we could ever have imagined.

These days we've been kept very busy as, rather to our surprise after barking in the wilderness for so long, eco is chic – and we have been tagged as green pioneers. The reward, perhaps for being regarded as crazy for a long, long time (especially in Craig's case; the 'old hippy' tag has been hard to shake off; he used to note wryly: 'You can tell the pioneers – they're the ones with the arrows sticking out of their backs'). And it is exciting. You can't *help* but be jumped up by an e-mail asking you to be in *Vanity Fair*'s green issue, or by an invitation from Buckingham Palace asking Jo to attend a Women of Achievement reception hosted by HM the Queen. Unfortunately, they were on consecutive days and on different sides of the Atlantic, but we were determined to find a way.

For the *Vanity Fair* shoot, the legendary Annie Leibovitz was due to photograph us, but had to cancel at the last minute (she had to head off to snap Leonardo di Caprio in Greenland, as it happens, so we'll let her off). She was replaced by Mark Seliger, who has hundreds of *Rolling Stone* covers to his name. There is something so establishment about *Vanity Fair* (Jo has bought every single copy for about the last twenty years, so this was A Very Big Deal in the Sams household; a pinch yourself moment). Not only were there timing issues, however, there was also an eco-dilemma, what with the photograph being taken in the States. This was a major conscience tussle because we really do try to keep our carbon footprint down.

Happily, we were due in the States on business, to launch Green & Black's Ice Cream, having finally sourced an ice cream partner (in Oregon) who could create a frozen dessert that was as creamy, thick and rich-tasting as our much loved UK version. We only fly long-haul for business, not for pleasure, and make sure to offset any flights. This can only be a short-term solution. We admire the stance of Rob Hopkins, founder of the Transition Towns movement, which aims to re-localise living, who now attends overseas conferences by sending a DVD of his speech. However, we were due for one-on-ones with food editors at *Gourmet*, *Real Simple* and *Natural Health* and virtual presentations just weren't going to work, so we spent a week in New York, in temperatures of 8 degrees below zero with a Siberian wind-chill factor, launching ice cream.

After a week of crystal-clear days in Boston and New York, we made our way just north of New York City to Stone Barns, on the historic Hudson River Rockefeller estate, which has been converted into a truly world-class learning centre for organic agriculture. You can 'eat the view' at Dan Barber's restaurant, Blue Hill (which focusses exclusively on seasonal and organic ingredients), and learn about organic farming from interactive displays. It is breathtakingly impressive.

We were the only UK-based organic foodies being photographed (they called us all 'The Nourishers'), alongside key names from the US organic market. We'd been asked to bring clothes in which we felt comfortable (Jo brought an embroidered and embellished waistcoat made by her Great-aunt Doris, aged ninety, who announced she 'didn't want to die with a full button tin', and so sewed the lot on what has become Jo's favourite ever garment). Craig was particularly chuffed when the grooming editor, Vaughn Acord, top stylist at New York hairdressers Bumble and Bumble, praised his haircut. 'I asked my hairdresser to cut it like Bill Clinton's,' Craig told him. 'Well, you can tell him he's done a good job.' Vaughn smiled. 'I should know; I cut Bill's hair.'

The shoot was outside, and it was getting colder and colder, with the sky developing that unmistakeable weird glow it gets before a snowstorm; a team of assistants was running around styling a cornucopia of fresh organic veg and fruit, behind which we would pose. Stand-ins took our places for the rehearsal shot. What you can't see, just out of the frame, is the vast and not at all green heaters blowing hot hair at us in the open air, to stop our teeth chattering. After each few frames Mark Seliger clicked, we'd be rushed back inside and plied with hot drinks, to defrost our extremities. As we posed, we counted a crew of thirty-five people on the other side of the camera. That's *Vanity Fair* for you.

We watched the ominously darkening sky nervously. Jo really had to be on that plane. In her hand luggage was a 'stiffie' from Buckingham Palace inviting her to the reception the next day, and a change of clothes so she could head for the palace straight from Heathrow.

Ironically, all the people in the shot for the annual green issue had been flown from the four corners of the USA (and Europe, in our case), and limo-ed up there. But if it truly highlights the importance of green issues, spreads the eco-word among movers and shakers, does it really matter? We told ourselves 'no', as we air-kissed the assembled foodie company and belted for the airport before the storm hit. In fact, snowflakes were falling heavily as we taxied down the runway, and the plane's wings needed to be de-iced before take-off. An hour or two later and we'd have been stranded at JFK, as thousands were.

At Heathrow, Jo kissed Craig goodbye and made the most of the Virgin arrivals facilities (showers, breakfast, comfy armchairs), changing into her palace finery. We don't really do finery. One of the VIPs in our life is the wonderful Audrey, our local 'clothes doctor', who rescues garments that are on the brink of extinction, turning collars, replacing linings and buttons and breathing life into favourite garments. Not to put too fine a point on it, if the human race is to survive, fashion must probably die, and clothes – dateless, timeless, much loved clothes – must be resuscitated whenever possible.

The cab dropped Jo at Buckingham Palace where she immediately bonded, in the queue, with Renée Elliot, a friend who'd founded Planet Organic, which made the experience of walking up the red carpet (without falling off her heels) much less scary. She says, 'Of all the times I have wished my parents were still alive, the reception at the palace was the most poignant. My mother – a flag-waving, souvenir-tea-towel-buying royalist – would have been so thrilled.'

Very efficient equerries ushered the guests into the suite of linked reception rooms, with just ten guests picked to be presented. Jo was one of them – along with Cath Kidston, the home-ware dynamo (a thrill in itself), a woman from the Hebridean smokery which had provided all the smoked fish for the Queen's eightieth birthday cruise, the former head of the Hong Kong and Shanghai Bank, and Sharon Osbourne (a huge fan of Green & Black's ice cream, as she lost no time in telling Jo).

The assembled line-up were lucky enough to meet not only the Queen, but also the Princess Royal, the Duchess of Cornwall, the Countess of Wessex and the Duchess of Gloucester. Sophie Wessex and Jo go back a long way, to when the countess was a very savvy young PR with clients Jo would write about for *You* magazine in her pre-Prince Edward days. 'I saw your name on the list,' Sophie said. 'We eat your chocolate all the time.' Jo can, like everyone who's ever met her, recall every word the Queen said, which focussed on her eightieth birthday cruise ('wet and blowing a gale in August'), the scariness of flying into Hong Kong airport ('you feel as though you could reach out and touch the washing lines') and the mosquito-beating power of Avon Skin So Soft ('my beaters wear it all the time and you get these great wafts of it, standing behind them'). Sadly, not a word about chocolate. We believe Her Majesty is still a Charbonnel & Walker devotee, and a royal warrant looks unlikely. Alas. The Queen shook hands with 180 women, made endless small talk, and – as Jo reported excitedly when she finally got home – the canapés, the Holbeins and the Queen's English rose complexion were *fabulous*.

Big Issues

Jo: Homelessness is something I care deeply about. It isn't an easy issue. It's ugly, and dirty and in your face, and people have all sorts of preconceptions about the type of people who wind up homeless which can be blown out of the water if you ever spend time in any homeless hostel, where you'll meet everyone from lawyers to school dropouts, who've all ended up without a roof over their head.

I've felt passionately about homelessness since the age of seventeen, when my best friend, a nice, middle-class girl from a comfortable home ended up homeless. Her mother died of cancer during her last year of school and her blind father remarried. Diane's new stepmother threw her out of the house and she ended up living in her car for a year, parked on smart suburban streets and coming to have all her meals and baths at our house, while feeling too proud to take up my mother's offer of our spare room. But if it could happen to her, it could happen to anyone.

So eight years ago, in my parallel life as a beauty editor, while chairing the Cosmetic Executive Women networking organisation, my friend Sharron Lowe and I set up a Make A Difference Makeover programme for young women at Centrepoint's homeless hostels, tapping into the huge well of generosity in the cosmetics industry. We've staged dozens of them, now, enlisting the help of companies like Estée Lauder, Elizabeth Arden, John Frieda, Michaeljohn hairdressers, L'Oréal. We recruit make-up artists, hairdressers and nail technicians to transform between eight to twelve women during a fun-filled evening. Most of the girls are reaching the end of their stay at Centrepoint, and are poised on the threshold of a new life. There are as many stories about how they ended up homeless as there are girls themselves: parental violence; tricky step-parents, acting like the cuckoo in the nest; horrendous sexual abuse; and then there was the girl whose entire family emigrated back to Jamaica without telling her, leaving her behind . . .

The makeovers are extraordinary. (It's a rare evening when we don't end up in tears, in-between all the laughter.) Girls who walk in with hunched shoulders or downcast eyes, sometimes giving off the kind of fear you more usually see in a beaten dog, walk out (float out?) feeling like princesses. (Their words, not mine.) And on a second evening (usually the night after), while they're still buzzing, we give them what we call their 'mind makeover', led by Sharron – a beauty industry life coach and leading trainer – or another colleague Anna DeVere who has a similar industry role. The young homeless women learn how to capture that feeling of confidence that looking so beautiful the night before gave them, and hang on to it without the need for powder and paint, about self-esteem, about how to set goals. At the end, we give them a workbook which they can refer to, time and again (and which often becomes really dog-eared, so we've heard). The workshops cost us nothing to stage (save a little bit on printing costs); they're funded purely out of the goodwill of cosmetic industry employees who want to spend an evening or two doing something hands-on that might just change someone's life, rather than just writing a cheque or putting a few pennies in a collecting box. So could Cadbury's have picked a better cause to support, in my eyes, than homeless-ness? I don't think so. Which is one very good reason why I was so happy that they were giving a home to Green & Black's . . .

Toledo Cacao Fest 2007

'Hi, I'm from England and me and my boyfriend here eat Green & Black's Maya Gold every day. Can you show us where it's grown?'

As sales of Green & Black's increased, so did the number of conversations like this multiply – more and more people who were on holiday in Belize or Guatemala would take the bus or a Maya Airways eight-seater aircraft to Punta Gorda to see for themselves what they'd been reading about since 1994 on the inside of Maya Gold wrappers.

There was still no real tourism infrastructure to deal with them on the ground so these choco-tourists would be pointed in the direction of the Toledo Cacao Growers' Association office on Main Street. It was sometimes left to the voluntary officers of the TCGA – who are working farmers – to take them up country to a village where cacao was grown and show them some trees. Alternatively, if nobody was available, they would be pointed towards the villages of San Antonio or San Pedro Columbia, up in the foothills of the Maya Mountains, where they could ask again and hope to find someone who could show them where cacao was grown: the villages, the forest, the pods growing out of the tree trunks, which never fails to fascinate. Either way, this was a real imposition on the volunteer time of the TCGA officers, but they felt obliged to act as unpaid tour guides because, as everyone understands 'the customer is king'.

Still, this was a haphazard and inefficient way to reward people's passion for our product. We know for certain that, once a Green & Black's customer has seen cacao growing, visited a Mayan village, met the growers, perhaps tasted the sweet pulp in a cocoa pod and the bitter purple insides of a fresh raw bean, their loyalty to our brand deepens and intensifies. They don't stop there though – they recommend it to all their friends and become proselytisers. Green & Black's becomes more than just chocolate for them, it becomes a mission.

Gregor Hargrove, who had led the Maya Gold Project to expand capacity through tree planting, started to lean on the rather sleepy south Belizean tourist industry to get their act together. This they slowly did. And in May 2007 they organised and hosted the first Toledo Cacao Fest. Craig was invited along.

Before the start of the festival proper, Jeff Pzena, owner of Cotton Tree, a newly opened jungle lodge set about 10 miles from town, organised a Chocolate Summit. The programme included talks on the history and current state of Belize cocoa and the growth of production. Attending were various important players in the world of chocolate, including Clay Gordon, the author of *Discover Chocolate*, subtitled *The Ultimate Guide to Buying, Tasting and Enjoying Fine Chocolates*. Clay also runs a website called chocophile.com that emphasises the distinction between chocoholics (chocolate addicts) and chocophiles (chocolate-lovers). Another guest was Chloe Doutre-Roussel, chocolate buyer at Fortnum & Mason's for three and a half years (until she fell out with them), and author of *The Chocolate Connoisseur*. Then there was Marcia Haimann, who organises 'Chocolate – A Culinary and Cultural Tour', which escorts drooling chocophiles on chocolate tours to Belize, Madagascar and Italy, and Melanie Boudar, a chocolatier from Hawaii. Green & Black's own invited guest was Alexandra Leaf, a culinary historian who conducts chocolate tours of New York City's finest chocolate boutiques and is the author of *Van Gogh's Table*.

Clay Gordon had brought along a cocoa winnower that he had made up from a drainpipe and a fan from an old computer, and Jeff Pzena, the organiser, produced a chocolate alchemy machine, which is a mini-grinder and concher to make chocolate on a very small scale. They were both actually making chocolate while we held the conference.

A Mayan woman called Cirila Cho, who made the journey to the conference from her nearby village of San Miguel, confided to Jeff that she'd love his machinery to help her to make chocolate. Cirila is one of a new breed of entrepreneurs who has emerged in the area. She has a nursery where she produces cacao seedlings which she sells to local farmers and she grows, ferments and dries her own cocoa. What sets Cirila apart is that she also laboriously winnows and mills that cocoa to make Brigadeiros, a toffee-ish truffle made from a recipe in the Green & Black's chocolate cookbook, which she then sells in bags with colour-laser printed labels to choco-tourists, as well as through local hotels and lodges. Cirila's daughter is the quality controller at the TCGA.

Throughout the conference, Chloe Doutre-Roussel kept asking questions about the Maya Gold story; she had an uncomfortable suspicion that the story was too good to be true, that there must be a cover up. Nana Mensah, country director from Sustainable Harvest International (an American NGO that works with farmers to help them farm without diminishing the rainforest) stepped in to protest, professing his organisation's complete independence. Nana explained to Chloe that SHI have clearly identified that the most effective way to help farmers prosper is to assist them in growing for reliable markets and that the market for cocoa in Belize is by far the best around. Chloe was still sceptical. Then Jack Armstrong, a Brit who has lived in Belize for decades stood up to say that the Maya are the only farmers in Belize who make any money, have security, get a good price, get paid on delivery (the government made rice growers wait seven months the previous year for payment) and that 'this is the best damn deal any farmer anywhere ever had'. Chloe settled down somewhat, after that. As part of the celebration, Jeff laid on a dinner of chocolate-based main course dishes and desserts. After dinner we came to the real reason we were there: a discussion about how chocolate and tourism can help each other. The tourist industry, it emerged, is waking up to the allure of chocolate and all the tour operators are now engaged in servicing this potentially huge market.

The next day we went to the TCGA and to Green & Black's new office in Punta Gorda, a nice green and white timber-frame building near the seafront, across from the fish market. Gregor's intern and assistant was Carolina Chun, the daughter of Juan Chun, a leading cacao farmer in the area who has been continuously grumpy, ever since we pulled up on the road outside his house in 1993 and urged him to go organic and sell us cocoa. Juan is the main and usually only voice of dissent, complaining about the price being too low, about 'These white guys coming down here and cheating us out of our cocoa,' while still, year after year, being one of our biggest suppliers. Having his daughter working for us was a surprise and Craig regaled her with highlights of some of his outbursts. She laughed knowingly. 'That's my father, all right.' Nonetheless, having a trenchant critic, a sort of leader of the opposition, keeps everyone on their toes and ensures that at an AGM or other meeting, the unspoken worries of farmers are articulated firmly, if somewhat aggressively. If we didn't have Juan Chun we'd probably have to invent him. The same goes for Chloe Doutre-Roussel. Many people have unspoken doubts or misgivings they're too shy or sensitive to voice so it always helps if there is someone outspoken enough to act as a lightning rod for those concerns. Once expressed, they can be channelled and dealt with in an open forum to everyone's satisfaction and this creates transparency, builds confidence and dissipates mistrust.

We headed off the next day to the remote village of Otoxha,

near the Guatemala border, where we were privileged to be invited
to attend the preparations for the Deer Dance – the same ceremony Craig had attended with his cousin Anthony in 1987, the
most sacred in the Mayan repertoire – and which involved burning
large amounts of copal incense while three musicians played
complex traditional rhythms on a single large wooden marimba.
Two of the dancers, costumed as a deer and a jaguar, held fretful
live chickens by their legs and swung them round their heads as
they followed the age-old steps of the dance in the square outside
the church. Dancing in a circle round them, Mayan women in
traditional dress steadily filled the air with more copal incense,
which rose slowly skywards, bridging the gap between mortals and
the gods.

Although it had been a clear day, it suddenly started to rain –
an auspicious sign as the Deer Dance is about invoking the rain
god Chac to start the rainy season and ensure crop fertility. Most
farmers had just finished planting their corn and were ready for
wet weather. We noticed that the sky was still blue in every other
direction: the rain seemed only to have fallen in the immediate
area of the ceremony. The dancers gently but firmly twisted the
dizzied chickens' necks to finish them off, then went into the church,
laid them down on palm leaves in the nave, cut their necks and
smeared chicken blood on the *marimbas*. The preparations were
done. The Catholic priest normally in charge of the church had
wisely chosen discretion and had made himself scarce. (At that
point, as a vegetarian, Craig felt like doing the same.)

That night the Cacao Fest opened with a big society do at the
Punta Gorda Sports Bar, on their open-air roof deck. *Le tout* Punta
Gorda was there: ladies in black dresses and jewellery, local business people, hoteliers, NGO representatives, Rastafarians, Garifunas,
TCGA leaders, Mayan cacao farmers and representatives of the
tourist trade. Every flight from Belize City had been filled with
people coming for this event. It was a balmy evening, light sea

breezes keeping us comfortably cool as a youth chamber quintet from Belize City played light classical music and show tunes.

The guests snacked on chocolate-covered pineapple and papaya (locally grown). There was chocolate *mole* sauce with local shrimp, a free bar operated by the local wine merchant, a selection of chocolates and a full display with generous sampling from Green & Black's. Such a splendid occasion – it was hard to believe this was happening in the normally unglamorous and sleepy Punta Gorda we knew and loved.

The governor general of Belize, Sir Colville Young, delivered an inspiring and thoughtful speech. He started by talking about Rachel Carson, whose 1962 book *The Silent Spring* is widely credited with sparking the modern environmental movement, leading to the ban on the use of DDT. He succinctly summarised the main point of the book (the silent spring referred to the disappearance of birds from the top of a food chain that had been destroyed by pesticides). Sir Colville went on to say that the future of Belizean agriculture had to be based on sustainability and biodiversity. He heaped praise on the Mayan farmers for showing the rest of the country the way forward. Justino Peck and the other cacao farmers were beaming and flushed with pride as the entire gathering respectfully applauded their achievement. The governor general then finished with a folk tale about a lizard which becomes an emerald and makes a farmer rich. The farmer returns the emerald to the land, it turns into a lizard and scampers away. Moral: if you take the earth's riches you must also give something back. It's clear that the whole country is fantastically proud of the cacao industry.

A 5 a.m. the next day Gregor Hargrove was in his office as a steady flow of last-minute entrants queued up for space at the Cacao Fest, eager to be part of the big event. The Deer Dance crew from Otaxha were at the back of the Toledo Cacao Growers' Association building: one jaguar, one dog, six deer, six Spaniards, one black-bearded Spaniard, an old lady, all resplendent in brilliantly radiant costumes, sequins shimmering.

In the main square of Punta Gorda were fifty stalls and displays; every school, NGO and farmers group had made an effort. Thousands of visitors – more than the entire population of Punta Gorda – were visiting, sampling, buying and tasting.

There was so much to take in. At one stall Gomier, a tall, vegetarian Rastafarian was selling soya ice cream from an Italian machine, using soya milk, carrageen moss seaweed, Maya Gold cocoa powder, spices and avocado purée. He had a permanent queue. Cirila Cho was also there with her homemade Brigadeiros, hot-chocolate powder, cold-chocolate drink – all made with her homegrown and home-processed cocoa. Mrs Ash, wife of Ignacio, a cacao farmer, was selling prepackaged balls of pure unsweetened chocolate. It was gratifying to see that many of the Maya had developing enterprises based on cocoa and had moved on from the embroidered handicrafts they traditionally sold tourists. However, because the Deer Dance was the central cultural event of the day, a stall selling carved wooden masks of deer, jaguar, dog, Spaniard and monkey was doing a roaring trade. The Punta Gorda library were selling Maya Gold cocoa and various books on Mayan culture. Sustainable Harvest International showed natural pesticides that can be made from widely available local plants. There was a whole area full of cocoa stuff for kids, offering prizes for the best drawings or for correctly guessing how many cocoa beans there were in a jar, and the TCGA themselves had created a big chart with a wheel that showed the whole process from growing a bean into a tree, to the pods, to fermenting, to drying, to a bean, to chocolate.

On the stage a *marimba* band played and the leader of the dancers from Otoxha danced alongside them on the stage. It was all a very far cry from that November day in 1993 when we first met a handful of debt-ridden, distrustful and disillusioned cacao growers in a part of the country that Belizeans called the forgotten district of Toledo.

The Maya, formerly the lowest and even pitied members of Belizean society, were being exalted with genuine respect, not least because, at last, there is some reason for tourists to come all the way south to Punta Gorda, which has no golden sandy beaches or flashy hotels to entice them. Eco-choco-tourism is the new holy grail and the Mayan cacao farmers are at the heart of it. For anyone who makes the dusty journey south, evidence of the entrepreneurial culture that has grown up in the last few years is everywhere. We still have to pinch ourselves that Green & Black's has come so far from that rainy night on the Portobello Road and has touched so many lives. And taste buds.

By Degrees

Jo: Two letters arrived out of the blue one day in 2005, one addressed to me, the other to Craig. Would we consider accepting an honorary business degree from Kingston University? Having established this wasn't actually a practical joke, I then had to pick myself up off the floor. Me, a homework-hating, knickers-up-the-school-flagpole, university-spurning rebel, being offered a degree! When we read more closely, the letter from the faculty asked us to provide details of our education. At that point, my heart sank. Despite Craig's reassurances (it was OK for him, he already had a degree!), I figured there was no way they'd award someone with a measly six O Levels an honorary business qualification.

It all went very quiet, and I put it to the back of my mind. Then another letter arrived, asking us to attend a ceremony at the Barbican, to which we were invited to bring guests, if we fancied. On 6 January 2006, Hon. Dr Sams and Hon. Dr Fairley were duly dressed up in pale blue robes and entered the concert hall to the sound of a trumpet fanfare. We gave a short ten-minute potted speech about the story of Green & Black's, and were handed our diplomas. My brother Alastair was beaming proudly from the audience, alongside our friend Deborah Garcia, the director of *The Future of Food*, a documentary about genetic engineering, who'd been at the Soil Association conference in London the previous weekend, and who thought it would be fun to join us for our Big Moment. Deborah is very big on fun, which is why we love her and, presumably, why her late husband, Jerry Garcia of the Grateful Dead, loved her, too. (Whether she thought it was *quite* so fun after 800 Kingston University undergraduates had made their way to the stage to collect their diplomas over the next two hours, I'm not so sure.

The commemorative photo from that day hangs on our downstairs loo wall alongside the programme for the Green & Black's Maiden Stakes at Goodwood (sponsored during an evening of organic racing organised by the glamorous Countess of March, a stalwart Soil Association supporter), our *Vanity Fair* picture, a cover of *Observer Food Monthly* on which Nigel Slater is tucking into a tub of Green & Black's Chocolate Ice Cream, and a prized letter from Bill Bryson. In 1998, he'd written a story about his memories of dark chocolate as a traveller in a Brussels train station so we thought we'd send him 70% Green & Black's, via his publisher. We were amazed to get a reply. 'Thank you very much for your letter and the wonderful chocolate – a very thoughtful and generous gesture and much appreciated. Please excuse any gurgly drool that may drip onto the page. It sounds like a wonderful thing you do. I congratulate you and wish you every success. You have certainly found a loyal customer in me, and I hope I have the chance to thank you in person one day.' After all, what are loo walls for?

Epilogue

If you're the kind of person who has the drive, enthusiasm and energy to create a business like ours, you're never going to be the type of person who's happy to sit with a gin and tonic and relax as the sun sets. We could have put our feet up, when we sold Green & Black's. Really put our feet up, gone on world cruises, pottered in our greenhouse, ricocheted from friend to relation, visiting all the people we had promised to get round to seeing (and neglected), during the Green & Black's years. We could have put our feet up – if we had been different people, which is how come, at the time when we were selling Green & Black's, we found ourselves starting a whole new venture: Judges Bakery. And why, most recently, we decided to open an eleven-room boutique natural health centre, in our home town of Hastings.

In 2003, Jo did an interview with Carole Bamford, wife of Sir Anthony Bamford, the JCB billionaire. She was opening a farm shop on the 1,500-acre Daylesford estate where she and Sir Anthony lived – although calling Daylesford a farm shop is a bit like referring to Karl Lagerfeld as a dressmaker, or the QE2 as a tugboat. Lady B was pleased with Jo's write-up, and invited us back for a more leisurely visit. The next time we happened to be in Oxfordshire, we made a detour to Moreton-in-Marsh so we could look round together.

Behind the scenes in the bakery, Craig instantly bonded with the

Daylesford baker, Emmanuel Hadjiandreou – they're both bread anoraks, au fait with eighteen-hour doughs and the practice of using sprouted wheat as a sourdough starter. While chatting to Emmanuel, Craig pronounced that he had 'always wanted to open a slow food bakery in Hastings'. The two of them stayed in occasional touch, sharing recipes and insights into baking, until one day Emmanuel e-mailed to say he'd resigned from Daylesford, and was anything happening with that slow food bakery? To which the honest answer was 'no'.

Then a few months later, out of the blue came a call from a neighbour in Hastings, who knew absolutely nothing of Craig's secret, flour-fuelled fantasy, but knew he had owned Ceres Bakery in the 1970s. Did we know that Judges – the bakery on our street – was up for sale, for the first time in thirty years? An amazing coincidence; one that it seemed almost rude not to investigate. We invited Emmanuel and his wife Lisa down to Hastings, to see whether they might be interested in being part of a new venture. They arrived on the most insane night of the town's calendar, our equivalent of the Venice Carnevale – Pram Race night, when groups of friends dress up in crazy costumes (some of which they've worked on for months), pushing homemade floats which have just one thing in common: their base is a set of pram wheels. Vast quantities of alcohol are involved. Tins are successfully rattled in aid of charity. The next day, everyone speaks very softly, conscious of the mass hangover that has the Old Town in its dyspeptic grip. Lisa and Emmanuel took one look and decided that yes, Hastings was definitely crazy enough for them to consider moving.

It took six long months to get the deal together to buy the bakery. In May 2005, we knew, we'd be getting our Green & Black's sale money from Cadbury's. Meanwhile, though we had a few properties to our name, we didn't actually have any cash or, at least, not enough to buy the bakery. So we had to borrow. Triodos Bank, the ethical bank, dragged their heels deciding whether to

In Praise of Farmers

Jo: It's a simple fact that *all* farmers deserve to be more fairly rewarded than they are, not just cocoa, sugar and tea growers. Our crusade at Green & Black's centred around raising awareness of the plight of Third World farmers, and to encourage shoppers to support them through buying produce that comes from small farmers, rather than giant farms owned by rich multinational corporations. But there are many, many farmers nearer home whose income is constantly being eroded by the world's enduring insistence on cheap food. Frankly, it's a bloody miracle there are any farmers left.

It blows Craig and I away that if someone buys a swanky BMW instead of a Ford, everyone pats him on the back and thinks he's done really well. Glossy magazines are awash with pictures of incredibly expensive hefty handbags, which we're meant to lust over and splurge on, in preference to an anonymous cheap nylon rucksack. (Which is much better for your back.) When a friend buys designer clothes in preference to something from Gap, we're meant to be jealous. And yet people actually drive out of their way to get 10p off the price of a packet of biscuits, or buy a chicken for £2 – and anyone who pays a higher price for food than their neighbour is considered a twit.

When supermarkets get into price wars, paring a few pence off here and there in order to lure customers away from the competition, the farmer pays, every single time. Cheap food makes for cheapened food production: chicken sheds are crammed to the rafters and necessitate mega-doses of antibiotics to stop flocks dying, vegetables are repeatedly sprayed with herbicides to avoid the cost of hand-weeding, and bread is laced with hydrogenated fat, a cheat that gives it body and texture which otherwise can only be achieved through time, as yeast ferments and puffs up the dough. What's more, land previously used for crops is now being given over to growing fuel for cars. To us, it seems insane.

front the cash, before coming up with an offer that was somewhat less than we needed. Our own bank manager dithered, despite the sight of the shareholder's agreement that showed we were due a windfall in just a few months, and only needed a short-term loan; he even told us we'd be better off asking for the money for a yacht or a Ferrari than a business. And actually, the short-term nature of our need was probably the problem. Banks like nice, leisurely lending periods so they can notch up lots and lots of interest from businesses. But, happily, a savvy commercial-banking manager from Barclays in Crawley called Melanie Collins got wind of our project via our personal bank manager, and moved heaven and earth to get us the cash we needed swiftly – for all of seven weeks, before we were in a position to pay off the mortgage, thanks to Cadbury's.

The pieces of the financial picture finally fell into place the day before Good Friday, which just happens to be one of the busiest days in the baking calendar. Lisa and Emmanuel had been working part-time at the bakery for a few weeks, alongside the previous owners. But suddenly, that Friday, the safety net was taken away and we actually had to run the place ourselves. Jo had never even worked a till before, but 1,200 hot cross buns later, had picked it up.

We had two major priorities from the start: to give the store a makeover and to change it over to organic. In order to decide how we wanted the shop to feel, Lisa and Jo (and sometimes Craig) trailed round almost fifty delis, natural food stores and gourmet emporia, taking notes on what they felt worked well, and what didn't. We couldn't help noticing how much wasted space there was above bottles of vinegar, or olive oil, space which was generating no income for the shop, at all. We also couldn't help noticing how little there was actually to eat in so many of the delis we visited: shelf upon shelf of fancy olive oils or balsamic vinegars, chutney and chilli sauces, which could languish in a pantry for years, but not much, frankly, that you could take home and eat that night.

Backstage in the bakery, Emmanuel was working on the organic conversion, with Lisa filling in literally hundreds of the required Multiple Ingredient Product Specification forms (MIPS, in Soil Association shorthand) which were required for our certification. Just as we had made organic accessible – and helped enhance its reputation for deliciousness – with Green & Black's, we wanted to popularise and even normalise organics with the bakery. Our goal, in fact, was to become the first high-street bakery in the world to be completely organic, down to the last Cornish pasty and fairy cake, keeping all the existing clientele while bringing serious food-lovers into the bakery for the first time.

This, however, was a major challenge. At Green & Black's, we had the advantage of starting with an organic product from day one, and could shape our new product development according to what was coming onto the market organically. At Judges, we didn't want to lose the loyalty of customers who were used to their Viennese hearts, their Bakewells, their crispy bloomer loaves and their sausage rolls. But in order to comply with organic regulations, we had to throw out all the emulsifiers, preservatives, bread improvers and E numbers, finding a new way to colour the meringue pigs, for instance (raspberry purée and beetroot juice work a treat, we discovered). You wouldn't believe the excitement when we stumbled upon organic hundreds and thousands, or managed to track down organic Smartie-style sweets for our scrummy cupcakes.

From the outset we realised that we didn't want to stop at sourdough and baguettes – we had the opportunity to create a one-stop 100% organic shop, with as much local produce as could be sourced organically. When food is being grown four miles down the road and can be delivered to a store still with the morning dew on it, taste, freshness and ripeness can again become the priority. In our organic shop, we sell local cheeses, wines, goat's milk, honey, eggs, meat (from Hen on the Gate, a nearby farm which has scooped no less than seven organic food awards for its chicken, beef, lamb and pork) and produce from a local organic farm taken over by a Dutch grower who (like many of his compatriots) has veg-growing in his DNA. We have seven of our own Soil Association-certified acres, Stonelynk Farm, just four miles from the bakery, with 180 fruit trees which will eventually supply all the apples, pears, plums (as well as peaches, apricots and quinces) for the bakery, not just to sell loose but for our pies and tarts. The two-acre field supplies potatoes, lettuces and salads, beets, pumpkins and literally dozens of other lines, which keeps customers interested, and so keeps them coming back, to see what's new, what's fresh.

As a result, we have locals who come in literally every single day (sometimes two or three times), to buy what they need, from a pint of milk to a single carrot. People really enjoy the flexibility. In a supermarket, organic carrots are sold in 2 kilo bags, which is a fortnight's supply for one of our pensioner customers. Not only would they have to lug 2 kilos back from the supermarket on the bus (virtually impossible when you use a stick); they also might die of carrot fatigue before reaching the end of the bag.

With Judges Bakery, our goal has been to offer a truly locally focussed, 100% organic alternative to the supermarket, to which ideally people could walk. Watching the bakery grow into such a thriving local store was incredibly rewarding, but we still weren't ready to put our feet up. People joke that when you sell your business, you can spend 'more time with your money'. Some people buy yachts, or second homes. For us, it's been about seeing what we could make that money do, rather than leaving it to languish in a bank. Since the advent of Judges and Stonelynk Farm (and even before, with our own back garden potager, and Craig's allotment), we have had ready access to organic food but to us, the missing part of the healthy living jigsaw in Hastings was that there was no first-class natural health centre.

How I Keep Going

Jo: If you're going to work this hard and not burn out, it takes a lot of self-care. Maybe caffeine, cocaine and staying up all night work for some people, but personally, I plan not to burn out. As well as eating a fresh, organic, pretty much macrobiotic diet with lots of wholegrains, a little fish occasionally, and literally tons of fresh vegetables every year, I religiously take the supplements Essential Balance, a blend of Omega 6 and Omega 3 essential fatty acids, AgeLoss (a mega-antioxidant), along with several drops on the tongue each day of a flower remedy called Women's Balance. I try to drink 2 litres of water a day (this is easier if you keep big bottles on your desk, as it's easy to lose track of the number of glasses glugged). I walk for half an hour at least five days a week (and even during that most manic time at the bakery, added a brisk stroll onto the thousands of steps taken in the shop, or running up and down to the stockroom). I try to keep my sugar intake as low as possible by restricting myself to a few squares of Green & Black's a day, but I have to admit: during the product development phase at Judges, tweaking those many recipes to organify them, a *lot* of sugar went down. (And it seemed like Craig walked in every time I had a Belgian bun or a doughnut stuffed in my mouth. Busted!) Although I may effortlessly spring out of bed in a 'hello clouds, hello world' kind of way at 5 a.m., I do not burn the candle at both ends. Indeed, I am physically incapable of doing so, as Craig and any of my friends and family – who long ago nicknamed me the Dormouse – will testify. Like a Maasai warrior, I'm primed for action within seconds of opening my eyes in the morning. But at the other end of the day, when sleep beckons, I simply collapse. If there's no bed handy, a train seat or a sofa (under a pile of coats, if necessary, with Black Sabbath pounding out from a nearby speaker) will do.

Neither of us even has a conventional doctor. In our house, if you're sick, the remedy is crushed *umeboshi* plums and pulverised *kudzu* root, or arrowroot, in a cup of hot water. Seems to cure most things – although this may be that it tastes so ghastly, you get better in order not to have to drink any more of the stuff.

The drug and surgery industry, like the agrochemical business (and we're often talking about the same companies, here) is worth billions. Just as we both think it's wrong that huge swathes of agricultural land have become ruined by pesticides, herbicides and fertilisers, polluting our rivers, poisoning the land (and, in many cases, the workers and growers who farm it), so we believe there has to be a better approach when it comes to human health than keeping taking the medicine. Yes, we'd head straight to Accident & Emergency, if we were injured. But through good diet (including a daily dose of dark chocolate), plenty of exercise and frequent cold dips in the sea, not to mention loving what we do, we are both (touch sustainably harvested wood) glowingly healthy. And when we have, very occasionally, been less than well, we have found the answer for us lay with gifted complementary therapists and/or rest, rather than trotting off to the GP for a prescription. What we felt was needed in our town was a place where experienced therapists and teachers could come together to offer yoga, Pilates, massage, nutritional therapy, acupuncture – all the therapies we ourselves have come to depend on, and more.

Both our careers have been built on the somewhat arrogant premise that we believe if *we* need a service or a product, then the chances are that many, many other people feel the same way. We're no different, except that we roll our sleeves up and try and fulfil the need, or plug the gap. The only (tiny) natural health centre in our town had closed, a few years earlier, and we tossed the idea back and forth, never really being able to find the right location. Then an auction catalogue landed on our desk, featuring (among many tumbledown and otherwise

How I Keep Going

Craig: As I don't work as hard as Jo, I prefer to take a cat nap when I feel a bit tired. I avoid coffee – it accelerates my metabolism a little too much and leaves me more tired and hungry than I can manage. (Jo would say murderous, but suicidal's more like it.)

I only experience two kinds of illness: tummy trouble and sniffles, both rarely. If I get the sniffles then I take a 100g zinc tablet two or three times over two days, along with a few 1000mg vitamin C tablets. Then I make sure I eat simply and infrequently and get some rest. I find *umeboshi* pickled plums with *kudzu* very good, too. It's a sticky concoction that lines the insides with a rich antifungal goo and knocks out yeast or anything else that's upset the balance of the intestinal flora. Personally, I *like* the taste.

Our fridge is full of what *Red* magazine – who did a story not so long ago on the contents of people's refrigerators – described as 'murky liquids'. This is because I like to use nettles, dandelion, burdock, hawthorn berries, angelica, fennel, artemisia, turmeric and seaweeds such as kelp when I cook. Some of these are seasonal so I either make them into teas, put them in the freezer or dry them to maintain a year-round supply. I grow them in our nearby smallholding, on my allotment and in our garden. About one third to one half of what I eat is brown rice, wholegrain seeded sourdough bread from our bakery or other wholegrains such as millet, buckwheat and oats. Another third is vegetables; raw, cooked or pickled (in particular beetroot and olives). For the final third I let my appetite lead me to anything else that appeals to me – once I've got the basics covered I trust my palate not to lead me too far astray.

For me breakfast is the most important meal of the day – *to skip*. If I eat an evening meal and don't eat again until the following early afternoon then I've given my digestion sixteen hours of peace. What's more, when you don't eat breakfast your body's blood sugar reserves are depleted and so it can only get more from one place: your fat reserves. It's the principle of the Atkins diet without the meat. Getting exercise in the morning, before your first meal of the day, helps accelerate the process. I also keep sugar consumption as low as possible – excess sugar turns to fat. I weigh myself every day and will eat less and exercise more if I'm gaining weight.

My favourite exercise is walking and there are plenty of challenging hills round here to get the heart pumping and the lungs wheezing. I see a Pilates trainer twice a week to maintain core strength in the pelvic floor and the muscles that support the back. As a result I haven't seen an osteopath for more than a decade, despite having whiplash and back injuries from two car accidents and a lot of heavy lifting when I worked as a baker and delivery van driver at Ceres Bakery. In the summer – actually, pretty much from April to November – we swim in the sea almost every day, sometimes even when it's raining.

dodgy buildings) an ex-council office in Hastings's most architecturally majestic square. The minute we stepped over the imposing Regency threshold, we started to get goose bumps: it would, with very few structural alterations, make the most amazing well-being centre: eleven spacious rooms, one perfect for a Pilates studio, another for yoga classes. Not a wall needed to be knocked down.

Less than a week later, we sat with pounding hearts in the auction room, and ended up with a seven-storey Regency building in the most beautiful square in town for, basically, a song. In addition to the amazing, huge windows and high ceilings, part of the appeal was that its design – already divided into offices – lent itself perfectly to the creation of a dozen consulting rooms. (Although Jo did have to spend a few nights trawling the internet, Googling 'big old doors' to find a pair that would partition off the rear of the reception area, in order to fill in a gap and create what is now our physiotherapy department – complete with replica skeleton.)

The renovations took six months of builders crawling all over the place and Jo scouring antique and junk shops for furniture, and we kept every local upholsterer, blind-maker and picture-framer rushed off his or her feet, while we tried to put ourselves in customers' shoes (which is how we always do things). What furniture would we like to find in a health centre? An eclectic mix of (inexpensive, locally sourced) antiques and earthy, natural pieces such as a long carpenter's bench, which (when sanded and waxed) has a wonderful, sculptural feel. A huge wooden panel painted with an image of Ganesh the Hindu god of overcoming obstacles came via a Yorkshire-based internet company, as did a huge studded wooden ceiling which we turned on its side to create a reception desk. We called in a feng shui person who told us exactly where we needed to have water, wood and stone elements, for optimum harmony and healing energy. (Whether you believe in feng shui or not, everyone comments on the centre's instantly calming vibe.) Natural paints were a must, in soft, blood pressure lowering neutrals. We wanted the centre to have a nod to spirituality, without coming over all rainbows and wind chimes. Everything had to look more than a notch above the average health centre: sumptuous pillows, organic wool duvets and organic towels. The wood-chip wallpaper definitely had to go. Lighting had to be dimmable. (And we declared it a whale-song-free zone.)

So with the help of a cracking team of builders and decorators, 'the world's first boutique well-being centre' – the Wellington Square Natural Health Centre – opened in June 2007. But anyone can create a beautiful space with a bit of help. Finding the people to work there ought to be tougher, but it wasn't. It was as if the therapists were magnetised to our building; we started with a small group of practitioners from our own personal positive health team, and in turn, they recommended others. The talented team was assembled as if by magic.

The great advantage of being serial entrepreneurs, meanwhile, is that when you have had one successful business, everyone wants to know what you're going to do next (something Richard Branson has long understood, and milked, albeit on a much, much grander scale). Once you've told a few key people about what you're doing, the publicity side (which helps bring customers through the door) is easier than for a first venture. Glossy magazines and newspapers clamoured to write about Judges Bakery. The *Daily Telegraph, You* magazine, even Australia's *Vogue Entertaining* showcased our Bakewell tarts. And the press have been equally interested in the Wellington Square Natural Health Centre. We managed to get onto www.vogue.com's and the *Daily Mail's* hot lists for 2008, and into *Tatler's* guide to the 103 top world spas within six weeks of opening, despite our protestations that no, we're *not* really a spa because we don't have a chill-out room, fluffy dressing gowns or a sauna. Success begets success. (Although, of course, there is always a small sector of humankind who seems poised to watch you fall flat on your face, but that's the price anyone who has even a modicum of achievement has to pay.)

But why do we bother? Why don't we just put those feet up, now? Because we're still doing what we believe in. We believe that natural food grown without artificial fertilisers, pesticides and herbicides, and without tantrum-inducing additives, is better for people and the planet. We believe that if food can be sourced from nearby, then it should be. We are convinced that natural therapies, exercise regimes and manipulation techniques can offer a real alternative to drugs, boosting someone's overall well-being while helping in the shorter-term with a specific chronic or acute problem: from sciatica to eczema, depression to asthma, panic attacks to migraines. In the bigger, wider, scarier world, science is trying to gain the upper hand: from genetically modified crops to biofuels, the ever-wider prescribing of statins and blood pressure pills. Personally, we think that nature already has most of the answers, and that the planet would be a lot better off if we stopped meddling.

But the meddling instinct is insistent and Craig's view is that it's sometimes better to meddle with nature and do the right thing than to leave it alone and let the wrong things happen. So he has founded a biochar company called Carbon Gold. They are turning waste biomass such as cocoa tree prunings and shade tree trimmings in Belize into biochar. They'll take olive prunings and olive pits froms Greek olive oil presses and turn them into biochar. They're taking chestnut coppice poles from overgrown woods in Kent and Sussex and turning them into biochar. What's the difference between biochar and charcoal? Well, charcoal is used for barbecues or in water filters so it has to be a certain type. Biochar is used as a soil improver – it makes the soil a more vibrant living environment for all the microorganisms, such as fungi and bacteria, that are essential for plant growth and health, particularly in organic systems, where chemical fertilisers and pesticides aren't used. Biochar improves soil structure, reduces the need for fertiliser, increases the water retention of soil, encourages soil biota and can increase plants' growth and health. Every time you put it in the soil it stays there. For a very long time. It's a natural way to take carbon dioxide out of the air and then turn it into carbon that doesn't go back into the atmosphere for hundreds of years. Biochar buys us time to get our act together with energy from sun, wind and tide that doesn't emit carbon and is the only way we can remove the carbon dioxide that we have already produced and which threatens us with runaway global warming.

Actually, we don't think of our approach as saving the planet, any more, but as saving the human race. A while ago, we heard the environmental campaigner Vandana Shiva speak. In the Q & A section, she was asked if she felt it was too late to save the planet. Vandana gave one of her wise smiles. 'Not at all,' she said, 'the planet will be just fine without us.' And it will. But what will happen to our grandchildren? And our great-grandchildren? How can we forgive ourselves if we don't do everything we can for them, at home and through our work and businesses?

So green may be the new black, but it shouldn't be the new bling, destined to go out of fashion just as swiftly as it came in, or we're all in deep trouble. What we hoped to do, with Green & Black's, was to show there is way of doing business that treads a little more lightly on the Earth. Our new ventures are just an extension of what we've done before. We're still trying to change the world. Only now, we're trying to change the world not with squares of chocolate, but one sourdough loaf, one pink meringue pig, one yoga class at a time . . .

Index

Abehsera, Michel 17
Acal, Leonardo 77
Acord, Vaughn 220
Adams, Vince 111
ADM (Archer Daniels Midland) 136, 139
ADM Cocoa 148
advertising 60, 143
AgeLoss 241
Agent Orange 133
air miles 81
Alderson, Maggie 37
Alfille, David 111
Alternative Trade Organisations 203
anandamide 56
Andreas, Dwayne 136
Annabel's 74
anti-stress tip 111
Antoniou, Dr Michael 133
apple juice as sugar substitute 20, 39
Aqua Manda 95–6
Argüelles, José, *The Mayan Factor* 75
Ark 36
Armstrong, Jack 227–8
aroma receptors 84–5
Arpège 91
ATOs 203
Austin, Richard 135
Aveda 215

awards 142–3
Aztec civilisation 45, 52, 85, 148

Bahanda, Pardeep 156, 161, 166
Bailey, Glenda 33
Baldry, Simon 213–14
Balfour, Lady Eve 130
Bamford, Sir Anthony 235
Bamford, Carole 235
BARC 149
Barclays Bank 238
Barry, Michael 93
Bart, Lionel 30
BBC 93, 95
BBC Good Food Show 94
Beart, Nick 156, 161–2, 166, 169, 175–82, 195, 211, 217–18
Beatles, The 18
    see also McCartney, Paul
Beckwith, Peter 161
Belgravia Imports 71–2, 188
Belize 46, 81–4, 86–91, 158–61, 190, 203–4
    cacao plantations 48
    Harmonic Convergence event 75–9
    Hurricane Iris 190–1
    impact of fair trade 198–200
    improvement in status of Maya 200

logging 206–7
tourism 96–8, 225–6
Belize Agroforestry Research Council
    149
Best, George 30
Big Issue 214–15
biochar 247
biodiversity, encouragement of 87
BioFach 69, 216
Bircher muesli 10
Bird, John 214–15
Bird, Neil 206, 207
Black, Charlotte 79
bloom 109
Blue Hill 220
Body Shop 34, 35, 75, 215
Boglione, Gael 37
Bol, Diego 82
Bolivia 80
Bolon, Maximo 77–8
Booker Tate Award for Small
    Businesses 142
Bordier 91
Boudar, Melanie 226
brand awareness 115
Brigadeiros 227, 231
British Airways 116
British Arkady Soy Products 136
Bromley High School 27–9
Brosnan, Pierce 36
Brown, Cluny 181
Brown, Tina 32
brownies recipe 124–5
Brynner, Yul 31
Bryson, Bill 234
Buckingham Palace 113, 219, 221–2
Buerk, Michael 93
Business Action on Homelessness
    214–15
Business Linkages Challenge Fund
    grant application 193–5, 197–8
Byng, John 138
Byrne, Charles 156

cacao
    Amazonian variety 45, 191–2
    Belize 78–9
    Central American variety 45
    criollo 47, 191–2
    diseases 49, 54
    domestication and cultivation
        47–9, 54
    on former rice-growing land 197
    geographical spread of growers
        53–4
    modern hybrids 191–2
    origins 45
    plantations 47–9
    time from planting to harvest
        190
    trade in 45–6
    use of pesticides in plantations
        54–5
    in the wild 46–7
Cadbury's 193
    buy Green & Black's 195, 198,
        211–15, 217–18
    corporate social responsibility
        213–15ethical sourcing team
        216
    discussion regarding milk
        chocolate packaging 120–2
    help with grant application 195,
        197–8
    Quaker origins 52
CaféDirect 90, 110, 203
CAFOD 92
Cantalou 170–1
capital, importance of 177
capsaicin 85
carbon footprint 219
Carbon Gold 247
Carluccio, Antonio 73
Carluccio, Priscilla 73
Carluccio's 73
carob 58–9
Caroline Walker Award 142–3

Carr-Hill, Micah 116
Carrarini, Jean-Charles 68
Carson, Rachel, *Silent Spring* 230
cash flow 153, 164
Centrepoint 223
Ceres Bakery 19, 20
Ceres Grain Shop 18–19
Charles, Prince of Wales 69, 74,
    123
'cherelle' 46
chilli pepper 85
Chinese angelica 107
Cho, Cirila 227, 231
Cho, Julian 206, 207
chocolate 22
    Belgian 138
    bloom 109
    chemical content 56
    consumption levels 53
    cultural associations 51–2
    European development 52–3
    history of 45–55
    industry standards 108
    manufacture 49, 50–3
    milk 53
    organic 22, 39
    70% cocoa solids 23–4, 39
    tasting technique 50
chocolate societies 64
Chocolate Society Journal 64
chocolate spread 78–9
Chocolate Summit conference
    226–8
Chocolaterie d'Aquitaine 81, 93–4, 95
Choisya ternata 84
Christian Aid 92, 96, 99–100, 110
Christian Aid News 96
Chun, Carolina 228
Chun, Juan 228
Clarence House 74
Clarke, Kenneth 142
Clipper Tea 110
clock-watching 163–4

Coady, Chantal 64
Coc, Ines 160
cocoa 51–2
    buying season 192
    forastero 80
    gene bank 151
    modern production 52–3
    organic sources 80–4
cocoa beans
    as currency 45–6
    drying 50–1
    fermentation 49
    grinding 51
    roasting 51
cocoa butter 51, 56
cocoa pods
    germination 49
    growth 46–7
    ripening and harvesting 49
    terracotta 46
cocoa powder 116
Cody, William 'Buffalo Bill' 188
Cohen, Mark 149
Coleman, Langston 69
Collins, Joan 36
Collins, Melanie 238
Collinson, Andy 165, 169
Columbia River Forest Reserve 82,
    206–7
Community Foods 57, 164–5, 166–8,
    169, 171–2
competition 63–4
conching 51, 53
Conforti, Anthony 75–7, 81–2
Conocado cooperative 190
Conran, Terence 73
contacts 73
contracts
    five-year rolling 87
    Toledo Cacao Growers
        Association 86–8
copper 56, 105
corporate culture 92

corporate social responsibility 173–4,
    213–15
Cortes, Hernando 52
Cosmetic Executive Women 223
cotton 55
count line 117–20
Cox, Cat, *Chocolate Unwrapped; The
    Politics of Pleasure* 65–6
Craven, John 93, 95
cream, organic 111–12
Crystal Skull of Doom 76–7
CSR 173–4, 213–15
customer service 109–10

Dagoba 218
Daily Mail 139
dairy farming, organic 112
Damsgaard, Lisbeth 22
Danone 74
dark chocolate (70%)
    decision to launch 39–40
    launch 57–74
    packaging 2–3
    prototype bar 22, 39
Dass, Ram 174
Davis, Bette 31–2
Dawson, Chris 140
Day of the Dead 51–2
DDT 54
Dean & DeLuca 72–3
Deberdt, André 22, 159, 164–5, 165,
    170–1
Deer Dance 76, 77–8, 84, 229, 231
dehydration 111
deliveries 144
DeLuca, Giorgio 72–3
Department for International
    Development 193–5
DeVere, Anna 224
DfID 193–5
diabetes 65
dichlorvos 54
Dick, Lillian 71–2

Dick, Ronnie 71–2, 188
dieldrin 54
Divine 192–3, 203
Dominican Republic 190, 204–5
dong quai 107
Doutre-Roussel, Chloe 226, 227–8
Dow Chemical 134
drinking chocolate 51
Drury, Mike 90, 91, 95
Duerr, Mark 169
Duerr, Tony 165
Duerr's 60, 144, 157, 164–5, 168–72,
    175, 176, 177
Dugstad, Lars Ole 7, 187
Dugstad, Ole 7–8
Dutching 53

eco-consciousness 25–6, 36–7
eco-tourism 96–8
    see also tourism
Eliot, Renée 221
Elkington, John 174
Elle 63
Environment Council 139
ES Magazine 37
Esom, Steven 140
Essential Balance 241
Ethical Consumer Association 142
Ethical Trade Mark 205
eugenol 85
Europe, sales in 201–2
Eurostar 116
Eve bar 105, 107
Ewé tribes-people 22, 80
expansion of business 101–24
    limits to 114–15
export 57–8
    markets 70–3
Eyadéma, General Gnassingbé 81
Eyes Wide Shut 154–5

fair trade
    certification 89–93, 95

and European sales 201–2
Fairtrade Foundation 89–93, 95,
    200–3
Fairtrade Labelling Organisation
    201, 202
importance of 198–200
Fairley, Alastair 102, 233
Fairley, Carson 102, 116
Fairley, Jo 2
    after selling the business 179–81
    eco-consciousness 25–6, 36–7
    education 27–9
    family 26–7
    freelance journalism 34–6
    as a green pioneer 218–22
    Hastings home 167–8
    health tips 241–2
    honorary degree 233
    magazine work 30–4
    office 155
    role models 41–2
    and Craig Sams 37–9, 106
    secretarial work 29–30
    support for WEN 66
Fairley, Paris 102
Fairtrade Foundation 91–3, 95
    certification 89–91
    and Green & Black's 200–3
Fairtrade Labelling Organisation 201,
    202
FAO 88
farmers 237
Fearnley-Whittingstall, Hugh 123
flavoured chocolate 103–9
FLO 201, 202
focus groups 182, 185
food, cheap 237
Food and Agriculture Organisation 88
Food Programme, The 93
Formentera 14
Foxen, Haley 123
Francis, John 76
Franks, Lynne 173

Friends of the Earth 138
Fry, Joseph 53
Fuchs, Nan 105

Garcia, Deborah 233
Garcia, Jerry 233
genetically modified crops 132–40,
    151–2
Ghana Wells Appeal 213–14
ginger 85
Girl Fridays 28–9
Glen House 174
glycemic index 65
GM crops 132–40, 151–2
Goldsmith, Ben 74
Goldsmith, Zac 74
Good Housekeeping Award 143
Goodman, Joy 30
Goodwood 233
Gordon, Clay 226, 227
Granny Takes a Trip 18
Green, Emily 62–3
Green & Black's
    awards 142–3
    capital investment in business
        175–8
    choice of name 1–2
    and Fairtrade Foundation 200–3
    financial problems 155–6, 161–3,
        165–72
    new lines 101–24
    new management 178–82
    offices 153–5, 181, 228
    potential flotation 176
    problems caused by power cuts
        155–6
    product range 144
    Punta Gorda office 228
    sold to Cadbury's 195, 198, 211–15,
        217–18
    use of Whole Earth supply chain
        40, 59–60
Green City Wholefoods 135

Green Consumer Guide, The 174
Greenpeace 138
Groucho Club 123
Gusto 195, 196

Hadjiandreou, Emmanuel 236,
    238–9
Hadjiandreou, Lisa 236, 238–9
Hailes, John 174
Hailes, Julia 174
Haimann, Marcia 226
Hampton Court Flower Show 110–11
Hanks, Tom 36
Harl, Neil 134
Hargrove, Gregor 226, 230
Harmonic Convergence 75, 77
Harmony 18
Harmony Foods 19, 20, 164
Harrison, Olivia 37
Hastings
    Judges Bakery 235–40, 246
    Wellington Square Natural
        Health Centre 235, 240, 242,
        244–6
Hawken, Paul 174
Hazelnut & Currant chocolate
    107–8
Hazelnut and Chocolate spread 116,
    180
health food stores 57, 58–9, 141
Henry, Bill 166–7, 168, 169
Hercules Ingredients 137, 139
Hershey 78, 83, 88, 218
Highgrove 69
Hirshberg, Gary 74, 173
Holden, Patrick 41, 138, 139
homelessness 214–15, 223–4
Honey 33–4
Hopkins, Rob 219
Hornett, Terry 30, 32
hot chocolate 116
Hurricane Iris 190–1, 194
husbands working with wives 106

ICAM 171–2
ice cream 110–13, 115–16, 219
Ico, Cayetano 199
ideas, capturing 106
IFOAM Organic World Exhibition
    Award 142
Independent 62, 139
independent retailers 145
Indica Books 17
interconnectedness in business 171
International Cocoa Gene Bank 151
International Food Exhibition 71
iodine 107
Istanbul 15
Ivory Coast 53–4

Jeremy, Caroline 179, 182, 185
Jessie Black Feather 188
JoJo Bar 119
Jones, John 112
Joseph Rowntree Foundation 92
Judges Bakery 235–40, 246

Kahn, Gene 195
Kallo Foods 185–6, 195, 196
Keenan, Lindsay 135
Kendall, William 156, 161–2, 175–82,
    195, 215, 217–18
Kennedy, John 197
Kidston, Cath 106, 221–2
Kingston University 233
kismet 75
Kuapa Kokoo cooperative 193
kudzu root 241–2, 243
kukuh 84

LaCroix, Neil 197
land rights of indigenous people
    82–3, 206–8
Lang, Tim 37
Lass, Tony 195, 197, 198
Launceston Place 123
launching products

Green & Black's 70% dark chocolate 57–74
  Maya Gold 91–6, 103
  time needed 93–4
Leaf, Alexandra 226
Leakey, Richard 36
lecithin 135, 137–9
Leibovitz, Annie 219
Leigh, Edna 13
Lennon, John 18
lindane 54
Lindt 23–4, 106
Lindt, Rudolphe 53
Little, Alastair 123
Long Wolf, Chief 187–9
Look Now 32–3
Lowe, Sharron 223–4
Lubaantun 46, 75–6, 77, 149

McCartney, Linda 36, 69, 123–4
McCartney, Paul 17, 36, 69, 123
McCartney, Stella 123, 125, 215
McCauley, Kay 38
macrobiotics 15–17, 18–20
Madonna 41
Magical Mystery Tour 18
magnesium 56, 105
mahogany 48, 87, 206, 208
Mailman, Josh 173
Make A Difference Makeover
  programme 223–4
Malcolm Electric Warrior 76
marketing 60–6, 113–14, 141, 211
Marks & Spencer 146–7
Mars 118, 218
Maya 45, 46, 47, 148
  Crystal Skull of Doom 76–7
  Deer Dance 76, 77–8, 84, 229, 231
  impact of fair trade on 198–200
  land tenure 82–3, 206–8
  and tourism 97–8, 225–6
  tribal culture 77
Maya Gold 72, 75, 84

contract for production 86–8
creation 86
Fairtrade mark 89–91, 201
growth in sales 194
launch 91–6, 103
organic certification 88–9
packaging 84, 86
secret of success 104
Maya Gold Project 197–8, 226
Maya Mountains Organic Farming
  Association 78–9
meditation 174
memorabilia 178, 233–4
Mensah, Nana 227
Meridian Foods 144
Meth, Hilary 123
methylxanthines 56
Mexico 45, 51, 52
Michaud, Michael 86, 87, 88–9
Miles, Barry 17
milk, organic spray-dried 101–2
milk chocolate 101–2, 120–2
mint chocolate 104–5
MIPS 239
Mitchell, Charlotte 131, 140–1, 144
Mitchell-Hedges, Anna 76–7
Mitchell-Hedges, Austin 76
mock orange 84
Monsanto 133–4, 136, 139, 151
Montezuma 52
Montignac, Michel, Dine Out and Lose
  Weight 64–5
Moon, Keith 30
Moss, Cliff 157–8, 158, 162, 164, 166,
  169–70, 172
mottos 58
Multiple Ingredient Product
  Specification forms 239
Music on a Summer's Evening
  113–14

naivety, benefits of in business 68
Native Americans 7, 83, 187–9

natural food movement 18–20
Natural Foods Union 57
natural health centre 235, 240, 242,
    244–6
Natural Products Expos 69–70, 71
Nesbitt, Chris 160–1
Nestlé 118, 212, 218
Nestlé, Henri 53
networking 173–4
New Covent Garden Soup Company
    178
New Woman 63
Newman, Nell 148
Newman, Paul 148
Newman's Own 148–9, 150–1
Newsround 93, 95
niches 104
Nilsson, Harry 30
NoCaf 115
Notting Hill 154
Nutella 116

OCP 148–51
ODA 88
offices 154–5, 181, 228
Oliver, Jamie 123
Olmec civilisation 45
Ono, Yoko 18
orders 144
organic certification
    Judges Bakery 239
    Maya Gold 87, 88–9, 91
Organic Commodities Project
    148–51
organic food 37, 38
    baby food 102
    Ceres Bakery 19
    chocolate 22, 39
    growing popularity of 129–32
    Harmony Foods 19
    peanut butter 21–2
    in supermarkets 140–1, 141, 143–5,
        146–7

Organic Food Awards 143
Osbourne, Sharon 113, 222
outsourcing 12–13
overseas aid 97–8, 193–5, 197–8
Overseas Development
    Administration 88
Oxfam 91, 92, 94, 95

packaging
    card sleeve 115
    dark chocolate (70%) 2–3
    eco-tourism promotion on
        wrapper 97–8
    Fairtrade Mark 89–93, 95, 200–3
    'health warning' note on wrapper
        59, 143
    makeover 122
    of the marketing material 62
    Maya Gold 84, 86
    redesign 182–5
    Soil Association logo 131
    Soil Association membership offer
        131–2
    use of inside of wrapper 182–3
    Whole Earth Foods 131, 182,
        185–6
Palmer, Mark 113
Paradox Restaurant 17, 77
Parents for Safe Food 37
partners, working together 106
partnerships with other businesses
    116
Passard, Alain 91
patents on crops 151–2
Paul, Irma 16
peanut butter 14, 19, 20–2, 77–8
Pearce, Dr Innes 130
Pearlfisher 183–5
Peck, Justino 82, 230
pesticides 37, 54–5
Peter, Daniel 53
phenethylamine 56
Phi Kappa Sigma 14

Phipps, Nigel 157–8
Phipps PR 179
photographic records 179
polyphenols 56
Powell, Tim 167, 168, 169
press coverage of launch
    Green & Black's 62–3
    Maya Gold 93
press cuttings 63
press releases 60–3, 64–5
prices, minimum guaranteed 87
pricing and independent retailers 145
Procter, Jane 30
product names 114–15, 118–19
promotion 97–8
public relations 60–3
publicity 60–6, 96
Punta Gorda 77, 97, 199, 228
    Toledo Cacao Fest 226, 229–32
'put and call' options 211
Pzena, Jeff 226, 227, 228

Quakers 52
Quatro, Suzi 31

Rapunzel 80, 148
Raven, Hugh 158, 160, 161, 207
Real Ice 111
recipe development 123–5
Reckitt, Mark 212–13
retailers 57, 58–9
rice-growing land, conversion to
    cacao 197
Robbins, Howard 99–100
Robinson, Howard 31
Roddick, Anita 34–5, 41–2, 75, 173
Roddick, Gordon 34, 173
Roddick, Justine 34, 35, 41
Roddick, Sam 34, 35, 41–2
role models 41–2
Romania 35
Ronnfeldt, Julia 187–8
Rowe, Bridget 31

Rudkin, Steve 145
Rumsfeld, Donald 133

Safeway 67, 131, 140
Sainsbury, Lady 67
Sainsbury, Sir David 69
Sainsbury's 67, 69, 81, 84, 93, 94,
    140–1, 144, 145, 146, 147
St Mary's Town and Country School
    10
sales 80
Sams, Craig 2, 41
    clothing enterprise 17–18
    education 10, 11–12, 13–14
    and Jo Fairley 37–9, 106
    family and early life 7–13
    food shops 18–19
    as a green pioneer 218–22
    Hastings home 167–8
    health tips 243–4
    honorary degree 233
    macrobiotic restaurants 17, 18
    office 155
    as president of Green & Black's
        179, 215, 216–17
    travels 14–16
Sams, Gregory 7, 9, 11, 13, 18, 19, 23,
    130, 176
Sams, Karim 39, 175–6, 196
Sams, Ken 8–9, 37
Sams, Margaret 8, 9, 187
Sams, Rima 39, 160, 175–6, 196, 206
San Pedro Columbia 191
Sao Tomé 52
Schmidt, Chet 77, 97
sea kelp 107
Seed 18
Seliger, Mark 219, 220
selling 99–100, 144–5
serendipity 75
SHI 227, 231
Shiva, Vandana 247
Sioux 7, 187–9

Slater, Nigel 113, 234
Smart, Larry 182
snack market 117-20
Social Venture Network 72, 173-4
Soil Association 69, 74, 86, 87, 88-9,
    130-2, 134, 201, 205
soya
    GM 132, 134-9
    identity-preserved 139
Spain, conquest of Mexico 52, 148
Spicy Apple Juice 84
Spurdens, Veda 9
staff recruitment and retention 163-4
Stamford Partners 195
starting a new venture 58
Steinbrecher, Dr Ricarda 133
Stephenson, Pamela 37
Stevenson, Rosemary 193
Stewart, Martha 41
    The Martha Rules 166
Stewart-Smith, Jane 158, 160, 161
Sting 36, 69, 72
Stone Barns 219-20
Stonehouse, Jane 38
Stonelynk Farm 240
Stonyfield Farm 74
Styler, Trudie 36, 69, 72
sugar, addition to chocolate 51
Suma 136
Sunday Times, The 63
supermarkets 67, 69
    empty shelves 81
    exclusivity agreements 84
    and organic food 140-1, 141, 143-5,
        146-7
    own-label brands 80
    selling to 99-100
    see also specific supermarkets
suppliers 80-4, 86-91
SustainAbility 174
Sustainable Harvest International
    227, 231
SVN 72, 173-4

taste, sense of 85-6
Taste magazine 63
Tatler 63
TCGA see Toledo Cacao Growers
    Association
telephone, answering 134
tele-working 164
Tennant, Tessa 174
Terra Verde 72, 73
Tesco 99-100, 147, 192-3
Textured Vegetable Protein 136-7
theobromine 56
theophylline 56
Tiddens, Katherine 72
timing, importance of 79
Tlaloc 84
TMCC 206, 207
Today 63
Togo 22, 80-1
Toledo Cacao Fest 2007 226, 229-32
Toledo Cacao Growers Association
    (TCGA) 82, 158-61, 190
    AGM 97
    and application to Business
        Linkages Challenge Fund
        193-5, 197-8
    approaches from other purchasers
        148-52
    contract with 86-8
    fair-trade certification 89-91,
        202-3
    impact of fair trade 198-200
    offices 228
    organic certification 88-9, 160-1
    and threat of logging 207
    and tourism 225-6
Toledo Maya Cultural Council 206,
    207
Toltec 84
tourism
    Belize 96-8, 225-6
    and chocolate 228
trade fairs and shows 69-74

trademarks 115, 118, 119, 120
Traidcraft 203
training of suppliers 87
Tramp 30
Transfair 201, 202
Transition Towns 219
tribal lands 82–3, 206–8
Triodos Bank 236, 238
triple bottom line 174
TRIPS 97
Turpin, Neil 181
TVP 136–7
Twiggy 37

UFO Club 17
umeboshi plums 241–2, 243
United States, export to 71–3, 148–9

Valrhona 63–4, 106
Valvona & Crolla 68
van Houten, Conrad 52–3
vanilla 108–9
vanillin 85, 108
vanilloid receptors 85
vanilloids 85
Vanity Fair 218–19, 219–21, 233–4
Vega Restaurant 13
vegetarian diet 13, 14
vendor remorse 178
venture capital 70
Villandry 68

Waitrose 131, 140–1, 144, 146–7
Wake Cup 115
weather, influence on chocolate sales 109–11
Wellington Square Natural Health Centre 235, 240, 242, 244–6
Welman, Karen 183, 184
WEN 65, 66
Wessex, Sophie, Countess of 222
Whinney, Joe 148–51
white chocolate 108–9

Whole Earth Foods 7
  capital investment in business 175–8
  cash flow 154
  demerger from Wilson King 79
  expansion 114
  financial problems 155–6, 161–3, 165–72
  launch 20
  and the Natural Foods Union 57
  new management 178–82
  'no added sugar' credo 39–40
  offices 153–5
  packaging 131, 182, 185–6
  peanut butter 20–2, 77–8
  potential buyers 195
  product range 129, 144
  profits 157
  sold to Kallo Foods 186, 195, 196
  in supermarkets 140
  Swiss-style muesli 93, 145, 146
  at trade shows 70
  use of facilities by Green & Black's 40, 59–60
  and WWAGM 136
Wholefood Wholesalers Against GM 135–7
wholesalers 57
Wickencamp, Jimmy 12
Williamson, Bob 162–3, 165–6
Wills, Alan 67, 94, 95, 99–100, 144, 155, 156–7, 162, 164, 165, 170
Wilson King 79
Winnebago Indian Reservation 7
wives working with husbands 106
Woman's World 30–2
Women of Achievement reception 219, 221–2
Women's Balance 241
women's chocolate 105–7
Women's Environment Network 65, 66

Women's Health Letter 105
Women's Institute 92
Wood, Beatrice 41
Wootton, Mrs 28–9
Worcester, Marchioness of 69
working hours 159
World Development Movement
    92
Worldaware 142
Wounded Knee 187
wrapper *see* packaging

Wright, Charles 207
Wright, Simon 119, 140–1, 144
WWAGM 135–6

Yates, Bill 91
Yin-Yang Ltd 18, 22
yoga 174
Young, Sir Colville 230
Young Methodists 96

zingerol 85

Acknowledgements

The authors would like to thank the following for their help with the book and/or for their belief in Green & Black's over the years . . .

Alexandra Thöring, Angela Mason, Christopher and Dawn Nesbitt, Cliff Moss, Cluny Brown, Gail Cohen, Darina Allen, Dee Nolan, Dominic Lowe, George Smith, Gordon and Anita Roddick, Gregory Sams, Hilary Meth, Ian Anderson, Jean-Charles Carrarini, John Kennedy, Jonathan Ford and Mike Branson and the team at Pearlfisher, Karen Welman, Karim Sams, Kay McCauley, Kenneth Sams, Lisbeth Damsgaard and Ronnie McGrail, Liz Hancock, Louise Campbell, Maggie Alderson, Margaret Sams, Mark Palmer, Micah Carr-Hill, Neil LaCroix, Neil Turpin, Nick Beart, Patrick Holden, Rima Sams, Riwa Foustok, Rodney Lochner, Ronnie and Lillian Dick, Simon Wright, Sophie Lazar, Stephen Philippsohn, Sue Peart, Tony Mackintosh, William Kendall.